The
Garland Library
of
War and Peace

The
Garland Library
of
War and Peace

Under the General Editorship of
Blanche Wiesen Cook, *John Jay College, C.U.N.Y.*
Sandi E. Cooper, *Richmond College, C.U.N.Y.*
Charles Chatfield, *Wittenberg University*

The Treaty Veto
of the
American Senate

by

Denna Frank Fleming

with a new introduction
for the Garland Edition by

Denna Frank Fleming

Garland Publishing, Inc., New York & London
1971

The new introduction for this

Garland Library Edition is Copyright © 1971, by

Garland Publishing Inc.

24 West 45 St., New York, N.Y. 10036

Library of Congress Cataloging in Publication Data

Fleming, Denna Frank, 1893–
    The treaty veto of the American Senate.

    (The Garland library of war and peace)
    Originally presented as the author's thesis,
University of Illinois, 1928.
    Includes bibliographical references.
    1. U. S.--Foreign relations--Treaties. 2. U. S.
Congress. Senate. I. Title. II. Series.
JK1170.F5   1972   328.73'07'46   72-147598
ISBN 0-8240-0359-4

Printed in the United States of America

Introduction

When this book was first published in 1930 the Preface said:

During the last thirty years the United States Senate has repeatedly stirred a large volume of controversy by refusing to approve, without extensive qualification, important treaties sponsored by the President. Bitter clashes, extending to the American people, have resulted, from which the writer has not been insulated. On the contrary, he has watched the greatest of these struggles with a degree of interest which will disqualify the present account from the standpoint of those believing that history must not be written by contemporaries who have had convictions upon the issues of their day.

Others not concerned about the final verdicts of history will feel, not unnaturally, that one who believes in the organization of world peace should not describe the action of Senators in opposition to this movement. The author can ask from these readers no greater effort to weigh all the evidence fairly than he has been able to put into his own work. It is his position that the failure of treaties for the advancement of peace in the administration of every President since Benjamin Harrison left office, in 1893, creates a situation which calls for study and appraisal. His findings are presented, not as a final word on the subject, but as a contribution to discussion. The reader is entitled to his own conclusion and to express them. Any new evidence bearing upon the

5

INTRODUCTION

*controversial questions discussed ought also to be added
to the record*

The passage of forty years has not changed my
belief that the constitutional requirement of a two-
thirds vote of the Senate for the approval of treaties
was a mistake and that it should be changed. The
scrutiny of treaties by the Senate is a proper
safeguard, but the two-thirds vote enabled a few
determined objectors or obstructionists to defeat a
long line of efforts to provide for the peaceable
settlement of disputes. In 1919-1920 it made it very
easy for partisan politicians to wield the power of life
and death over the greatest proposal ever conceived
by man, up to that time, for the orderly handling of
international conflicts—the League of Nations.

In an Epilogue written for this edition I have
sketched the disasters which followed our failure to
make peace after World War I, and I have tried to ask
the ultimate questions which confront us.

D.F.F.

Nashville, Tennessee
March 8, 1971

Editor's Note:

Denna F. Fleming (1893—) is a productive, if controversial, historian of American foreign policy, particularly as it relates to the structure and values of American politics. Having taken his advanced studies at the University of Illinois, he joined the department of political science at Vanderbilt University in 1928, becoming chairman in 1940. By the time he became professor emeritus in 1961 he had influenced a generation of students and had produced several important books, including The United States and the League of Nations *(N.Y., 1932) and* The United States and World Organization *(N.Y., 1938),* While America Slept *(Nashville, 1944),* The United States and the World Court *(Garden City, N.Y., 1945), and the two-volume* The Cold War and Its Origins, 1917-1960 *(Garden City, N.Y., 1961). Since that time he has written* The Origins and Legacies of World War I *(Garden City, N.Y., 1968), and* America's Role in Asia *(N.Y., 1969).*

THE TREATY VETO
OF
THE AMERICAN SENATE

By

DENNA FRANK FLEMING, Ph.D.

ASSISTANT PROFESSOR OF POLITICAL SCIENCE
IN VANDERBILT UNIVERSITY

NEW YORK : LONDON
G. P. PUTNAM'S SONS
The Knickerbocker Press
1930

THE TREATY VETO

OF

THE AMERICAN SENATE

∾

Copyright, 1930

by

D. F. Fleming

∾

Published, January, 1930
Reprinted, September, 1930

Made in the United States of America

To

MY MOTHER AND FATHER

PREFACE

DURING the last thirty years the United States Senate has repeatedly stirred a large volume of controversy by refusing to approve, without extensive qualification, important treaties sponsored by the President. Bitter clashes, extending to the American people, have resulted, from which the writer has not been insulated. On the contrary, he has watched the greatest of these struggles with a degree of interest which will disqualify the present account from the standpoint of those believing that history must not be written by contemporaries who have had convictions upon the issues of their day.

Others not concerned about the final verdicts of history will feel, not unnaturally, that one who believes in the organization of world peace should not describe the action of Senators in opposition to this movement. The author can ask from these readers no greater effort to weigh all the evidence fairly than he has been able to put into his own work. It is his position that the failure of treaties for the advancement of peace in the administration of every President since Benjamin Harrison left office, in 1893, creates a situation which calls for study and appraisal. His findings are presented, not as a final word on the subject, but as a contribution to discussion. The reader is entitled to his own conclusions and to express them. Any new evidence bearing upon the controversial questions discussed ought also to be added to the record.

I am glad to record my obligation to Professors James W. Garner, John A. Fairlie, Clarence A. Berdahl and Laurence M. Larson, of the University of Illinois; to Professors James T. Shotwell, Arthur W. Macmahon and Joseph P. Chamberlain, of Columbia University; also to Walter L. Fleming and Frank L. Owsley, my colleagues. They have all given their time liberally to the improvement of the survey. None of them should be held in any sense responsible, however, for any opinions expressed or errors that remain; both are my own. I am further indebted to President T. H. McMichael, of Monmouth College, for generous leave of absence and to my wife, Doris Anundsen Fleming, for constant assistance.

D. F. F.

Nashville, Tennessee,
    January 1, 1930.

CONTENTS

THE TREATY VETO OF THE
AMERICAN SENATE

CHAPTER I

THE ORIGINS OF THE SENATE'S POWER OVER TREATIES

A SURVEY of the constitutional systems of the world does not reveal a counterpart of our plan of associating only one house of the legislature with the executive in treaty making. How did our constitution happen to break with the long established custom of leaving full control over treaties to the executive? Why did it give the Senate power over treaties and exclude the House of Representatives? And why did it require a two-thirds majority of the Senate for their approval?

The first direct answers to these questions are to be found, naturally, during the Revolution and the Confederation. The Declaration of Independence may be said to have asserted the creation of thirteen independent states—not one. It was solemnly published and declared that "these United Colonies are, and of right ought to be free and independent states . . . and that, as free and independent states, they have full power to levy war, conclude peace, and contract alliances, establish commerce, and do all other acts and things which independent states may of right do." To the extent that this was a proclamation of the sovereignty of the individual states, the propriety of their direct representatives, the Senators, having a share in treaty making was obvious.

The national view which generally prevailed in later times of course stressed the statement that the above declaration was made "in the name and by the authority of the good

3

people of these colonies" by "the representatives of the United States of America, in general Congress assembled." In the words of Justice Story, "It was not an act done by the State governments then organized, nor by persons chosen by them. It was emphatically the act of the whole *people* of the United Colonies—an act of original, inherent sovereignty by the people themselves." [1]

Whatever the agency of the signers of 1776 may have been, we find the Articles of Confederation, signed two years later, providing that "Each state retains its sovereignty, freedom, and independence, and every power, jurisdiction, and right, which is not by this Confederation expressly delegated to the United States in Congress Assembled." Such express delegation of the power to determine peace and war, and to enter into treaties and alliances was made to Congress in Article 9, but under the restriction that no treaty of alliance nor declaration of war could be made without the assent of nine states. [2] All voting was by states, each state having one vote.

The framers of the Constitution, then, were used to a Congress in which the States, declared to be sovereign and independent, voted as such and upon a complete equality in the making of treaties. Furthermore, to make a treaty, or exercise several of the other fundamental powers of government required a majority slightly larger than two thirds. Finally, no separate executive or judiciary existed. Congress was the sole organ of government. All treaties were negotiated by agents appointed by and responsible to it alone. There was nothing else to represent.

[1] Joseph Story, *Constitution of the United States* (4th Ed.), Boston, 1873, Vol. I, p. 149. The state governments previously formed had been created in compliance with a recommendation of Congress (148).

[2] Neither could any of the following things be done without the vote of nine states: coin money or regulate its values, emit bills, borrow money, appropriate it, or even ascertain sums and expenses necessary for the defense and welfare of "the United States, or any of them." The same majority was required to agree upon the acquisition of warships, the creation of land forces or appointment of a Commander-in-Chief.

THE DEBATES UPON TREATY MAKING IN THE
CONSTITUTIONAL CONVENTION

It is not strange, therefore, that the members of the Constitutional Convention thought of treaty making as a legislative function. None had been made in any other way. The first proposal, however, the Randolph plan, submitted immediately upon organization, seemed to revert to the traditional practice of executive treaty-making. At least its seventh resolution, providing for a national executive, concluded with the observation that "it ought to enjoy the executive rights vested in Congress by the Confederation." [3] The Pinckney draft, introduced the same day, agreed with Randolph's on the creation of an executive and an upper legislative body but lodged the control of foreign affairs almost wholly in the Senate. That body was to "have the sole and exclusive power to declare war; and to make treaties; and to appoint ambassadors and other ministers to foreign nations. . . ."[4] The only powers granted to the President were to receive the ministers of foreign nations and to correspond with "the executive of the different states"— presumably foreign. Otherwise the Confederation idea of legislative control of foreign relations was kept intact.

The necessity of a national executive was admitted in the Randolph draft, but its enumerated powers were few. They embraced only the power to grant pardons, to command the armed forces, and execute the laws. Further than that there was only a limited power to appoint officers and to recommend measures to Congress. It was difficult for the men of 1787 to look with confidence on a powerful executive. They had been engaged for generations in a constant warfare with the Royal Governors of the colonies, gradually wresting rights and powers from them, and finally they had

---

[3] Jonathan, Elliot, *Debates on the Federal Constitution*, Philadelphia, 1891, Vol. I, p. 144.
[4] Ibid., 148.

risked their lives in defiance of King George III to preserve these rights. [5]   More than half of the Declaration of Independence is taken up with a recital of the King's misdeeds —"A history of repeated injuries and usurpations, all having in direct object the establishment of an absolute tyranny over these states."   Throughout the long enumeration of abuses suffered there is no attempt to attach the blame to the King's ministers or agents.   The nearest they came to dividing his responsibility was in the preface of the longest catalogue of oppressions where it was said that "He has combined with others . . ."   The King himself was named some eighteen times, and the indictment closed with the personal thrust that "A prince, whose character is thus marked by every act which may define a tyrant, is unfit to be the ruler of a free people."   Everything preceding this long arraignment of the King is quite introductory; when it is finished there remains only a word to "our British brethren" and the formal Declaration.

When this background is considered, the executive was perhaps fortunate in the opening plans submitted to the Convention to get the power to shake the hands of foreign ambassadors and to write letters abroad. [6]

Gradual Return to the Rule of Treaty Making by the Executive.—The first suggestion of transferring the conduct of foreign relations to the executive came from Alexander Hamilton on June 18.   After listening to intermittent de-

---

[5] "The conflict between the colonial executives and legislatures had embittered the men of that time against the exercise of executive authority. . . . Hence the executive was rendered weak and inefficient both in organization and function.   As Madison succinctly expressed it in the Convention of 1787, 'The Executives of the states are in general little more than ciphers; the legislatures omnipotent.'"   J. M. Mathews, *American State Government*, N. Y., 1926, p. 143.

[6] Patterson's plan, submitted on June 15, was silent on the allocation of the treaty power, but the failure to mention it among the few powers given to the Executive presumably left it wholly in the hands of Congress.   No Senate was contemplated.   James Madison, *Journal of the Debates in the Constitutional Convention of 1787* (Hunt Edition), N. Y., 1908, Vol. I, p. 140.

bate for three weeks on proposals for a plural executive for a three year term or a seven year period, Hamilton arose to plead for a strong executive and to hold up the English Kingship as the only good model to aim at. While praising the hereditary principle he recognized it to be politically out of the question and so suggested a President to be elected for life. For such an executive he proposed substantial powers in his plan submitted at the close of the speech. The Senate was still to have the sole power of declaring war, but in addition to a negative on all laws, the President was to be given the direction of war once begun, the sole appointment of the Secretaries of Foreign Affairs, War, and Finance, the appointment, subject to confirmation, of all other officers and the power of making all treaties "with the advice and approbation of the Senate." [7]

At the close of Hamilton's presentation, the Convention rose and adjourned, but there is no record that it did so with any loud applause or as a mark of respect for the proposals made. Nor was any fruitage of his ideas apparent when the Committee of Eleven reported two months later, on August 23, 1787. The Senate was still to have the power to make treaties and to appoint Ambassadors. [8] Then, however, Mr. Madison observed that the Senate represented the States alone, and that for this as well as other obvious reasons it was proper that the President should be an agent in the making of treaties. Gouverneur Morris did not know whether he would refer the making of treaties to the Senate at all, but for the present proposed that no treaty should be binding which was not ratified by a law.

The first debate then took place on the propriety of ratification by the whole legislature. [9] Madison suggested the inconvenience of requiring such ratification of treaties of al-

[7] Madison's *Journal of the Debates in the Constitutional Convention of 1787*, I, 152-164.
[8] Ibid., II, 238.
[9] The assumption was still for making treaties in the Senate. .

liance for the purpose of war. Mr. Gorham thought that
many other disadvantages must be experienced if treaties
of peace and all negotiations were to be previously ratified,
and if not previously, the ministers would be at a loss how to
proceed. American ministers, unlike others, would have to
go abroad not instructed by the same authority which was
to ratify their proceedings. He could hardly suppose the
King of Great Britain proceeding in such a manner. Mr.
Wilson thought that the necessity of Parliamentary execution
of treaties placed the King under the same fetters, but Doc-
tor Johnson challenged the parallel. Full and complete
power was vested in the King, and if Parliament should fail
to provide the necessary means of execution the Treaty would
be violated. [10]

Mr. Morris was not eager to facilitate the making of
treaties. He wished none to be made with Great Britain until we should be at war. Then a good bargain might be made
with her. So with other foreign powers. The more difficulty
in making treaties, the more value would be set on them.[11]

Madison finally "hinted for consideration" whether a distinction might not be made between different sorts of treaties,
allowing the President and Senate to make some treaties [12]
and requiring the concurrence of the whole legislature for
other treaties—the principle later adopted in Europe. [13]

The Adoption of the Two-Thirds Requirement.—The provision regarding treaty making was then referred to a Committee of Five and on August 31, along with sundry other
postponed articles, to a new Committee of Eleven. This
Committee reported, on September 4th, the solution that
went into the Constitution. The President was given power
to make treaties and to appoint ambassadors, other public

[10] Madison's *Journal*, 238–9.
[11] Madison in a later debate "observed that it had been too easy in the
present Congress to make treaties although nine states were required
for the purpose." Ibid., II, 334.
[12] For example, treaties of alliance.
[13] Madison's *Journal*, II, 240.

ministers, etc., by and with the advice and consent of the Senate. The making of treaties, but not appointments, required the consent of two thirds of the Senators present. [14]

The clause being taken up on September 7, James Wilson, consistent believer in popular control of government, at once moved that the advice and consent of the House of Representatives be also required. As treaties, he said, are to have the operation of laws, [15] they ought to have the sanction of laws also. The circumstance of secrecy formed the only objection; but this, he thought, as far as it was inconsistent with obtaining the legislative sanction, was outweighed by the necessity of the latter. Roger Sherman held that the need for secrecy was more important and the Convention agreed with him by a vote of nine states to two.[16]

Mr. Wilson then objected that the requirement of a two-thirds majority put it in the power of the minority to control the majority. He was supported by Roger Sherman who remarked that the joining of the executive in the business provided a check which did not exist in Congress where the concurrence of two-thirds was required. Wilson argued the next day that if the majority could not be trusted it was proof, as observed by Mr. Gorham, that we were not fit for one society. Moreover, if two-thirds were necessary to make peace, the minority might perpetuate a war against the sense of the majority. [17]

[14] Madison's *Journal*, II, 240, 262, 299.
[15] No objection appears to have been made to giving treaties the full force of law. Their execution had of course suffered under the Confederation for lack of a Federal judiciary. "It is unquestionably true that the very most pronounced evil in connection with the Confederacy —aside from its inability to tax—was its inability to enforce the treaties then made and existing with foreign states." Speech of Rep. Sherley, of Kentucky, in the House of Representatives, June 22, 1907, p. 8.

This condition must have existed, for Pinckney's plan, at the start of the convention, made treaties "the supreme law of the land" and Patterson's scheme later gave them the status of "the supreme law of the respective states." Butler, *The Treaty Making Power of the United States*, N. Y., 1902, 178.
[16] Madison's *Journal*, II, 327.
[17] Ibid., II, 329, 333.

Madison had offered two amendments to the clause designed to make it easier to conclude treaties of peace. First
he "moved to insert after the word 'treaty' the words 'except
treaties of peace', allowing these to be made with less difficulty." The motion was apparently generally agreed to,
but not put. He then moved to authorize a concurrence of
two-thirds of the Senate to make treaties of peace, without
the concurrence of the President. The President, he said,
would derive so much power from a state of war that he
might be tempted to impede a treaty of peace. Mr. Butler
seconded this motion and supported it strenuously as a necessary security against ambitious and corrupt Presidents, citing
historical examples as proof of the danger. Morris and
Gorham thought the elimination of the President unnecessary, since they regarded him as the general guardian of the
national interests. Their view prevailed on roll call, seven
to two. [18]

A vote was then had on Madison's first motion to except
treaties of peace from the two-thirds rule and the amendment
carried eight to three. The next day, however, King moved
to strike out this exception and the Convention reversed itself, seven to three, after an argument by Mr. Williamson
that in the Senate a majority vote of the states might not represent a majority of the people. Eight men might be a
majority of the quorum and decide the conditions of peace.
"Mr. Gerry enlarged on the danger of putting the essential
rights of the Union at the hands of so small a number as a
majority of the Senate, representing, perhaps, not one-fifth
of the people." The Senate would be corrupted by foreign
influence. [19]

A special status for peace treaties being defeated, Wilson
and Dayton forced a vote on the whole two-thirds rule, los-
ing nine to two, after which Rutledge and Gerry sought to

[18] Madison's *Journal*, II, 330.
[19] Ibid., II, 331, 333.

raise the requirement to two-thirds of all the members of the Senate. They were likewise outvoted, eight to three. Sherman then made the compromise motion [20] that no treaty should be made without a majority of the whole number of the Senate. The reported debate on this proposal consists of two sentences. Mr. Williamson warned that "This will be less security than two-thirds as now required," to which Sherman replied: "It will be less embarrassing," a comment which future Presidents struggling to secure approval of their treaties may well have regarded as prophetic. The vote on the question was negative, six states to five.[21] If one or two men had happened to vote differently—enough to change the vote of one state—we would now look upon the requirement of a majority of all the Senators elected as hallowed by time and wisdom instead of venerating, as we generally do, the two-thirds vote thus finally adopted by the narrowest of margins.

Attempts failing to define a quorum and to provide for special notice to Senators of the time of treaty votes, the consideration was finally closed by a vote of eight to three on the whole clause.

Convention Motives As Reflected in *The Federalist*

Long continued reliance on legislative action in the Colonial and Confederation periods made it natural for the Convention to rely upon legislative supervision of treaty-making —and even to assume that it was a legislative function to make treaties. Coupled with that was the deep-seated distrust of the executive described above. This more active side of the general feeling crops out all during the debates, and is found afterwards in the battle for ratification. In the issue of *The Federalist* on the treaty-making power

[20] Seconded, rather curiously, by Gerry.
[21] Madison's *Journal*, II, 334.

written by Hamilton the discussion begins with a general justification of the division of the power, maintaining that it is neither a legislative nor an executive function and therefore belongs properly to neither of these departments.[22]

Hamilton's first definite argument is based upon the danger of entrusting the power to the President alone. His attribution of a substantial share of the power to the President in his plan submitted to the Convention had been predicated on a life term for that official. He had thought the President should have but little power if appointed for a seven year term.[23] When, therefore, the Convention adopted his distribution of the treaty power and also agreed upon a four year presidential term he naturally valued the Senate check quite highly. The interests of an hereditary monarch were perhaps so great as to prevent his corruption, "But a man raised from the station of a private citizen to the rank of a Chief Magistrate, possessed of but a moderate or slender fortune, and looking forward to a period not very remote, when he may probably be obliged to return to the station from whence he was taken, might sometimes be under temptations to sacrifice his duty to his interest, which it would require superlative virtue to withstand. An avaricious man might be tempted to betray the interests of the State to the acquisition of wealth. An ambitious man might make his own aggrandizement, by the aid of a foreign power, the price of his treachery to his constituents." [24]

Somebody apparently had to watch the President. The electoral college, select and deliberative as it was to be, might still make a mistake. Besides the whole theory of checks and balances required a counterpoise to the President in this important matter. Who should it be?

Legislative Approval Without Sacrificing Secrecy and Despatch.—The answer was, an agency which could assist in

[22] *The Federalist* (Ford Ed.), N. Y., 1898 No. 75; p. 500.
[23] Madison's *Journal*, I, 160.
[24] *The Federalist* (Ford Ed.), p. 501.

treaty framing at any time on short notice and without publicity. These two things, secrecy and despatch, had been held all along to be vital to successful diplomacy. "It seldom happens," wrote John Jay in an earlier number of *The Federalist,* "in the negotiation of treaties of whatever nature, but that perfect secrecy and immediate despatch are sometimes requisite. There are cases where the most useful intelligence may be obtained, if the persons possessing it can be relieved from apprehensions of discovery." [25]

No matter whether the motives were mercenary or friendly, such persons would rely on the secrecy of the President, whereas they could not be persuaded to whisper in the ear of the Senate and certainly not that of a large popular assembly. Obviously, too, when the President passed on the secret information it had to go to a safe repository. It is not recorded that the idea occurred to anyone at the time that secrecy in diplomacy was not a good thing or that there could be too much of it.

Then there were tides in the affairs of men to be reckoned with, "tides very irregular in their duration, strength, and direction, and seldom found to run twice exactly in the same manner or measure. To discern and to profit by these tides in National affairs, is the business of those who preside over them; and they who have had much experience on this head inform us that there frequently are occasions when days, nay, even when hours are precious. The loss of a battle, the death of a Prince, the removal of a minister, or other circumstances intervening to change the present posture and aspect of affairs, may turn the most favorable tide into a course opposite to our wishes. As in the field, so in the cabinet, there are moments to be seized as they pass, and they who preside in either, should be left in capacity to improve them." [26]

[25] Ibid., No. 64, p. 429.
[26] *The Federalist* (Ford Ed.), No. 64, p. 429.

The President might have some difficulty in catching these tides if encumbered with a small Senate; certainly the crest would be far out before he could also bring with him the popular assembly.

The House of Representatives was to have about sixty-five members [27]—far too many in the opinion of both the Convention and *The Federalist,* to entrust a secret to. But there were only twenty-six Senators. The President carrying on all "preparatory and auxiliary" negotiations could call in the Senate when any special points were to be decided [28] and settle the matter much as the King had acted in Council for ages and as the Colonial Governors had done habitually —in fair weather. If there were a disagreement over what to do it would be necessary to mobilize only eighteen minds at the most, which, done quietly and quickly, the conclusion of the treaty could proceed. Thus the Senate composed of "able and honest men" would be in close touch with our foreign affairs at all times, and moreover, being a continuous body they would become "perfectly acquainted with our national concerns" and by greatly extending their political information render "their accumulating experience more and more beneficial to their country." [29]

We find here no plea for control of diplomacy by the people. It was too complicated even for their direct representatives. The Senate was to be as far removed from them by indirect election as the President. The circle of power and responsibility was to be enlarged a little—just enough to give us the benefit of the accumulated wisdom of the Madisons and Franklins who should sit in the Senate, without injuring the conduct of the public business. No

---

[27] David Ramsey, Member of the Convention, in an address to the people of South Carolina urging support of the Constitution asked who else might be trusted with the treaty power. "Can the Continental House of Representatives? When sixty-five men can keep a secret, they may." Ford, *Pamphlets on the Constitution,* Brooklyn, 1888, p. 376.

[28] *The Federalist* (Ford Ed.), No. 64, p. 430.

[29] Ibid.

wonder that Hamilton thought this "one of the best digested and unexceptionable parts" of the Constitution.[30] We should have, agreed Jay, "every advantage which can be derived from talents, information, integrity and deliberate investigations, on the one hand, and from secrecy and despatch on the other." [31]

And withal there would be enough collaboration to prevent the President from seizing a sceptre and a crown, especially in the making of peace. "The usurpation of power on the part of a single executive was a present and continuing danger. No one anticipated that there was any occasion for the slightest apprehension that the Senate would ever mar any provision of the constitution." [32]

[30] *The Federalist* (Ford Ed.), No. 74, p. 499.
[31] Ibid., No. 64, p. 430.
[32] B. M. Thompson, "The Power of the Senate to Amend a Treaty," *Michigan Law Review*, April, 1905, Vol. III, p. 441.

CHAPTER II

THE RELATION OF THE SENATE TO THE NEGOTIATION OF TREATIES

THE discussions of the treaty making power attending the adoption of the constitution reveal many fears that were natural at the time but which have since turned out to be groundless. The debates show, too, with even greater clearness, as Mr. Walter Lippman has observed, that the Fathers had no very prophetic idea of how they meant Article 2, Section 2 to work.[1] Nor was this strange. They were departing from the beaten paths of government in this matter as in many others and though they had some real statesmen among them they could not hope, being only human, to have everything work out just as they had guessed it would.

Making Treaties in Council. Certainly the initial attempt of the new government to operate the treaty making machinery did not result in the orderly association of the best minds that had been anticipated. The often quoted account in Senator Maclay's journal foreshadows vividly the difficulties inherent in the President's task of securing in advance the advice and consent of an independent legislative body. [2]

A treaty being in prospect with the Southern Indians, President Washington came down to the Senate on August 22, 1789, to settle upon its terms. The Senate had just

---

[1] "Concerning Senator Borah," *Foreign Affairs,* January, 1926, Vol. IV, p. 218.
[2] Wm. Maclay, *Sketches of Debate in the First Senate,* Harrisburg, Pa., 1880, p. 122.

taken up the Coasting Bill when the doorkeeper informed it
of the arrival of the President who was introduced and took
the Vice-President's chair according to the procedure
adopted by the Senate the day before.   Then without further ceremony "He arose and told us bluntly that he had
called on us for our advice and consent to some propositions
respecting the treaty to be held with the Southern Indians.
Said he had brought General Knox with him, who was well
acquainted with the business.   He then turned to General
Knox, who was seated on the left of the chair.   General
Knox, handed him a paper, which he handed to the President of the Senate, who was seated on a chair on the floor
to his right.   Our Vice-President hurried over the paper.
Carriages were driving past, and such a noise, I could tell
it was something about 'Indians,' but was not master of
one sentence of it.   Signs were made to the doorkeeper to
shut the sashes.   Several heads, as we have since learned,
were stated at the end of the paper which the Senate were to
give their advice and consent to.   They were so framed that
this could be done by aye or no. . . ." [3]

The noise of the carriages had been so great that Mr.
Morris asked to have the paper read again.   It was so read.
Then the President of the Senate proceeded to ask the advice and consent of the Senate on the first proposition.
Mr. Maclay felt sure that if he did not interpose no other
would, "and we should have these advices and consents
ravished, in a degree, from us," so he reluctantly rose and
asked for the reading of the treaties and documents mentioned in the paper.   "The business labored with the Senate"
until Mr. Maclay again took the floor and moved a postponement until Monday.   The question was put and "actually
carried."

Then it was Mr. Morris' turn again.   At an early stage
Mr. Maclay had whispered to him that he thought the best

[3] Ibid.

way to conduct the business was to have all the papers referred to a committee. His reasons were that he "saw no chance of a fair investigation of subjects while the President of the United States sat there, with his Secretary of War, to support his opinions and overawe the timid and neutral part of the Senate." Mr. Morris now rose, and moved that the papers be referred to a committee of five directed to report as soon as might be. He was seconded by Mr. Gunn. Several members grumbled objections, however, and Mr. Butler contended at length that they were acting as a council and "no Council ever committed anything."

Mr. Maclay supported the mode of doing business by committees, arguing that they were used in all public deliberative bodies—a generalization which did not apply because the Senate on that occasion was to have been a secret executive commission, not a public legislative assembly. His contention that no possible harm could be done by a postponement over Sunday was of course plausible enough. The whole speech, spoken in a low tone of voice, "did the subject justice" in such a manner that "Peevishness itself," he thought, could not have taken offense at anything he said.

Imagine the Senator's surprise, therefore, when, as he sat down, "the President of the United States started up in a violent fret. 'This defeats every purpose of my coming here,' were the first words that he said. He then went on that he had brought his Secretary of War with him to give every necessary information; that the Secretary knew all about the business, and yet he was delayed and could not go on with the matter. He cooled, however, by degrees. Said he had no objection to putting off the matter until Monday, but declared he could not understand the matter of commitment. He might be delayed; he could not tell how long. He rose a second time and said he had no objection to postponement until Monday at ten o'clock. By the looks of the Senate this seemed agreed to—a pause for some time ensued. We waited for him to withdraw. He did so with a discontented air. Had it been any other man than the man whom I wish to regard as the first character in the world, I would have said with sullen dignity." [4]

Evidently his Council had behaved in a manner totally unexpected by the President. Perhaps he had been thinking more of securing consent than advice. On the other hand the saving of time seemed to require some analysis of the proposed treaty that would give the Senate something definite to act upon. He had come prepared to give full information and settle the business according to the common understanding of the required procedure; the Senate had halted discussion and refused to continue it in his presence. He returned with General Knox on Monday, August 24, however, and after a long and tedious debate all the seven propositions were voted on by the Senate. [5] It must have been after this second session that the President resolved that "he would be damned if he ever went there again." [6]

The feeling of Senators that they could discuss the treaty much more freely if the great man were not present is also understandable. It was natural, moreover, that the Senate should desire to uphold its full dignity and rights in the case. It was proper that it should not give perfunctory approval to the draft. That any such summary action was intended by the President is disproved by his statement to

---

[4] Maclay, *Sketches of Debate in the First Senate*, 122–24.

[5] *Senate Executive Journal*, Vol. I, p. 23. (Two of the seven propositions had been acted on in the first session.)

[6] John Quincy Adams, *Memoirs*, Phila., 1874, Vol. VI, p. 427. It may be added that the President would have done well to have remembered to ask Senator Maclay to dinner before the consideration of the treaties. He bethought himself of it after the first session, and sent him an invitation on Monday to dine at four on Thursday, but it was apparently too late. "I was really surprised at the invitation. It will be my duty to go; however, I will make no inferences whatever. I am convinced all the dinners he can now give, or ever could, will make no difference in my conduct. Perhaps he knew not of my being in town. Perhaps he has changed his mind of me. I was long enough in town, however, before my going home. It is a thing, of course, and of no consequence; nor shall it have any with me." Maclay, p. 126.

the Senate Committee which conferred with him on August 8, only two weeks previous, about the manner of treaty consideration.   He had said then "In all matters respecting treaties, oral communications seem indispensably necessary; because in these a variety of matters are contained, all of which not only require consideration, but some of them may undergo much discussion; to do which by written communications would be tedious without being satisfactory." [7] Nominations to office, on the other hand, he thought had best be made by written message.   His choices of men were to be taken or left; accommodation of views was not necessary.   So, in making "the fullest and freest inquiry into the character of the person nominated" the Senate should not be "under the smallest restraint" from the presence of the President.

Here was no evidence of a desire to prevent full and free consideration of treaties in the Senate.   However, in a second interview with the Committee two days later the President had stated that "The Senate, when this power is exercised, is evidently a Council only to the President, however its concurrence may be to his acts."   It, therefore, seemed "incident to this relation between them that not only the *time* but the *place* and *manner* of consultation should be with the President."   The President would probably often wish to summon the Senate to his residence. [8] The Senate accordingly being notified on August 21 that the President would visit it the next day, adopted a rule (which still exists as Rule 36), permitting the President to convene the Senate wherever he liked. [9]   While granting the President's wish the Senate may not have liked altogether his reference to it as a "Council only."   What happened in the Senate on August 22 was probably not so spontaneous as

[7] *The Writings of George Washington* (Ford Edition), N. Y., 1891, Vol. XI, p. 417.
[8] Ibid., 418.
[9] J. W. Foster, *The Practice of Diplomacy*, N. Y., 1906, p. 265.

Senator Maclay's record would indicate. That gentleman and others had ample time to decide what they would do when the President came with a treaty.

At any rate after the incident there could be no doubt in Senator Maclay's mind as to the wisdom of the rebuff given to President Washington. He could not "now" be mistaken. "The President wishes to tread on the necks of the Senate. Commitment will bring the matter to discussion; at least in the committee where he is not present. He wishes us to see with the eyes and hear with the ears of his Secretary only. The Secretary to advance the premises, the President to draw the conclusions, and to bear down on our deliberations with his personal authority and presence. Form only will be left to us." [10]

Whatever the reason for the Senate's refusal to sit in council with the President, it is probable that that method of considering treaties would have broken down before many years. Postponement and further investigation by the Senate would have been inevitable in many cases.

In any event the incident shows the friction inherent in the attempt to give two independent bodies power over treaties.

PROCEDURE DURING NEGOTIATIONS

After the experience narrated, President Washington confined his communication with the Senate on the subject of treaties to written messages, though he still adhered to the practice of asking the advice of the Senate before negotiations were opened and during their course. Negotiations with England over the northeastern boundary were suspended until the President could consult the Senate, and the Senate agreed in advance to approve the proposed terms of a treaty with Algiers. [11]

[10] C. A. Beard, *The Journal of William Maclay*, N. Y., 1927, p. 128.
[11] Foster, *The Practice of Diplomacy*, 267-70.

Even this method of consulting the Senate during negotiations lapsed with Washington, however, and seems not to have been resumed until 1838 when President Van Buren asked the Senate to disapprove of a proposed commercial treaty with Ecuador before negotiations rather than after. Polk, in 1846, asked the Senate's approval of suggested terms of peace with Mexico, and similar requests were forwarded by Buchanan and Lincoln in 1861, Johnson in 1868, Grant in 1872 and 1874 and Arthur in 1884. [12]

An indirect method of securing advance approval of the Senate was to nominate an envoy to negotiate a treaty and attach an outline of proposed terms. Confirmation of the appointment then automatically approved the treaty project. This device was used by Washington and Adams repeatedly and by Jefferson at least once. The President has also sought the advice of the Senate on questions of treaty interpretation. [13]

Full Executive Responsibility the Rule. Ample precedents exist, then, to justify a President in asking the Senate's advice at any time he sees fit. The precedents, however, do not alter the rule that the President is responsible for the negotiation of treaties at all stages. He may keep in informal touch with influential Senate leaders, indeed it is customary to do so, but the extent of this collaboration will depend largely on political conditions, and to a lesser extent on the personality of the President. Conversely the Senate has a right to offer advice to the President at any time either by formal action or quietly through its leaders, and the President should consider well such advice, but in all cases he is free to accept or reject it as he sees fit. If he fails to accept the advice of the Senate his treaty may be rejected by that body; he must always consider that probability, but

[12] Foster, *The Practice of Diplomacy*, 267–70.
[13] Ibid., pp. 271–73.

the Senate has no means of enforcing its views on the Executive until the treaty comes before it.

Claims of the Senate to a Share in Negotiations. A claim to participation in the negotiation of treaties is occasionally set up in the Senate. In 1901, after the Senate had altered the Hay–Pauncefote Treaty with England relative to the Isthmian Canal with the result that considerable irritation was aroused in English circles, the occasion was seized by Senator Henry Cabot Lodge, of Massachusetts, to assert the right of the Senate to negotiate. He declared in *Scribner's Magazine*, January, 1902, [14] that "The treaty so-called is . . . still inchoate, a mere project for a treaty, until the consent of the Senate has been given to it." The English Foreign Minister, Lord Landsdowne, did "not seem to have realized that the Senate could properly continue the negotiations begun by Mr. Hay and Lord Pauncefote by offering new or modified propositions to his Majesty's Government." "What actually happened was that these propositions were offered at a later stage of the negotiation by the other part of the American treaty-making power in the only manner in which it could then be offered. . . ."

Whether Mr. Lodge intended these statements as a full fledged claim to the right to a share in all negotiations may be questioned. If so, as was freely charged at the time, the Secretary of State would indeed serve two masters—or more likely become the errand boy of the Senate. He would need first to find out what Senators wanted, then open negotiations, stopping at each important point in the discussions to secure the approval of Senators while foreign ambassadors waited. This would not be very dignified, and it would bring diplomatic business nearly to a standstill. "Diplomacy is at best, a leisurely affair; this plan would make it a veritable Dead March." [15]

[14] Vol. 31, p. 34.
[15] Editorial, *The Nation*, January 30, 1902, Vol. 74, p. 84.

The Senator was not unwilling, it is true, to claim a wide range of power for the Senate. He maintained the right of the Senate to advise the opening of a negotiation or against its opening, and cited many Presidents as asking the Senate's advice at various stages in the discussions. His chief purpose appeared, however, to be a defense of the Senate's right to propose amendments to treaties. The main concern was that no treaty should be considered as made until the Senate had approved it. Foreign diplomats and others must expect the Senate to make changes as freely as it wished and they must not charge it with bad faith or destructive tactics. A treaty was by no means made when it was signed; this act signified nothing except that one step in the negotiations had been taken. The Senate might be expected to reopen the parley at its pleasure by modifying propositions previously agreed upon or presenting new ones.

Clearly if people would think of Senate changes in treaties as merely a continuance of negotiations criticism of such action must abate.

Moreover, if this concept of negotiations could be established the right of the Senate to take a hand in the earlier stages also would be difficult to contest. Senator Bacon, of Georgia, in a Senate debate a few years later, admitted the right of the President "to suggest a treaty to a foreign power—or receive a suggestion from a foreign power that a certain treaty should be made, or to discuss with a foreign power the subject or the terms of a proposed treaty," in short to start negotiations. This was necessary because "undoubtedly the power to negotiate within that narrow limit is one which can only be exercised by the President, since he alone under this clause can have direct communication with the foreign power. No other officer or authority on the part of the United States can submit a proposed treaty to a foreign power. No other authority can discuss with a foreign power the terms of a proposed treaty, or come to a preliminary agreement with the foreign power regarding the same." [16]

Plainly this statement of the necessities of the case is true, but it applies in its entirety to all later negotiations as well as to the preliminary ones. The Senate cannot really negotiate at any time. It can only have contact with a foreign power through the agency of the President. It ordinarily deals with a treaty in secret session. But whether its deliberations are public or secret, if it questions an article or a phrase it is not in a position to ask for information from the other party; it can suggest no proposition to his ambassador—cannot come to terms with him. [17]

That the Senate may advise the President at any time is undisputed—as may anyone who is in contact with him—but by its very nature advice is not binding on anybody. The Senate can only enforce its advice by threats to withhold its consent and by the very nature of consent it can be withheld or given only when it is asked for. The President may ask the consent of the Senate on a part of a treaty at a time if he desires, or only on the completed document. He is at all times the maker of the treaty, even at the time the Senate is engaged in amending it. That body may lay down any conditions for its consent that it desires; the President may accept them, make them his own and ask the other party to the contract to assent to them before the seals of ratification are set. If the conditions laid down impair too much his purposes in making the treaty [18] he can abandon the whole project, as he has repeatedly done. Then certainly the Senate has done no treaty making. Neither has it when it refuses its consent to a proposed treaty entirely. The power to make treaties remains in the Executive from first to last.

[16] *Congressional Record*, Vol. 40, Pt. 3, p. 2125–26, Feb. 6, 1906.
[17] H. L. Nelson, "The Ratification of Treaties," *Harper's Weekly*, June 22, 1901, Vol. 45, p. 623.
[18] They may advance them.

The actual situation was well described by Senator Spooner, of Wisconsin, in the Senate on January 23, 1906, as follows:

"The words 'advice and consent of the Senate' are used in the Constitution with reference to the Senate's participation in the making of a treaty and are well translated by the word 'ratification' popularly used in this connection. The President negotiates the treaty to begin with. He may employ such agencies as he chooses to negotiate the proposed treaty. He may employ the ambassador, if there be one, or a minister or a chargé d'affaires, or he may use a person in private life whom he thinks by his skill or knowledge of the language or people of the country with which he is about to deal is best fitted to negotiate the treaty. He may issue to the agent chosen by him—and neither Congress nor the Senate has any concern as to whom he chooses—such instructions as seem to him wise. He may vary them from day to day. That is his concern. The Senate has no right to demand that he shall unfold to the world or to it, even in executive session, his instructions or the prospect or progress of the negotiation. I said 'right.' I use that word advisedly in order to illustrate what all men who have studied the subject are willing to concede—that under the Constitution the absolute power of negotiation is in the President and the means of negotiation subject wholly to his will and his judgment." [19]

[19] Continuing, Senator Spooner said: "When he shall have negotiated and sent his proposed treaty to the Senate the jurisdiction of this body attaches and its power begins. It may advise and consent, or it may refuse. And in the exercise of this function it is as independent of the Executive as he is independent of it in the matter of negotiation.

"I do not deny the power of the Senate either in legislative session or in executive session—that is a question of propriety—to pass a resolution expressive of its opinion as to matters of foreign policy. But if it is passed by the Senate or by the House or by both Houses, it is beyond any possible question purely advisory, and not in the slightest degree binding in law or conscience upon the President." *Congressional Record,* Vol. 40, Pt. 2, p. 1418.

The speeches of Senator Spooner and Senator Bacon referred to, are given in convenient form in S. E. Corwin, *The President's Control of Foreign Relations,* Princeton, 1917.

INDIVIDUAL SENATORS AS NEGOTIATORS

If the Senate has no right to a share in the negotiation of treaties, can the same be said of individual Senators? Are they to be debarred altogether from the making of treaties? Rather may not their use by the President as negotiators form a bridge to unite the Senate and the Executive and prevent conflicts when treaties are to be ratified?

When powerful Senate leaders act as negotiators of a treaty they acquire a paternal interest in the document and are likely to defend it vigorously. They are able to do so effectively, moreover, because of the extensive information of the reasons for the terms of the treaty which they can give in an intimate way. Other Senators, too, are likely to look upon the treaty as made by capable, friendly hands and therefore to be attacked with much more restraint. The very fact that a couple of leaders on the Foreign Relations Committee are engaged in defending the treaty instead of criticising it will have an important bearing on the result. What better means of securing harmonious action can be advanced?

In the view of some Presidents this device has offered the easiest and best way to secure the approval of treaties. It has naturally appealed especially to Presidents who have been Senators and who owe their elevation in large part to fellow Senators whom they know well. Thus President McKinley named three members of the Senate Committee on Foreign Relations to the commission of five appointed September 13, 1898, to negotiate a Treaty of Peace with Spain, and he continued the practice later, with the feeling no doubt that a desirable and proper unification of the treaty making power was being achieved.

Criticism in the Senate. It must have given him considerable surprise, therefore, when on two different occasions strong criticism of the practice arose in the Senate, led by

members of his own party. Senator Hale, of Maine, opened
the second of these debates by protesting vigorously that he
did not want any more Senators to appear in the Senate advocating the adoption of treaties which they themselves had
negotiated as representatives of the Administration. Senator
Tillman, of South Carolina, followed him to recall the almost
unanimous vote to prohibit the practice at the time Senators
Cullom and Morgan were sent to Hawaii, a vote rescinded
to prevent reflection on the Senators concerned, and proposed new legislation to forbid it. Senator Foraker, of Ohio,
did not like the practice. He thought the Senate had a right
to the services of Senators in that body, but felt the debate
would effect the purpose in view without a formal vote.
He could not but feel that the President might sometimes
do well to appoint a Senator. Senator Aldrich, of Rhode
Island, made similar remarks and Senator Platt, of Connecticut, thought no restrictions should be laid on the practice
at all. Senator Bacon, of Georgia, then quoted the constitution to show that such an appointment was illegal and
pointed out that the only escape was to rule that a negotiator was not an officer. Senator Hoar of Massachusetts
closed the debate by reviewing the case at length.[20]

Senator Hoar's Protest. Later, in his autobiography, Senator Hoar again condemned the custom. In his judgment the
meaning of Article I, Section 6, of the Constitution was
clear.[21] At the time the Senate had refused to take any ac-

---

[20] February 26, 1903. *Congressional Record*, Vol. 36, Pt. 3, p. 2695, ff.
[21] The Constitution provides, in Article I, Sec. 6: "No Senator or
Representative shall, during the time for which he was elected, be appointed to any civil office under the authority of the United States, which
shall have been created, or the emoluments whereof shall have been increased, during such time; and no person holding any office under the
United States shall be a member of either House during his continuance
in office."
Senator Hoar thought it "beyond dispute that the intention of that
provision was to protect the members of the legislative branch of the
Government from Executive influence. The legislator was not to be
induced to create a civil office, or to increase its emoluments, at the
request of the Executive, in the hope that he might be appointed. He
was to preserve his independence of Executive influence and to approach

tion on the appointment of Cullom and Morgan to the Hawaiian Mission an eminent member had pertinently asked: "If these gentlemen are to be officers, how can the President appoint them under the Constitution, the office being created during their term? Or, how can they hold office and still keep their seats in this body? If, on the other hand, they are not officers, under what Constitutional provision does the President ask the advice and consent of the Senate to their appointment?" [22]

The suggestion that Senators so appointed were not officers seemed to him the merest cavil.

"They exercise an authority, and are clothed with a dignity equal to that of the highest and most important diplomatic officer, and far superior to that of most of the civil officers of the Country. To say that the President cannot appoint a Senator or Representative postmaster in a country village, where perhaps no other person can be found to do the duties, because that would put an improper temptation in the way of the legislator to induce him to become the tool of the Executive will, and then permit the President to send him abroad; to enable him to maintain the distinction and enjoy the pleasure of a season at a foreign capital as the representative of the United States, with all expenses paid, and a large compensation added, determined solely by the Executive will; and to hold that the framers of the Constitution would for a moment have tolerated that, seems to me utterly preposterous.

"Besides, it places the Senator so selected in a position where he cannot properly perform his duties as a Senator. He is bound to meet his associates at the great National Council Board as an equal, to hear their reasons as well as to impart his own. How can he discharge that duty, if he has already not only formed an opinion, but acted upon the

all questions in which he might have to deal with matters which concern the Executive power, or Executive action, absolutely free from any bias." Geo. F. Hoar, *The Autobiography of Seventy Years*, N. Y., 1903, Vol. II, p. 49.
[22] Ibid., 50.

matter under the control and direction of another department
of the Government? . . . If that practice continue, it will
go far, in my judgment, to destroy the independence and
dignity of the Senate." [23]

After considerable discussion and the introduction of
several bills and resolutions to prohibit such appointments in
the future the matter was finally referred to the Judiciary
Committee of which Mr. Hoar was a member. It transpired,
however, that three members of that Committee had been
already appointed on the Alaskan Boundary Commission.
One of them had accepted the appointment without reflection and was satisfied the practice was wrong, but the Committee disliked exceedingly to make a report which might
reflect on its members, so Senator Hoar was instructed to
call upon President McKinley and tell him the Committee
hoped the practice would not be continued. He did so,
and writes of the interview that the President "said he was
aware of the objections; that he had come to feel the evil
very strongly; and while he did not say in terms that he
would not make another appointment of the kind, he con-
veyed to me, as I am very sure he intended to do, the assurance that it would not occur again." At the same time the
President explained that it was little understood "how few
people there were in this country, out of the Senate and
House of Representatives, qualified for important diplomatic
service." [24]

[23] Hoar, *Autobiography of Seventy Years*, 47-50. In describing the
extent to which the practice had gone Senator Hoar said:
"The President has repeatedly, within the last six years, appointed
members of the Senate and House to be Commissioners to negotiate and
conclude, as far as can be done by diplomatic agencies, treaties and other
arrangements with foreign Governments, of the gravest importance.
These include the arrangements of a standard of value by International
agreement; making the treaty of Peace, at the end of the war with
Spain; arranging a treaty of Commerce between the United States and
Great Britain; making a Treaty to settle the Behring Sea controversy;
and now more lately to establish the boundary line between Canada and
Alaska." p. 49.
[24] Ibid., 50. Senator Hoar thought that sooner or later some emphatic

The service of a Senator as a negotiator puts him in an equivocal position, to say the least, as was pointed out again in 1920 by Ex-Governor McCall of Massachusetts. A Senator as negotiator receives his instructions from the Executive, instructions which probably by no means coincide in all details with his own views. Then afterward, in the exercise of his independent office as a Senator he is called upon to pass upon his work done while acting as an agent of the Executive, and since it is hardly thinkable that he would fail to approve what he had already solemnly executed, he in effect exercises his function as Senator as an instrument of the President. "An amiable executive, or one who was more concerned to get his treaties ratified than to perform his own independent constitutional function, might view such a practice with complacency; but it is none the less an abuse, and it deprives the country of that safeguard, of vast importance, which comes from the independent action of two branches of the government." [25]

The Harding Revival. From a desire to have negotiators undivided in their allegiance, or for other reasons, McKinley's successors in the Presidency did not appoint Senators to conduct major negotiations until in 1921 President Harding revived the custom in appointing Senators Lodge and Underwood as delegates to the Washington Arms Limitation Conference.

After intimate observation in the Senate of what happened to the Treaty of Versailles when President and Senate were at odds, he cannot perhaps be severely blamed for desiring to recognize that body signally, or purchase its good will, in behalf of the Conference treaties. He could well reason that the end justified the means whether you construe

---

action would be taken to stop such appointments though he recognized that there would always be men in either branch who desire such honorable employment and others certain to follow wherever the President might lead. p. 48.

[26] S. W. McCall, "Again the Senate," *Atlantic Monthly,* September, 1920, p. 399.

the means as an insidious attack upon the integrity and independence of the Senate or as public surrender to its dominance. The success of the Conference would mean the saving of many sorely needed millions to each of the great naval powers besides removing dangerous rivalry among them and displacing suspicion and distrust in the Orient and around the world. By the side of these great gains the objections to the appointment of Senators as negotiators may well have appeared to be worth incurring.

The same conclusion may be reached often in the future. If the approval of important treaties by the Senate can be secured in no other way there is much to be said for the practice in spite of its apparent illegality. If, on the other hand, the President should find himself increasingly unable to use talented and highly qualified men outside the Senate in negotiating weighty treaties the country might well be deprived of services which it should have.

CHAPTER III

THE SENATE'S ASSERTION OF A RIGHT TO PROPOSE AMENDMENTS

THE practical difficulty of its complete isolation under the constitution from any contact with foreign powers made it impossible for the Senate to establish a right to take part directly in the negotiation of treaties. The makers of the Constitution, as we have seen, undoubtedly intended that the Senate should act as a council to the President in framing proposed treaties, but after that experiment proved a failure the Senate found no feasible method of sharing in the negotiations. The President had in his hands the explicit power "to make treaties" and the Senate found no new way of making the limiting clause "by and with the advice and consent of the Senate" mean anything in advance of the time when the remainder of the limitation, "provided two thirds of the Senators present concur," became effective.

The Senators assumed from the very beginning, however, that a treaty was not made until two thirds of them had formally approved it and that any changes they saw fit to make in the negotiated document were in order.[1] Amending is a legislative habit and it would be natural for any Senator to assume that if a provision of the treaty did not suit him the thing to do was to propose an amendment. During the consideration of the treaty with the Southern Indians on August 24, 1789, described above, Senator Maclay moved to

[1] For the purpose of amending a treaty the requirement of a bare majority only of the Senators present was adopted.

33

have the words "in failure thereof by the United States" struck out. The words objected to bound the United States to pay a stipulated purchase price in case the State of Georgia did not, and the arguments against the stipulation were so plain to Mr. Maclay that he thought he "need not set them down" in his Journal. In spite of the clarity of his case the proposed amendment was not seconded, although three Senators had spoken on the same side with him. "A shame-facedness, or I know not what, flowing from the presence of the President, kept everybody silent."[2]

Since President Washington never returned to seek the "advice and consent" of the Senate about treaties his presence did not thereafter deter the Senators from supporting amendments. The removal of the executive from treaty deliberations made it easy to follow the ordinary legislative process.

Yet the first alteration of an important treaty was made with some hesitation. The twelfth article of the famous Jay Treaty of 1794 was "suspended," in part, as a means of preventing outright rejection of the whole treaty.[3] After this conditional approval was accepted by both the President and a foreign power it was easier to resort to the same expedient in the future when strong objection arose to a provision in a treaty, and from such cases it was easy to go on to the moving and passage of proposed amendments designed not to prevent rejection of the whole treaty, but simply to improve it a little as it happened to appear defective to Senators.

Minor Amendments Usually Accepted. Thus the Senate approved a treaty with Bavaria on March 15, 1845, after striking out from the third article the words "real and." A treaty with the same country was approved July 12, 1854,

[2] Beard, *The Journal of William Maclay,* 129.
[3] The Senate acted on June 24, 1795. *Senate Executive Journal,* I, 186. *The American Secretaries of State and Their Diplomacy* (Bemis Editor), N. Y., 1927, Vol. II, p. 172.

after changing "nine" to "fifteen" in article 6.[4] Similarly the Behring Sea Arbitration Treaty with Great Britain was approved March 29, 1892, with a request that the arbitrators be acquainted with English, and a Congo treaty was approved January 24, 1891, after taking the words "His Excellency" from the title of the President of the United States.[5] Two similar treaties with Guatemala and Nicaragua were altered March 31, 1871, by striking out "things and" and changing "on" to "or," while a Belgian treaty was amended June 15, 1880, by leaving out the word "alone" and an extradition treaty with Great Britain, February 18, 1890, by inserting "voluntary" before "manslaughter." [6] Many other treaties have been approved conditionally in like fashion.

Changes like these are likely to be accepted by both the President and the other party to the treaty as not worth arguing about or at least not worth jeopardizing the larger aims of the treaty on account of them. Occasionally, however, even the change of one word has caused the failure of a treaty. President Roosevelt dropped nine general arbitration treaties signed with European powers in 1904 because he felt that the substitution by the Senate of the word "treaty" for "agreement" made the treaties useless.[7] A few years later, President Taft pocketed arbitration conventions with England and France because of more extensive Senate changes.[8]

[4] Senate Executive Journal, Vol. 6, p. 447; Vol. 9, p. 353.
[5] Ibid., Vol. 20, p. 197; Vol. 28, p. 121.
[6] Ibid., Vol. 18, p. 51; Vol. 22, p. 372; Vol. 27, p. 470.
[7] S. B. Crandall, Treaties, Their Making and Enforcement (2nd ed.), Washington, D. C., 1916, p. 98.
[8] W. H. Taft, The Presidency, N. Y., 1916, p. 102.
Other instances of amended treaties dropped by the President could be cited. The Senate amended a commercial treaty with Venezuela to such an extent, on March 10, 1857, that President Buchanan decided to negotiate an entirely new treaty instead.

On the other hand, the Executive has often considered the device a convenient arrangement. Presidents from Washington down to Roosevelt have more than a dozen times recommended amendments at the time treaties were sent to the Senate. Crandall, Treaties, pp. 95-98.

Important Changes Likely to Prevent Ratification.   The acceptance by the other powers of minor amendments to their treaties as originally agreed upon perhaps made it somewhat easier to concede more important advantages when claimed in a proposed amendment.   The Senate is likely to make substantial new claims or to withdraw concessions already given by the Executive as the price of its agreement and these terms are sometimes accepted by the foreign power. For example, a proposed treaty with China was amended, July 24, 1867, by rewriting Article 8 on the subject of educational privileges in the two countries in a way which perhaps gave a clearer guarantee to our schools in China, and a treaty with Venezuela was altered, June 26, 1860, by striking out Article 3 which gave up all American claims to Aves Island.[9]   Somewhat later a reciprocity treaty with Hawaii was successfully amended, March 18, 1875, to prevent the alienation of any Hawaiian harbors and a similar treaty was modified on January 20, 1887, to get for us the use of Pearl Harbor.   An article added to a commercial treaty with Persia, March 11, 1852, guaranteed most favored nation treatment to the citizens of both countries.[10]

Weak nations will probably accept additional terms prescribed by the Senate in this manner, and strong ones may also agree under a feeling that the need for the remainder of the treaty justifies them in yielding.   In one case out of three, however, the proposal of amendments to a treaty in the Senate leads to the failure either of the President or of the foreign power to complete ratification.   Up to the opening of the 70th Congress, in 1928, the Senate had altered the terms of 146 treaties by amendment or reservation out of a probable total of 900 treaties approved by it.   Of the 146 treaties modified by the Senate, 48 were dropped by the President or rejected abroad.   The number of treaties

[9] *Senate Executive Journal,* Vol. 16, p. 356; Vol. 11, p. 222.
[10] Ibid., Vol. 20, p. 42; Vol. 25, p. 709; Vol. 8, p. 373.

changed in the Senate has naturally increased in recent years with the greater volume of treaties made necessary by increasing international contacts. From 1794 to 1901 there were 88 treaties approved conditionally, of which number 27, or 30%, failed to be accepted. The number approved with changes from 1901 to 1928 was 58, of which 21, or 38%, failed.[11] The alteration of treaties in the Senate seems to be increasing both extensively and intensively. The Senate not only proposes more changes in treaties but kills a larger percentage in the process.

The Mexican Purchase Treaty Made in the Senate. The proposed treaty most completely re-written in the Senate, the Gadsden Purchase Treaty of 1853, was, however, ratified. In that year President Pierce sent James Gadsden to Mexico to secure a release from our expensive promise made in the Mexican Treaty of Peace of 1848 to protect Mexico against incursions from our newly acquired Indians. He was also to secure additional territory for a transcontinental railroad and compose other serious disputes. The negotiation was complicated by the activities of two rival groups of American promoters who held grants from Mexico of rights to build a railway across the Mexican isthmus and

[11] The figures quoted are taken from a list of amended treaties compiled by the Foreign Policy Association, 18 E. 41st St., N. Y., and published in its *Information Service*, Vol. IV, No. 16, October 12, 1928. It was based upon the Holt, Lodge and Tansil lists of amended treaties and checked with Malloy's *Treaties, Conventions, Etc., Between the United States and Other Powers.* The treaties amended since 1901, the present terminal date of the *Senate Executive Journal*, were listed with the assistance of the Executive Clerk of the Senate from Senate records of treaties from which the injunction of secrecy has been removed. Few treaties are still held under this injunction so the list is probably quite complete. It is difficult to compile a list which will be wholly accurate. Prof. Tansil has shown that Senator Lodge's list of 68 treaties amended is too long by some eleven treaties. See H. C. Lodge, *Scribner's Magazine*, January, 1902, pp. 42–3; C. C. Tansil, "The Treaty Making Powers of the Senate," *American Journal of International Law*, 1924, Vol. 18, pp. 477–81.

The estimate that 900 treaties have been approved by the Senate is based upon the fact that Malloy's compilation contains approximately 700 treaties made up to 1909. On this basis the Senate has approved five out of every six treaties laid before it without change.

the treaty resulting was very unsatisfactory to President Pierce who recommended its extensive amendment by the Senate. [12]

That body accepted the amendments advised by the President and evolved other changes of its own in a bitter six weeks battle which finally ended in ratifying only a shadow of the Gadsden Treaty.[13] Article 1 describing the territory to be purchased was entirely recast and the size of the cession greatly reduced. Article 2, which was a compromise on the question of Indian incursions, was changed so as to relieve the United States of all responsibility under Article 11 of the Mexican Treaty of Peace. Article 3 as negotiated gave $15,000,000 to Mexico for the ceded territory and in a lengthy paragraph extinguished all claims of the citizens of each country against the other; the Senate struck out the whole article and wrote instead merely that $10,000,000 should be paid. Article 4 provided a claims commission to be set up by the United States to hear claims of its citizens against Mexico, assumed in Article 3, and pay them up to a limit of $5,000,000; the Senate struck out the article entirely. The next three articles were left intact, but the Senate eliminated Article 8 which bound each country to prevent revolutionary movements against the other from hatching in Its territory so far as possible, and if not prevented, to use its military and naval forces, when requested, to capture the filibusterers on the high seas, captives in all cases to be judged and punished by the laws of the captors.

Article 9 was changed to Article 7 and a lengthy and entirely new Article 8 was inserted giving to the United States all the "stable benefits" of the proposed Mexican railway across the Isthmus of Tehuantepec. No charges were to be higher for the United States than for other countries, no interest in the railroad or its revenue was ever to be trans-

[12] P. N. Garber, *The Gadsden Treaty*, Philadelphia, 1923, p. 116.
[13] Ibid., Chapter 5.

ferred to a foreign government, no customs duties or other charges by the Government of Mexico were to be levied on the property of the Government of the United States or of its citizens while crossing, and no passports were to be required for transit only. Mexico was to be further bound to open an additional port of entry on the Atlantic coast and to make arrangements later for the prompt transit of United States troops and munitions. Finally the United States was to have the right to protect the railroad "as it shall judge wise to it when it may feel sanctioned and warranted by the public or international law." In Article 9 the dates of ratification only were changed. [14]

What the Senate did in fact was to make a new treaty and submit it to the President and to the Mexican Government for their acceptance or rejection. Both accepted, the latter because it feared war and badly needed the funds assured it, but Mexican bitterness against the United States was further intensified by the attempt at a settlement thus carried through. [15]

This result suggests the grave objection to the Senate's practice of amending treaties—that any considerable change in the terms of a treaty as agreed upon strikes the other party as an unjustified ultimatum. When for example, the United States through the President negotiates a treaty with Holland, the parties meet as equals, each arguing for certain provisions and accepting others in return for them, or after persuasion during discussion. The bargain is eventually satisfactory enough to both parties that it is concluded and signed, with the proviso that it is to become effective if ratified by both parties within a specified period. [16] Holland has almost certainly been warned that the Senate must

---

[14] *Senate Executive Journal*, Vol. 9, p. 312-15.
[15] Garber, *The Gadsden Treaty*, 147.
[16] This waiting period was originally designed to allow each home government to examine the acts of its agent and see if he had exceeded his instructions. Probably it is coming more and more to be a period during which the consequences may be further weighed.

pass upon the treaty and yet when in doing so, it strikes out a vital clause and especially if it adds a new proposition, the Dutch government is likely to take the attitude that the onus of accepting or rejecting a changed draft is improperly placed on it without any opportunity being given to state and argue the merits of both sides of the question. [17]

Refusal of the Other Party to Permit Amendment. This was the objection made by Lord Landsdowne in his note of February 22, 1901, with reference to the Hay-Pauncefote treaty to which amendments were proposed by the Senate in December, 1900. The purpose of this treaty on our part had been to secure the cancellation of Great Britain's right, guaranteed by the Clayton-Bulwer Treaty of 1850, to participate in any canal joining the Atlantic and Pacific in Central America. The Treaty apparently did this successfully except that it did not assert the right to fortify the canal, and since the Clayton-Bulwer treaty forbade fortification the Senate proceeded to propose the abrogation of that treaty by the simple expedient of inserting after mention of it the words "hereby superseded."

When the American Government communicated that action to Lord Landsdowne he replied that "The Clayton-Bulwer treaty is an international contract of unquestioned validity, a contract, which, according to well-established international usage, ought not to be abrogated or modified save with the consent of both the parties to the contract. His Majesty's Government find themselves confronted with a proposal communicated to them by the United States Government without any previous attempt to ascertain their views, for the abrogation of the Clayton-Bulwer treaty." [18] He therefore refused to ratify the treaty, though he was not strongly opposed to abrogating the Clayton-Bulwer treaty,

---

[17] W. W. Willoughby, *Constitutional Law of the United States*, N. Y., 1910, Vol. I, p. 464.
[18] Ibid., 465.

and thereby assenting to the fortification of the canal, for he suggested a new treaty, which was signed on November 18, 1901, specifically granting the points insisted upon by the Senate. [19]

The British Government had become used to having treaties changed by the Senate many years before, but it had not grown to like the practice through familiarity with it. In 1824, it had presented its views on the subject quite plainly in refusing to accept a convention for the suppression of the slave trade after it had been materially modified by the Senate. On that occasion the British Foreign Minister, Mr. George Canning, wrote to Mr. Rush, the American Minister, that "a treaty of which the basis was laid in propositions framed by the American Government was considered here as so little likely to be made a subject of renewed discussion in America that not a moment was lost in ratifying it, on the part of his Majesty; and his Majesty's ratification was ready to be exchanged against that of the United States when the treaty came back; not as it had been sent to America, but with material variations; variations not confined to those stipulations or parts of stipulations which had been engrafted upon the original project, but extending to that part of the project itself which had passed unchanged through the negotiations."

"The knowledge," he continued, "that the Constitution of the United States renders all their diplomatic compacts liable to this sort of revision undoubtedly precludes the possibility of taking exception at any particular instance in which that revision is exercised; but the repetition of such instances does not serve to reconcile to the practice the feelings of the other contracting party whose solemn ratification is thus rendered of no avail, and whose concessions in negotiation having been made (as all such concessions must be understood to be made) conditionally, are thus accepted as positive and ab-

[19] C. E. Hill, *Leading American Treaties*, N. Y., 1922, p. 357.

solute, while what may have been the stipulated price of those concessions is withdrawn." [20]

A reply to this tart note was made by Henry Clay, Secretary of State, in which he refused to admit "that any just cause of complaint can arise out of the rejection by one party of a treaty which the other has previously ratified. When such a case occurs, it only proves that the consent of both, according to the constitutional precautions which have been provided for manifesting that consent, is wanting to make the treaty valid. One must necessarily precede the other in the act of ratification; and if, after a treaty be ratified by one party, a ratification of it be withheld by the other, it merely shows that one is, and the other is not, willing to come under the obligations of the proposed treaty." [21]

The most recent case of refusal to permit alteration by the Senate appears to be the case of the Halibut Fisheries Treaty with Canada in 1923. This was the first treaty ever concluded by a Canadian commissioner alone, without the signature of a British ambassador, and the Canadians naturally took a great deal of pride in it as an evidence of their arrival at full nationhood. They felt, therefore, that the Senate entirely misunderstood the situation when it attached an amendment to the treaty in the form of a reservation saying "that none of the nationals . . . of any other part of Great Britain shall engage in halibut fishing contrary to any of the provisions of the treaty." The Canadian Government accordingly refused to accept the reservation, though it proceeded to enact legislation to give the assurance desired by Senator Jones, of Washington, who had moved the reservation. The treaty was then submitted to the Senate again in its original form, and after due consideration it consented to ratification without reservation. [22]

[20] *American State Papers, Foreign Affairs,* Vol. 5, p. 365.
[21] Ibid., 783.
[22] N. A. M. Mackenzie, "The Treaty Making Power in Canada," *American Journal of International Law,* 1925, Vol. 19, p. 498.

The Government of the Netherlands has, on two widely separated occasions refused to ratify proposed treaties amended by the Senate on the simple ground that its procedure did not allow such alteration. Extradition treaties signed May 29, 1875, and November 24, 1903, failed for this reason. In both cases new treaties were negotiated and submitted to the Senate. [23]

If an attitude similar to that of Holland were taken by all nations the Senate would practically lose its power to qualify proposed treaties since amendment would be tantamount to killing the treaty. That in the majority of cases the other signatories have accepted proposed Senate amendments does not seem sufficient justification for the continuance of a practice which is regarded abroad as both irritating and unfair.

The proposing of amendments in the Senate is deeply grounded in custom and it would be difficult to attack in law. Article II, Section 2, of the Constitution says: "He shall have power, by and with the advice and consent of the Senate, to make treaties, provided two thirds of the Senators present concur; and he shall nominate and, by and with the advice and consent of the Senate, shall appoint ambassadors, —" From this phraseology almost any action which the Senate might take on treaties may be justified. [24] This fact should not, however, bar serious consideration of the effects of the practice upon our international relations.

[23] Crandall, *Treaties, Their Making and Enforcement*, p. 81. The Senate has been especially active in amending extradition treaties. In one instance, however, when urged by President Polk to revise an extradition treaty with Prussia, signed January 29, 1845, it was too busy to do so. The President after waiting a couple of years decided that the Senate thought even less of the treaty than he did and negotiated a new one that suited him better. He was not a little astonished, therefore, when the Senate returned the first treaty to him more than three years after its conclusion, duly approved without amendment. Needless to say he did not ratify it. *Sen. Exec. Jour.*, Vol. VII, pp. 7, 433, 462.

[24] See the argument to the contrary by B. M. Thompson, "The Power of the Senate to Amend a Treaty," *Michigan Law Review*, April, 1905, Vol. III, pp. 432–41.

Shall We Have Senatorial Courtesy for Treaties? The record of the Senate indicates that something amounting almost to a senatorial courtesy for treaty making is developing. It is, of course, well known that however clearly the Constitution may have given the power of making appointments to office to the President alone, the Senate has seized a very large share of that power for itself by the simple agreement not to confirm appointments, as a rule, unless the Senators of the ruling party in whose state the official will work are willing. While this custom constitutes a serious limitation on the President's power it is in large measure justified by the fact that the President must turn over a major part of the great burden of selecting thousands of federal employees to some one, and it may be maintained that no official is better fitted to fill the positions local to his state than the Senator of that state. Perhaps the Civil Service Commission should receive this delegation of power more largely than the Senators, but there are extenuating circumstances for a senatorial courtesy on appointments that would not apply to a senatorial courtesy on treaty making.

The tendency of such a new "courtesy" to develop is strongest when commercial or reciprocity treaties are being considered. Then Senators begin to insist that the treaty be amended to make it acceptable to certain towns, trades, or local industries in their states and if the Senate listens to one such plea it probably must accept many of them. "Judging from the course taken in the Senate during the last few years, the time will come, if the hour has not already struck, when no reciprocity treaty can be negotiated by the President which will be concurred in by the Senate before amendments have thoroughly impregnated it with the smell of codfish or some other pungent local odor." [25]

It will not be contended that any treaty ought to be

---

[25] B. M. Thompson, "The Power of the Senate to Amend a Treaty," *Michigan Law Review*, 1905, Vol. III, p. 438.

adopted which adversely affects the interests of large blocks of people or regions of the country. If such is the case the Senate should veto the treaty. But probably no commercial treaty could be made without a good many comparatively minor groups objecting to something in it, and the interests of the country at large should certainly not be sacrificed or imperilled by an attempt to please everybody who may think his interests adversely affected. It cannot be done without moving plainly in the direction of requiring unanimous consent, or giving each Senator a free veto over commercial treaties, and if over reciprocity treaties why not over others? The tendency of individual Senators to demand conditions whenever a peace or arbitration treaty comes up is as clearly marked.

The President is Not Irresponsible as a Negotiator. Can the Senate, then, rightfully do nothing except give a perfunctory "yea" or "nay" to any treaty project submitted to it? Must the supreme law of the land be evolved and shaped "alone in the brain of the President, alone in his suggestion and deliberation, and alone in his judgment?" [26] Stated thus the need for remedial or surgical treatment of treaties in the Senate seems likely to be urgent at any time. But is it? The President is the responsible officer of all the people. In the main he works through the Cabinet, the State Department and the diplomatic officers. He is advised by all these and by the leaders of his party in Congress and elsewhere, not to mention the press and his personal advisors, and is forced to remember at all stages of making a treaty that the draft must stand the scrutiny of his political foes in the Senate who usually have the votes to defeat it and certainly the will to pin upon him any responsibility for errors discoverable in it.

[26] As phrased by Senator Bacon in the debates quoted above, *Congressional Record*, Vol. 40, Pt. 3, p. 2126.

The Senate's Right to Advise is an Important Check. But if the Senate has no power except to withhold consent, what becomes of its right to advise? Is it worth no more than the President's right to advise Congress about legislation? There seems no present reason why it should be. The Constitutional Convention clearly intended the Senate to act as a council in treaty making, a relation, which, as we have seen, never effectively came into being. The picture the Convention had in mind when it wrote "by and with the advice and consent of the Senate" dissolved on the first exposure. The concept of the Senate advising and consenting to the terms of a treaty proposed to them by the President in person, or his direct representative, was based upon the ancient English institution, the King (or the Governor) in Council. It involved no dispute over the meaning of advice and consent; the two terms referred to one act, not two, the act of giving final shape to measures through council discussion. With the failure of this method in our experience the one function was split into two by the practical necessities—the right to advise and the power to consent, each exercised in new ways and at different times.

In this separation the advice element of the original function did not entirely perish. The general obligation to make use of the advice of the Senate remained. New means of securing this advice had to be invented and a very effective means of compelling their use was at hand, that is, the power finally to withhold consent. This is no mean power. It compels the Executive to heed the probable views of Senators and to seek to ascertain them either by formal request, by conferring with influential individual Senators or by consultation with the Foreign Affairs Committee. The ever present threat of a Senate veto does generally compel the President to shape important treaties with the views of that body in mind, just as the threat of a Presidential veto of laws often forces their modification to suit his views.

Undesirable Treaties Should Be Rejected. When the Senate rewrites a treaty, and if it can change one provision it can change any number, it exceeds both its right to influence and its power to check and takes the power to make treaties out of the hands of the President. There appears to be no logical reason for such action. It is not necessary to make the power of the Senate over treaties dignified and important. There is no reason why the approval of a treaty need be perfunctory any more than the signing of bills by the President is, and the Senate veto once given is even more deadly and final than that of the Executive. If the treaty, due to the failure of the President to seek or heed advice, or for any other reason, is in the opinion of the Senate a bad treaty it should be rejected outright, leaving the President free to attempt to meet the views of the Senate in a new treaty, if he sees fit, just as Congress is free to frame a new law to satisfy the judgment of the Supreme Court or the veto objections of the President if in either case it appears feasible to do so.

The practice of proposing amendments to treaties is a device for confusing and escaping responsibility. The best talent and skill that the country affords may have labored for weeks in framing a treaty which secures important concessions and advantages to us, and the President may be ready to stake his reputation on it, but when it reaches the Senate the Foreign Affairs Committee is free to offer any amendment designed to make the treaty unpalatable to the President or to the foreign power or to secure some credit for a party. Other amendments honestly intended to remedy a defect, or an omission, are put forward, and still others are likely to be offered by individuals whose chief desire is "to send their names ringing down the grooves of time affixed to a vital amendment of a historic treaty." [27] The result has

[27] H. L. Nelson, "The Ratification of Treaties," *Harper's Weekly,* June 22, 1901, Vol. 45, p. 623.

been that the President frequently would have preferred an outright rejection to having his work imperilled or nullified by proposed Senate amendments.

The results of the amendment of treaties in the Senate down to 1900 were not very disastrous, nor very impressive. Since that date proposed Senate amendments to treaties, particularly those negotiated for the peaceable settlement of international disputes, have kept us quite perpetually at odds or out of touch with our international neighbors. Mr. Roosevelt's arbitration treaties were changed by the Senate until he dropped them in disgust; Mr. Taft's patient effort to make an advance in arbitration was nullified by Senate changes so completely that he also abandoned one of the chief measures of his administration. Mr. Wilson's League of Nations was so qualified by the Senate that he would not accept the result and the Harding-Hughes proposal of entry into the World Court was so altered that it was unacceptable to the members of that body and abandoned by President Coolidge. [28] The recent passage of the Multilateral Anti-War Treaty without alteration or addition suggests, however, that it is possible for the Senate to express its objections and reservations in an informal declaration. [29] This method at least permits the treaty to be tried out and adds a means of interpreting it which, though not legally binding, will have some weight. Why should this device not be more generally used when the imperfections almost certain to exist in any treaty, from the standpoint of absolute national self interest, are not serious enough to justify outright rejection?

Some real errors in treaties have been undoubtedly corrected by the Senate and material advantages obtained on different occasions as a result of Senate demands, but it is at

---

[28] Mr. Coolidge was apparently more impatient with the Powers than he was with the Senate. See his Armistice Day Address, November 11, 1926. He at length expressed a willingness, however, on November 25, 1928, to reopen negotiations with them. N. Y. *Times*, Nov. 26, 1928.

[29] *Congressional Record*, January 15, 1929, p. 1783.

least a question whether the good results obtained could not have been achieved by simple rejection of some of the treaties with reasons stated and without the internal and international friction which Senate amendments have increasingly caused. It may be that the President and the foreign state involved would not have enjoyed re-negotiation of a treaty any more than they have the acceptance of unpalatable Senate amendments, but the feeling which comes from having to approve a distasteful rider would have been less acute at least.

The adoption of this policy would eliminate the Senatorial objections of a minor character, the bulk in fact, with attendant saving of the valuable time necessary to present, discuss, and vote upon them, and with a gain rather than loss of dignity to the Senate. The incentive of the negotiators to meet the probable or stated objections of the Senate during negotiation would also be sharpened.

CHAPTER IV

TREATIES REJECTED BY THE SENATE

THE power to alter treaties laid before it has often been used by the Senate to secure desirable changes; in many other cases the results have been trivial; in still others positive harm to carefully thought out agreements has been done. The results of the Senate's activity in this respect have, however, not been quantitatively large. As noted in the preceding chapter, the Senate has amended about one hundred and fifty treaties or sixteen per cent of the total number submitted to it. Five-sixths of all treaties laid before it have been approved unconditionally.

The proportion of treaties which the Senate has refused to approve in any manner whatever is still smaller. Search of the *Senate Executive Journal* and other records shows only thirty treaties as failing altogether. Of these, ten failed to come to a final vote and twenty were definitely rejected by a failure to command the two-thirds majority. Seven had a majority but not two-thirds. The treaties defeated comprise a very small per cent of those considered. The failure of a single important treaty, however, may determine the course of our foreign relations for many years. It is still, therefore, of importance to examine the vetoes which the Senate has put upon proposed treaties. Have they had good results or bad? In particular has the operation of the two-thirds rule been an advantage or a disadvantage?

The First Rejection

The earliest case of outright rejection of a treaty occurred in 1825 when a convention with the Republic of Colombia for the suppression of the slave trade was rejected by a vote of 40 to 0. [1]

The British Treaty of 1824. Of far greater importance than the rejection of the Colombian treaty, however, and leading directly to it, was the failure of the treaty of 1824 with England for the same purpose, a failure due to Senate amendment rather than outright refusal to ratify, but so important as to justify detailed consideration in any list of treaties killed by Senate action. This treaty was the result of a sustained agitation against the slave trade expressed especially in the House of Representatives. House committees had urged action four times between 1817 and 1822; a law of May 15, 1820, had declared slave trading piracy, punishable by death; and a House resolution of February 28, 1823, had requested the President to enter into negotiations with the maritime powers of Europe with the object of denouncing the slave trade as piracy.[2]

At the same time an even stronger movement against the slave trade was in progress in England. In 1814–15, when the settlements following the Napoleonic wars were being made, the English public had been so thoroughly aroused that in the thirty-four days beginning June 27, 1814, some 772 petitions demanding the general suppression of the slave trade, and bearing nearly a million signatures, were presented at the House of Commons. Even today, with all our knowledge of propaganda methods, that would be considered a remarkable expression of sentiment. At that time, when the population of Great Britain numbered only

[1] *Senate Executive Journal,* Vol. III, p. 446.
[2] *Revised Statutes of the United States,* Second Edition, Washington, 1878, p. 1042; J. B. Moore, *Digest of International Law,* Vol. II, p. 922.

thirteen millions, it measured a feeling of the British people which was one of the mysteries of the time hardly understood by themselves and widely misunderstood abroad. [3]

With opinion against the slave trade very strong in both countries it nevertheless proved impossible for decades to secure any effective cooperation between them to extirpate the slave trade.   The difficulty came in arranging for the mutual right of search which was necessary to the suppression of the traffic.   The activity of the British Navy in searching American ships during its great struggle with France was so keenly remembered on this side that the American Government resisted granting the right of search until 1823.   After the almost unanimous House resolution of that year, John Quincy Adams, Secretary of State, at length sent a draft of a treaty to England in which he conceded the mutual right of search on condition that the captor be held to strict accountability for his conduct and that the alleged slavers be returned to their own country for trial.   These stipulations were adopted by England with the added agreement that citizens of either country captured under the flag of a third power should be sent home for trial. [4]

The convention thus agreed upon was submitted to the Senate April 30, 1824.   Mr. Adams thought it differed only in a few unimportant particulars from his own original draft.   He was therefore greatly mortified by unexpected opposition to it in the Senate.   President Monroe was likewise "much astonished" at the prospect of its failure. [5] He had hoped in his annual message "that this odious and criminal practice will be promptly and entirely suppressed." [6]

Opposed in the Senate. The causes of the opposition in the

[3] F. J. Klingbery, *The Anti-Slavery Movement in England,* Yale Historical Studies, New Haven, 1926, p. 146.
[4] *American State Papers, Foreign Affairs,* Vol. V, pp. 333–7.
[5] J. Q. Adams, *Memoirs,* Vol. VI, pp. 311, 330, 338.
[6] *The Writings of James Monroe* (Hamilton Edition), N. Y., 1903, Vol. VI, p. 329.

Senate were several. Probably the principal one was the
sore matter of visit and search. British naval strength was
so great that most of the searching under the treaty was
likely to be done by English warships. Might they not
interfere with our legitimate commerce with Latin America?
The rivalry with English trade after the war and the overthrow of Spanish rule in America was keen. Stoppage and
search might seriously hamper American competition if
delay only resulted.. Moreover, the fact that first news of the
treaty came from England, when the English Foreign Minister asked Parliament to pass the law requested by the
United States making the slave trade piracy, created an impression of English initiative and of surrender on our part
which the facts did not really justify.

The treaty came before the Senate, also, when the four
cornered contest for the Presidency in 1824 was under way.
Secretary Adams was one of the candidates, and, according
to testimony quoted by him, the Crawford men in the
Senate "made of it a bitter and rancorous party matter."
John C. Calhoun is quoted as saying that sixteen or seventeen Senators were systematically hostile to the Administration and prepared to manifest their dislike by any
opposition that had a chance of success. [7]

Furthermore, some of the Senators from the Southern
states had become alarmed at recent speeches in the British
Parliament looking to the abolition of slavery itself and
were therefore opposed to making any concert whatever
with the British Government on the subject of slavery. [8]

Amendments Voted. In this atmosphere the Senate began
to propose amendments to the treaty, the first being that
either party might terminate it on six months notice. This
proposal was adopted by a vote of 36 to 2, all Senators apparently desiring to be able to denounce the right of search

[7] J. Q. Adams, *Memoirs*, VI, 338, 339, 348, 350.
[8] Rufus King as quoted by Adams, *Memoirs*, VI, 321.

if its use should prove too obnoxious to us. A second amendment, likewise motivated, excepted the waters of "America" from the operation of the treaty and a third struck out the clause applying the right of search to vessels of a third nation chartered by English or American citizens. The vote on this motion was 22 to 21, after which the treaty thus altered was approved 29 to 13. [9]

While these amendments were being voted, President Monroe sent a strong message to the Senate, on May 21, reviewing our domestic legislation against the traffic, citing our pledge in the Treaty of Ghent to use our best endeavors to abolish it, quoting the House resolutions on the subject and showing that it was as a necessary corollary to our insistence that the slave trade be branded as piracy that the right of search was granted. [10]

Having done the best he could to get the treaty through the Senate, he then ratified it and forwarded it to Great Britain with a letter attempting to minimize the effect of the excisions made by the Senate. He reasoned that the treaty really could not confer the power of capturing slave traders under the flag of a third party, that the coasts of the United States needed very little watching and that the right of denunciation on six months notice would undoubtedly be given up when the public mind had become used to the practical operation of the treaty. He had been prepared to ratify it as signed but hoped the high end in view would enable the British Government to accept the conditions made by the Senate.[11]

Rejected by Great Britain. The Government of Great Britain, however, refused to accept the altered draft returned to it.[12] It could agree to the majority of the changes

[9] *American State Papers, Foreign Affairs*, Vol. V, p. 361.
[10] Ibid., 344.
[11] Moore, *Digest of International Law*, II, 924.
[12] Mr. Canning's protest against the practice of altering treaties after they had been concluded is quoted at length in the preceding chapter.

made by the Senate, "better satisfied as his Majesty's Government undoubtedly would have been if they had not been made," but refused to permit the coasts of America to be excepted from the operation of the treaty. "The right of visiting vessels suspected of slave trading," wrote Mr. Canning, "when extended alike to the West Indies and *to the coast of America,* implied an equality of vigilance, and did not necessarily imply the existence of grounds of suspicion on either side. The removal of this right as to the coast of America, and its continuance to the West Indies, cannot but appear to imply the existence on one side and not on the other of a just ground either of suspicion of misconduct, or for apprehension of an abuse of authority."

The Colombian Sequel. In the meantime the United States had invited several nations to denounce the slave trade as piracy and to cooperate in suppressing it. Among them was the United States of Colombia, to which our Minister, Mr. Anderson, expressed "the certain belief that the Republic of Colombia will not permit herself to be behind any Government in the civilized world in the adoption of energetic measures for the suppression of this disgraceful traffic." The Colombian Government returned a cordial reply and as a project for a treaty Mr. Anderson, on November 4, 1824, offered the proposed British Treaty as amended by the Senate earlier in the year. This draft was accepted by Colombia with only minor alterations which Mr. Anderson felt were immaterial.[13] Careful reading of the texts supports him in that judgment, yet on March 9, 1825, the Senate rejected the treaty by the unanimous vote previously noted. After the failure of the British treaty the Senate was in no mood to approve any treaties on the subject.

Results. This first failure of treaties through Senate action indicated clearly the extent to which strong feelings

[13] *American State Papers, Foreign Affairs,* V, 729–35.

could be concentrated in the Senate against a treaty designed to carry out an admittedly good purpose. It may be that the Senators were right in refusing to approve the treaty with England as it was negotiated. Many who were not animated either by prejudice or politics doubtless felt that the principle so recently fought for could not be safely modified so soon by the young and comparatively weak Republic.

In any case the failure of the treaty left the matter in contention for many years. The search of American ships continued and so did the slave trade. According to Du Bois, who cites official sources in detail, it proceeded in such volume that many hundred thousands of negroes were landed in the Americas during the succeeding thirty-five years. What proportion of this flow was protected by the long continuance of our controversy with the British over searches is difficult to say. Mr. Du Bois' study indicates that it was a heavy one.[14] Others would no doubt contend that the operation of the proposed treaty would have resulted in more international friction than slave trade suppression.

THE COLOMBIAN CANAL TREATIES

Two canal treaties negotiated with Colombia in 1869 and 1870 also failed to become law. Secretary Seward, recognizing the drift of canal sentiment, planned a treaty with Colombia to secure the Panama rights, and was so desirous of making an agreement that he sent Mr. Caleb Cushing, twice Attorney General, to Bogota to conduct the negotiation. After prolonged discussion the treaty was concluded on January 14, 1869, but was summarily rejected by the Colombian Congress [15] and never brought to a vote in the American Senate.

[14] W. E. Du Bois, *The Suppression of the Slave Trade*, Harvard Historical Studies, N. Y., 1896, pp. 141–44.
[15] H. Arias, *The Panama Canal*, London, 1911, p. 38.

President Grant coming into office soon after, sent a new minister to Colombia, Mr. S. A. Hurlbut, charged with negotiating a new treaty. The second draft fared little better than the first, however, being subjected to so many amendments by the Colombian legislature that it was apparently never discussed in the United States Senate,[16] notwithstanding some efforts of the Colombian minister at Washington to secure its consideration. Perhaps this was due to the fact that the canal was to revert to Colombia after a hundred years. [17] On the Colombian side the chief difficulty seems to have been the question of Colombia's status during an American war. [18]

MEXICAN TREATIES DEFEATED

The La Abra Silver Mine. Two treaties with Mexico likewise lacked Senate approval. The more interesting of the two is the Convention for Reopening and Retrying the Claims of Benjamin Weil and the La Abra Silver Mining Company against Mexico. A joint claims commission which concluded its labors on January 31, 1876, had awarded approximately a million and a quarter dollars to these two American claimants. The Mexican Government protested both awards, especially the latter, on the ground of fraud. After much correspondence, Congress finally ordered an investigation on June 18, 1878, which resulted in an indecisive report. President Arthur suspended payments to the claimants in 1881 and in July, 1882, a convention for rehearing the cases before a new commission was signed.[19] This convention was rejected by the Senate on January 15,

[16] J. C. Rodrigues, *The Panama Canal,* N. Y., 1885, p. 36; *Sen. Exec. Jour.,* Vol. 17.
[17] N. Thomson, *Colombia and the United States,* London, 1912, pp. 42–44.
[18] Rodrigues, *The Panama Canal,* p. 36.
[19] J. B. Moore, *Digest of International Law,* Washington, 1906, Vol. VII, p. 65.

1883, by a vote of 33 for and 20 against, and again on April 20, 1886, by a vote of 32 to 26. [20]

The matter was kept before Congress, however, and in December, 1892, the Court of Claims was given full power to pass upon the charges of fraud. After five more years, it decided, on June 24, 1897, that the La Abra case was a fraud, that the American individuals promoting the claim had been dispossessed of no silver mines, and that the whole case was based on perjury. Consequently, the United States returned to Mexico, in 1900, the undistributed installments on the claims and, in 1902, the sum of $412,572.70 was appropriated to repay to Mexico the earlier installments which the fraudulent claimants had received. [21] Thus after nearly thirty years a miscarriage of justice was at length rectified.

The Mexican Commerce Treaty of 1859. An earlier Mexican treaty in the Senate grew out of the disturbed state of Mexican affairs which later resulted in the French occupation of Mexico during the Civil War. The United States had recognized the Jaurez government in 1859 and had sent Robert M. McLane as minister to it. This government was based on Vera Cruz, while Mexico City was in the hands of the Miramon faction. Feeling that the Jaurez government was the constitutional one and also friendly to us, Mr. McLane believed that the condition of anarchy and threatened European intervention could best be met by a treaty with the Jaurez government giving the United States a limited right of intervention for the support of its treaty rights and the protection of its citizens. He therefore negotiated a treaty of transits and commerce which was calculated to avert the necessity of general American or European intervention.

After attempts to modify a clause which provided for the

[20] *Senate Executive Journal*, Vol. 25, p. 429.
[21] Moore, *Digest of International Law*, VII, 68.

entry free of duty of lists of American and Mexican goods, the Senate rejected the whole treaty by a vote of 18 to 27, on May 31, 1860, though it reconsidered and postponed action until the December session, when more urgent business occupied it. [22] The slavery issue probably had something to do with the failure, the northern senators generally voting against it. An amendment to provide for the mutual surrender of fugitives from service and justice was lost, 22 to 20, and the fear of an expansion of slave territory in the Mexican direction most likely determined the attitude of the northern Senators. In any event, the Jaurez Government triumphed over its Mexican enemies only to be forced to suspend, in July, 1861, all payments on the public debt, the act which furnished the excuse for the European intervention and the Maximilian monarchy.[23]

The Cuban Claims Convention of 1860. A convention with Spain signed March 4, 1860, for the settlement of certain claims of American citizens arising under a provisional decree issued for the Island of Cuba was also rejected in the last year of Buchanan's administration by a vote of 24 for to 18 against, the alignment of Senators being substantially the same.[24]

THE JOHNSON-CLARENDON TREATY OF 1869

The tendency of Senators to oppose treaties because of party or personal hostility to the Administration responsible for them was especially marked after the Civil War. The first treaty to fall before the antagonisms growing out of the war was one which the American Minister to England had finally succeeded in concluding with England for the

[22] *Senate Executive Journal*, Vol. XI, p. 199.
[23] J. M. Callahan, "The Evolution of Seward's Mexican Policy," *West Virginia University Studies in American History*, Vol. IV, June, 1909, pp. 10-18.
[24] *Senate Documents*, Vol. 14, 66th Cong., 1st Sess., p. 169.

settlement of our claims against Great Britain due to the operations of the Confederate cruiser *Alabama* and others. Secretary Seward had largely dictated the terms and both he and President Johnson were much pleased with the convention, feeling "confident that if it were ratified and executed this country would recover every dollar due to it. . . ." But it was not to be ratified, for two reasons: "One was the hateful spirit of faction, which was just then raging at a pitch unknown since the days of the elder Adams, seventy years before. Nothing that President Johnson and his associates could do would be acceptable to his political foes who were in full control of Congress." [25]

The other reason for the treaty's rejection was the claim for "national" or "indirect" damages put forward by Senator Charles Sumner and others. Mr. Sumner, as chairman of the Senate Foreign Relations Committee, reported against the treaty in one of his most carefully prepared orations in the course of which he maintained that British recognition of the belligerent rights of the Confederacy had prolonged the Civil War for at least two years, during which our large share of the world's carrying trade had passed into the hands of the British. Great Britain should therefore pay for the loss of our merchant marine and for half the cost of the war, a total of $2,500,000,000.[26]

This preposterous proposal so impressed the Senate that only one man out of fifty-five had the courage to vote for the Johnson-Clarendon treaty when it was rejected by the Senate on April 13, 1869. [27] To complete the mischief, Sumner and his friends had the injunction of secrecy removed and the treaty published, with the result that "American expectations of the ultimate award were expanded to an impossible degree, and British suspicions and antago-

[25] W. F. Johnson, *America's Foreign Relations*, II, 78.
[26] C. R. Fish, *American Diplomacy*, N. Y., 1919, p. 340.
[27] *Sen. Exec. Jour.*, Vol. 26, p. 333.

nisms were similarly exaggerated." [28]   Further attempts to
settle the controversy were, of course, useless until the feeling on both sides of the ocean had had time to subside.
This took some time, particularly since Sumner was influential with the new Minister to London, Mr. John L. Motley.
Sumner's influence in Washington declined, however, so in
spite of his amazing demand, in January, 1871, that the
British give up Canada and all their possessions in this
hemisphere, a protocol providing for arbitration of the
claims was signed, in February, 1871, and the definitive
treaty ratified on May 25. [29]

The American Government felt compelled to make some
show of presenting the indirect claims for loss of merchant
marine, however, and for another six months there was a
fresh crop of alarms, charges of bad faith, and counter-
charges, which ended only when an American member of
the Geneva Tribunal, Charles Francis Adams, induced that
body to declare that it would not consider the indirect
claims. [30]   Our direct claims to the extent of $15,500,000
were allowed.   This sum proved to be considerably in excess
of the claims of individuals who had lost directly from the
operations of the Confederate cruisers. [31]

TREATIES OF ANNEXATION REJECTED

Still another of Secretary Seward's treaties was destined
to receive scant courtesy at the hands of the Senate and of
the Grant Administration.   Mr. Seward, impressed by the
need during the war for a naval coaling station in the West
Indies, had persuaded Denmark to conclude a treaty, on

[28] Johnson, *America's Foreign Relations,* II, 78.
[29] Ibid., p. 81.   Sumner seems to have had the idea at the time he first
made his huge claim of later exchanging it for British America. Fish,
American Diplomacy, 341.
[30] Fish, *American Diplomacy,* 348.
[31] Moore, *International Law Digest,* VII, 52.

October 24, 1867, for the sale of the Islands of St. Thomas and St. Johns at a price of $7,500,000.

The Danish Islands Treaty of 1867. The story of this treaty and the implications of its failure were pungently given in *The Nation* of May 30, 1872, as one of several illustrations of "the growing tendency to make the management of our international relations subservient to the purposes of party politics—which is another way of saying, of growing indifference to national reputation." Denmark, "was literally teased by the American Department of State into consenting to sell the Island of St. Thomas. She was unwilling to do so—at first refused to do so—but was finally pressed into consenting. The bargain was closed, as far as the Administration could close it; the vote of the islanders was taken on the scheme, was given in the affirmative, and the King formally released them from their allegiance—the American people and the Senate all the while looking on, to all outward appearance approvingly; and the treaty was sent to the Senate. The Senate was then, however, out of temper with Mr. Seward, and it determined to punish him. Now, it is a well-settled principle of international law that, when the ratification of one branch of a government is necessary to the validity of a treaty concluded with a foreign power by another, the ratification should not be refused for 'mere reasons of convenience', to use Martens' phrase, but for strong and solid reasons, going to the merits of the case, and based on considerations of justice and right. Well, it seems hardly credible, but it is nevertheless true, that the Senate not only did not ratify this treaty framed under these extraordinary circumstances, but it never gave itself the trouble even to discuss it, and has to this day never discussed it at all."

"In other words, to punish Seward, it has inflicted on Denmark, a small but friendly power, one of the grossest insults ever inflicted by one nation on another, and has

committed as gross a breach of faith as could well be
imagined; and in this performance it has had the connivance
of the present Administration, for General Grant has actually refused to take up the St. Thomas matter, on the
ground that it was an 'affair of Seward's' with which he
had nothing to do—thus presenting the American Secretary
of State who represented the American people to foreign
nations during the most momentous period of its existence,
as a kind of interloper, whose acts were not binding on any
of his successors."

In defense of the Senate it should be said that the country
was having a reaction from the expansion policy. The
opponents of the Alaskan purchase were still unconvinced
that we had bought anything beside an iceberg, and the
House voted that it would not appropriate the money to buy
the Danish Islands. [32] Nevertheless, political rancor seems
to have been the determining motive of the Senate in refusing to consider the treaty. [33] According to Willis Fletcher
Johnson, "the best judgment of the country was that the
Senate greatly erred, and that the acquisition of St. Thomas
would have been a highly commendable and profitable
achievement." [34] Moreover, as the same writer noted, we
should have been in an awkward predicament if Denmark
had entertained a proposal of sale to another power. We
should then have been compelled either to repudiate the
Monroe Doctrine, to reverse the Senate, or to assume the
merest dog-in-the-manger attitude.

The Dominican Annexation Treaty. Strangely enough, it
was not long before President Grant himself fell afoul of
Senator Sumner and the Senate on a new annexation project.
Secretary Seward had failed to come to a bargain with

[32] Fish, *American Diplomacy*, 361.
[33] Johnson, *Amer. For. Rel.*, II, 63. Three years and three months
after the treaty was referred to the committee it was reported adversely,
March 17, 1870, though not discussed. *Sen. Exec. Jour.*, Vol. 17, p. 405.
[34] Johnson, *Amer. For. Rel.*, II, 63.

President Baez, of the Republic of San Domingo, who wanted to sell that derelict republic while it had a going value, though Mr. Seward had sounded sentiment in the House and President Johnson had commended the acquisition in his annual message of 1868. [35]

For some reason little understood, President Grant fastened upon the idea of annexing San Domingo and made it his chief objective. A treaty negotiated by one of his private secretaries was sent to the Senate with the strongest possible recommendations for its ratification. Senator Sumner, however, who had so lately demanded possession of all the Caribbean possessions of Great Britain, could see no virtue in San Domingo. So, in spite of the President's picture of the capacious harbors, salubrious climate and most valuable products of forest, mine, and soil, he opposed the annexation. The President felt that its possession by us would in a few years build up a coastwise commerce of "immense magnitude" which would go far toward restoring to us our lost merchant marine, that it would expand our markets throughout the Caribbean while reducing our imports, and that it would make slavery insupportable in the Spanish islands and ultimately in Brazil by creating such a demand for labor that they would have to abolish slavery to keep their negroes. [36] But even this prospect failed to win the abolitionist Mr. Sumner who ridiculed the whole project and combined with the Democrats to defeat the treaty on June 30, 1870, by a vote of 28 to 28, with 7 paired for and 4 against. [37]

The brunt of reasoned opposition to the treaty was borne by Senator Carl Schurz who thought it would lead, step by step, to the extension of our borders to the Isthmus. He was convinced that "labor, if left free, inevitably ran to

[35] Fish, *American Diplomacy*, 361-2.
[36] Message of May 31, 1870, to the Senate. Richardson, *Messages and Papers of the Presidents*, Washington, 1898, Vol. VII, pp. 61-2.
[37] *Sen. Exec. Jour.*, Vol. XVII, p. 503.

shiftlessness in the tropics" and that republican institutions could not be built up under a tropical sun. Opposed to negro slavery as he was, he dreaded the introduction of a new mass of negroes into American citizenship. The prospect of incorporating still other millions of people "who have nothing in common with us; neither language, nor habits, nor institutions, nor traditions, nor opinions, nor ways of thinking; nay not even a code of morals—people who cannot even be reached by our teachings, for they will not understand or appreciate them"—this project appalled Mr. Schurz, as well it might. [38]   With all our progress in sanitation and communication today the handling of tropical lands and peoples is a problem which the Nordic peoples cannot claim to have solved.

Notwithstanding the weight of these arguments and the unusual irregularity of the Dominican negotiations and occupation, many have since felt that the annexation would have been a good thing. Senator Shelby M. Cullom was later of that opinion. [39]   In any event it must have given Mr. Seward some satisfaction to see the men who had ignored his Danish Islands annexation defeat each other in mortal combat over an annexation project which had far less to commend it. We have seen some aspects of Grant's defeat; Sumner's came in March 1871, when, standing in the road of the Washington Treaty with England for the settlement of the Alabama claims, Fisheries dispute, etc., he was deposed by the Republican senatorial caucus as chairman of the Committee on Foreign Relations. [40]

[38] Speech in the Senate, Schurz, *Speeches, Correspondence and Political Papers*, N. Y., 1913, Vol. II, pp. 71-122. (p. 93 quoted). See also, Schurz, *Reminiscences*, N. Y., 1908, Vol. III, pp. 323-38.
[39] S. M. Cullom, *Fifty Years of Public Service*, 391.
[40] Schurz, *Reminiscences*, 329.
     In 1911, Secretary Knox negotiated a treaty with Honduras on January 10, and another with Nicaragua June 6, establishing financial protectorates over those countries similar to the protectorate established over San Domingo by President Roosevelt. These treaties failed in the Senate. Latane, *The United States and Latin America*, 283-4; Wright, *The Control of American Foreign Relations*, 283.

The Annexation of Texas. An earlier example of an annexation treaty defeated by domestic politics is to be found in the treaty signed with the Republic of Texas on April 12, 1844. That republic, which had succeeded in maintaining its independence for eight years, was persuaded by President Tyler to sign the treaty of annexation on promise of full protection against Mexico. Unfortunately for Tyler's purpose, however, he filled a vacancy in the Secretaryship of State by appointment of John C. Calhoun, whose identification with the slavery cause alarmed the Northern Senators, many of whom felt it was primarily a scheme to increase slave holding territory. On June 8, therefore, all but one of the Whigs voted against the treaty and were joined by seven Democrats, making a total of thirty-five nays to sixteen ayes. [41]

Unpopularity of President Tyler in the Senate contributed to the result, but was not sufficient to prevent annexation by joint resolution of Congress after the election of Polk on an annexation platform, though it is true that some Senators voted for the resolution with the understanding that Polk would be left to conclude the entry of Texas. The resolution was adopted on March 1, 1845, three days before the end of Tyler's term, with twenty-seven for and twenty-five against, but whatever the understanding of Senators, Tyler despatched the offer to Texas post haste and Texas came into the Union during the year on much better terms than the rejected treaty had conceded. [42]

"No acquisition of territory by the United States," says John Bassett Moore, "has been the subject of so much honest, but partisan misconception as that of the annexation of Texas. By a school of writers whose views have had great currency, the annexation has been denounced as the

[41] J. W. Foster, *A Century of American Diplomacy*, N. Y., 1900, pp. 299-301.
[42] Ibid., 302.

result of a plot of the slave-power to extend its dominions. But, calmly surveying the courses of American expansion, we are forced to conclude that no illusion could be more complete. It would have been more nearly correct to say that, but for the controversy concerning slavery, there would have been no appreciable opposition in the United States to the acquisition of Texas." [43]

EXTRADITION TREATIES

A much less controversial subject, that of the extradition of criminals, but one upon which national sensibilities are somewhat acute, has occasionally led to the failure of treaties in the Senate. The earliest case of this kind appears to be the Treaty with Belgium of February 11, 1853, which failed to come to a vote. [44]

A convention with Great Britain on the same subject, dated at London June 25, 1886, was before the Senate for two years, only to be rejected on February 1, 1889, by a two-thirds majority, 15 to 38. Various petitions for and against it were received by the Senate. The Father Matthew Total Abstinence Society of Lawrence, Mass., prayed its defeat; bankers of Boston and Pittsburgh urged its ratification to facilitate the return of defaulters; two St. Patrick's Societies of Audenreid, Pa., and the Tom Moore Literary Society of Honey Brook, Pa., remonstrated against it, as did citizens of Iowa and Minnesota. Various minor amendments were proposed and adopted as late as the date preceding rejection, but they did not win a majority for it. [45] Probably the political and anti-British atmosphere which had defeated the more important Fisheries Treaty with Great Britain a few months before accounted in part for the failure of this treaty.

[43] *J. B. Moore, American Diplomacy,* N. Y., 1905, p. 234.
[44] *Sen. Doc.* Vol. 14, 66th Cong., 1st Sess., p. 170.
[45] *Sen. Exec. Jour.,* Vol. 26, p. 446 and preceding.

Somewhat later, on May 11, 1892, an extradition treaty with France was defeated by a tie poll of 23 to 23 after having been amended in four particulars. [46]

THE CANADIAN FISHERIES TREATY OF 1888

The principal political battle over a treaty between the close of the Civil War period and the Great War was the Fisheries Treaty dispute in President Cleveland's first administration.

The rights of American fishing vessels in Canadian ports and waters had been in almost constant dispute since the creation of the Government. A treaty of 1818 had attempted to define the rights in question, but had left many points in dispute. Later supplementary treaties of 1830, 1854, and 1871, had been limited in terms and had not settled the disputes. [47] The last of these conventions expired on June 30, 1885, leaving the situation as in 1818. Soon after two American fishing vessels were seized by Canada, whereupon the American Government made vigorous diplomatic protest, condemning the conduct of the Canadian officials severely and demanding full redress. [48] Somewhat later, the Senate Foreign Relations committee presented a resolution, promptly adopted by Congress, which empowered the President to exclude all Canadian vessels from our ports as well as to bar fish or "any other product" of Canada from the country. "This was making straight for trouble. Had the

---

[46] *Sen. Exec. Jour.*, Vol., 28, p. 237.

More extradition treaties are killed by amendment than by rejection. Up to 1928, the Senate amended 35 extradition treaties, eleven of which were rejected abroad or not presented by the President to the Foreign Power for ratification. See the list of amended treaties published by the *Foreign Policy Association, Information Service,* October 12, 1928, Vol. IX, No. 16, pp. 328–336.

[47] President's Message, *Sen. Exec. Doc.,* Vol. 14, 66th Cong., 1st Sess., p. 238.

[48] Robert McElroy, Grover Cleveland, *The Man and the Statesman,* Vol. I, p. 294.

President acted according to this resolution, relations with Great Britain would have reached perilously near to the breaking point. Fortunately, however, he exercised a wise discretion. Instead of resorting to the measures of retaliation he appointed commissioners to confer with British representatives in seeking settlement of the whole dispute." [49]

The President's Analysis. They concluded a treaty in Washington on February 18, 1888. Mr. Cleveland submitted it to the Senate five days later as a "just, honorable and therefore satisfactory solution." After an historical survey of the controversy from 1818 on, he presented the gains made in the new treaty over all preceding ones in detail and urged ratification.[50]

---

[49] Johnson, *America's Foreign Relations,* II, 99.

[50] He said, in part: "The proposed delimitation of the lines of the exclusive fisheries from the common fisheries will give certainty and security as to the area of their legitimate field; and the headland theory of imaginary lines is abandoned by Great Britain, and the specification in the treaty of certain-named bays especially provided for gives satisfaction to the inhabitants of the shores without subtracting materially from the value or conveniences of the fishery rights of Americans.

The uninterrupted navigation of the Strait of Canso is expressly and for the first time affirmed, and the four purposes for which our fishermen under the treaty of 1818 were allowed to enter the bays and harbors of Canada and Newfoundland within the belt of 3 marine miles are placed under a fair and liberal construction, and their enjoyment secured without such conditions and restrictions as in the past have embarrassed and obstructed them so seriously.

The enforcement of penalties for unlawfully fishing or preparing to fish within the inshore and exclusive waters of Canada and Newfoundland is to be accomplished under safeguards against oppressive or arbitrary action, thus protecting the defendant fisherman from punishment in advance of trial, delays, and inconvenience and unnecessary expense.

The history of events in the last two years shows that no feature of Canadian administration was more harassing and injurious than the compulsion upon our fishing vessels to make formal entry and clearance on every occasion of temporarily seeking shelter in Canadian ports and harbors.

Such inconvenience is provided against in the proposed treaty, and this most frequent and just cause of complaint is removed.

The articles permitting our fishermen to obtain provisions and the ordinary supplies of trading vessels on their homeward voyages, and under which they are accorded the further and even more important privilege on all occasions of purchasing such casual or needful provisions and supplies as are ordinarily granted to trading vessels, are of great importance and value.

The licenses which are to be granted without charge and on appli-

Foreign Relations Committee Report. The Committee on
Foreign Relations returned a majority report, on May 7,
advising rejection of the treaty. The report denied that
the President had authority to negotiate the treaty without
previous consent of the Senate, held that it had not been
approved by the Senate, contended that the matters considered in the treaty were not fit subjects for negotiation
with Great Britain, declared that the time for negotiation
with that Government on these subjects had passed, and
demanded retaliation instead. [51]

Senate Debate. This report was accompanied by Republican caucus action which compelled consideration of the
treaty in open session. [52] After one of the votes to proceed
to the consideration of the treaty in open executive session,
Senator Riddleberger, Republican, of Virginia, summed up
the result of the debate in advance, saying: "Mr. President,
the vote just taken I think conclusively settles the only question that can possibly be in controversy from this time on
in respect to this treaty, and that is, that the Republican party
of this country is opposed to the ratification of the pending
treaty, and that the Democratic party is in favor of its
ratification."

Feeling therefore, no doubt, that it would be a waste of
time to discuss the treaty itself, the Senator proceeded to

---

cation, in order to enable our fishermen to enjoy these privileges, are
reasonable and proper checks in the hands of the local authorities to
identify the recipients and prevent abuse, and can form no impediment
to those who intend to use them fairly.

The hospitality secured for our vessels in all cases of actual distress,
with liberty to unload and sell and transship their cargoes, is full and
liberal.

The right of our fishermen under the treaty of 1818 did not extend
to the procurement of distinctive fishery supplies in Canadian ports and
harbors; and one item supposed to be essential, to wit, bait, was plainly
denied them by the explicit and definite words of the treaty of 1818,
emphasized by the course of the negotiation and express decisions which
preceded the conclusion of that treaty."   *Senate Executive Documents,*
Vol. 14, 66th Cong. 1st Sess., p. 239.

[51] *Congressional Record,* 50th Cong., 1st Sess., Vol. 19, Part 8, p.
7156-7.

[52] *Congressional Record,* 50th Cong., 1st Sess., Vol. 19, Part 8, p. 7163.

declare that the Secretary of State had said in a private conversation that the ratification of the treaty would lead to free trade, quoted a dozen editorials from English newspapers approving the President's tariff message, branded the Administration and the Democratic party as a pro-English organization, delivered a page attack on England and English institutions and closed with a few columns on Catholicism, Protestantism and the travels of Representative Cox of New York.[53]

Senator Morgan, of Alabama, the Democratic leader, agreed, that the country had already been advised through the action of the Republican caucus that the treaty was doomed to defeat. He spoke only in an effort to mitigate, if possible, the peculiar position the Government would be in after the rejection of the treaty. He noted that neither Presidents Lincoln, Johnson, Grant, Hayes nor Arthur had ever attempted to resort to the retaliatory law of 1850 even though more than 300 cases of seizure of our fishing vessels had occurred and the situation had often been as aggravated as of late. He thought the door of negotiation ought not now to be shut in an effort to force Mr. Cleveland to the sole alternative of retaliation and invited the Senate to amend the treaty in any way it saw fit. "If the treaty does not suit us," he said, "let us write one, to which two-thirds of the Senate will agree, that does suit us and advise the President to submit it to Great Britain for ratification or rejection." [54]

Usually a proposal to amend a treaty would have been received by the Senate sympathetically enough, but this time the majority not only refused to permit amendment but also to allow postponement until December. After keeping the subject before the Senate and the country in thirty

---

[53] Ibid., 7154-56.
[54] *Congressional Record* 50th Cong., 1st Sess., Vol. 19, Part 8, pp. 7158–60.

days of debate scattered through the months of May, June, July and August the final blow was given on August 21, 1888, by a strict party vote of 28 for to 30 against. [55]

RECIPROCITY AND COMMERCIAL TREATIES

Swiss and Zollverein Treaties. The largest group of treaties failing to pass the Senate have attempted to establish reciprocal tariff relations with other countries. The first reciprocity treaty falling before the Senate was a Swiss treaty, rejected June 10, 1836, 14 to 23. [56] The next was a treaty with the German Zollverein, lost April 17, 1854, 26 to 18. [57] The gains of customs union to the States of the Zollverein had been so clearly shown that other nations, including the United States, wanted to share its benefits. The treaty negotiated by the United States was commercially very favorable to it.

The Senate Committee on Foreign Relations, however, opposed the treaty on the ground that the President had no right to negotiate it, the right to control taxation belonging exclusively to Congress. Calhoun, as Secretary of State, vigorously maintained that such rate-making was a well established practice. Just how deeply the constitutional objection animated the objecting Senators would be difficult to say. The unpopularity of Tyler and the objection of the Whigs to lowering any customs duties played a part. [58] Probably "the constitutional argument was a plausible and soothing apology for a refusal largely dictated by the wishes of interests which feared to find their profits reduced by foreign competition." [59]

---

[55] *Sen. Exec. Jour.,* Vol. 26, p. 333; McElroy, *Grover Cleveland, The Man and Statesman,* 295.

[56] *Sen. Exec. Jour.,* Vol. IV, p. 559.

[57] Ibid., Vol. VI, p. 347.

[58] Fish, American Diplomacy, 225.

[59] J. L. Laughlin and H. P. Willis, *Reciprocity,* N. Y., 1903, 9.

Hawaiian Treaties. A treaty for Commercial reciprocity with Hawaii, negotiated by Secretary Marcy on July 20, 1855, soon after he had secured the ratification of our first effective reciprocity agreement, that with Canada in 1854, was apparently pushed aside by the press of business in the Senate,[60] though it was reported adversely on March 11, 1857.[61] A new treaty to establish reciprocity was negotiated with Hawaii in 1867, but rejected by the Senate, 20 to 19, on June 1, 1870, after being pigeon-holed for three years. [62] Five years later a third treaty vigorously promoted by a group of Americans who had acquired sugar lands in Hawaii was ratified by the Senate and the necessary enabling law passed by Congress, the leading motive was, however, political rather than economic, that is, to keep the islands out of the hands of Great Britain and France. [63]

Canada, Cuba and San Domingo. A new reciprocity treaty with Canada was negotiated at Washington in February 1874, but was rejected by the Senate in 1875.[64]

Ten years later President Arthur sent John W. Foster to Spain to negotiate a reciprocal tariff arrangement between the United States and Cuba. Mr. Foster succeeded in his mission and Secretary Frelinghuysen negotiated a similar pact with San Domingo in the same year. Both treaties failed to receive Senate approval in Arthur's term partly because of election politics, both Blaine and Cleveland throwing their influence against them. The latter recalled them as soon as he was inaugurated President, so these are not true cases of Senate rejection. [65]

The Kasson Treaties. A little later, Mr. Blaine espoused the cause of reciprocity and negotiated a series of treaties which proved popular. In the campaign of 1896, spellbind-

[60] Ibid., 72.
[61] *Sen. Exec. Jour.*, Vol. X, p. 237.
[62] Ibid., Vol. XVII, p. 446.
[63] Laughlin and Willis, *Reciprocity*, pp. 75–85.
[64] Ibid., 65.
[65] J. W. Foster, *Diplomatic Memoirs*, N. Y., 1909, p. 239, pp. 258–60.

ers excited the enthusiasm of their audiences by references to these treaties, and according to W. E. Curtis, "There is not the slightest doubt that the hope and expectation of a renewal of these arrangements, endorsed with cordial confidence by Mr. McKinley, contributed very largely towards his election——," [66] The party leaders in Congress, however granted the President, in the Dingley Tariff Act, only very limited authority which he exercised through a special commissioner, Mr. J. A. Kasson, to a surprisingly successful degree. Mr. Kasson managed to negotiate treaties with France, Argentina, the Dominican Republic, Denmark (for St. Croix) Ecuador, Nicaragua and Great Britain (for various American colonies.) [67]

These treaties were presented to the Senate in December, 1899. Popular interest in them was keen and they had the cordial support of the Administration. The manufacturing interests were divided; those on an export basis such as the iron, steel and agricultural implement trades backed the treaties while domestic producers who feared foreign competition opposed them. Aided by those who saw in them only an infringement of the principle of protection, the latter interests won and prevented any action on the treaties in 1900 and 1901, although they were consistently supported by President McKinley who expressed himself more strongly than ever in favor of the policy of reciprocity in his last speech at Buffalo.[68] President Roosevelt likewise held the same views, but he also found it impossible to secure Senate approval. Senator Cullom, Chairman of the Com-

---

[66] W. E. Curtis, "A Brief History of The Reciprocity Policy," *Annals of the American Academy*, Vol. 29, pp. 459–60.

[67] U. S. Tariff Commission, *Reciprocity and Commercial Treaties*, 1919 p. 30.

[68] He said at Cincinnati, on October 30, 1897: "Commerce is a teacher and a pacificator. It gives mankind knowledge one of another. Reciprocity of trade promotes reciprocity of friendship. Good trade insures good will.—Abating none of our interest in the home market, let us move out to new fields steadily and increase the sale of our products in foreign markets." *Speeches and Addresses of William McKinley*, N. Y., 1900, p. 54.

mittee on Foreign Relations, favored the treaties, but did not succeed in getting them reported from his committee until June, 1902, after he had threatened to "carry them out in a basket." Even then two were withheld and discussion was permitted only on the French Treaty. None of them ever came to a vote.

A vigorous, determined fight by President Roosevelt did, however, secure the approval of a reciprocity treaty with Cuba in 1902, which was, says Mr. Cullom, the third in all our history, which actually went into effect. [69]

The Lausanne Treaty of Amity and Commerce. The most recent case of treaty failure occurred on January 18, 1927, when the Senate rejected the treaty of amity and commerce signed with Turkey at Lausanne on August 6, 1923, by a vote of 50 for to 34 against, 6 votes short of a two-thirds majority. The reasons for opposition appeared to be the absence of definite guaranties concerning naturalized American Citizens of Turkish origin, and sympathy for the Armenians whose national aspirations had been sacrificed by the Allied Powers at Lausanne.[70]

SOME REASONS FOR THE FAILURE OF TREATIES

Sectional and occupational interests undoubtedly caused the defeat of some of the treaties here considered, as might be expected. Sometimes, again, the defeat was due to politics alone. These causes for failure are clearly apparent, and yet many votes have undoubtedly been cast against treaties because Senators honestly believed them to be bad.

The danger of vitiation by amendment is always greater

[69] S. M. Cullom, *Fifty Years of Public Service,* Chicago, 1911, pp. 368–75.
[70] *American Journal of International Law,* July 1927, p. 503. A number of commercial treaties have failed because of amendments in the Senate. Up to 1928, the Senate had amended 40 treaties dealing with commerce, navigation, tariffs, consuls, etc. Nine of these were rejected abroad or dropped by the President. *Foreign Policy Association, Information Service,* October 12, 1928, Vol. IV, No. 16, pp. 328–36.

than the chance of outright defeat. There are always likely to be lawyers in the Senate who can think of something that ought to be changed. There are always some who are of the opinion that the Executive must be watched, or it will betray us. This detective habit of mind was most aptly described by Mr. H. L. Nelson at the close of the century when it was especially active. At that time Mr. Nelson wrote:

"Many Senators are invariably of the opinion that the executive department has not guarded sufficiently the rights of the United States, or that it has not obtained for American citizens as much as should have been wrung out of the foreigner. A well-known idiosyncrasy of a certain type of Congressional mind is suspicion of the loyalty and good faith of the Executive. It is especially the habit of this type of mind to believe that all the employees of the State Department are in collusion with the governments with whose diplomatic representatives the department is naturally in almost daily communication. When it is understood that there are a number of men in the Senate who are certain that the Executive ought always to be suspected of lack of patriotism in his intercourse with foreign powers, and that the duty rests upon them to protect the country against the wiles and snares of cunning foreign diplomats, and when it is also understood that there is also a good deal of human vanity among Senators, and that some of the lawmakers cannot resist the temptation to attach to a treaty of importance amendments which will go down into history as monuments to their own greatness—when all this is understood the difficulty of reaching an agreement with the foreigner will be apparent." [71]

[71] H. L. Nelson, "Chamberlain's Tripartite Understanding," *Harper's Weekly*, Dec. 30, 1899, Vol. 43, p. 1316.

CHAPTER V

THE ACTION OF THE SENATE ON ARBITRATION TREATIES

In addition to an adverse attitude toward commercial reciprocity with other countries, the Senate began to develop a habit of opposition to any effective efforts to promote the arbitration of international disputes. Perhaps it would be more correct to say that a minority of the Senate consistently maintained this attitude, but under the operation of the two-thirds rule the effect was the same—no step could be taken without the approval of the minority.

THE OLNEY-PAUNCEFOTE TREATY OF 1897

In 1897, Secretary Olney signed a treaty of arbitration at Washington with Lord Pauncefote for the arbitration of disputes between the United States and England. The treaty concluded was in response to the formally expressed desire of the legislatures of both countries. Congress, in 1890, had requested the President "to invite from time to time, as fit occasions may arise, negotiations with any government with which the United States has or may have diplomatic relations to the end that any differences or disputes arising between the two governments which cannot be adjusted by ordinary diplomatic agency may be referred to arbitration and be peaceably adjusted by such means." Three years later the British House of Commons had adopted a resolution expressing satisfaction with this proposal and the hope that the British government would coöperate to that end. [1]

The treaty thus motivated was designed to effectively carry out the expressed wish of the two parliaments. It provided for the reference to carefully constituted arbitration tribunals of all matters in difference not involving title to territory.

Supported by Two Administrations. No action was taken on the treaty in the Senate during the remainder of the second Cleveland Administration, but after President McKinley had been inaugurated and had added his cordial support, it was taken up in the Senate, on March 18, 1897, and considered at intervals for six weeks, with the result, one might confidently expect, that it would be approved with minor amendments. With the idea fathered by a Senate resolution concurred in by the House, accepted by the foreign government and heartily endorsed by Presidents of both political parties it would seem to have been endowed with enough wisdom and careful consideration to make its approval in the Senate a foregone conclusion. But the event was otherwise. The Senate would have none of it.

Amended and Rejected by the Senate. That body began with a proviso from the Foreign Relations Committee that every agreement to submit a question to arbitration under the treaty must be submitted to the Senate and receive the approval of two-thirds of that body. The Senate would not agree to arbitrate at all; it would merely consent to consider submitting a future question to arbitration after the dispute had become so advanced and so notorious that it could not be settled by ordinary diplomatic means.

The chance of two-thirds of the Senators finding themselves in a conciliatory and pacific state of mind in such a contingency was remote enough, but the Senate evidently

[1] Elihu Root, *Addresses on International Subjects,* Boston, 1916, p. 234–5.

feared it might sometime have a moment of weakness and agree to the submission of a dispute to the tribunal, for it proceeded to forbid the President to send in to it any proposal to arbitrate a question that might be of importance. It voted by a majority of 54 to 13, "that no difference shall be submitted under this treaty which, in the judgment of either power, materially affects its honor, the integrity of its territory, or its foreign or domestic policy." The treaty had excepted from arbitration all questions involving title to territory, but this was not enough; the "integrity" of our territory must be preserved. When also any question that in the heat of the controversy either party might conclude affected its "honor" was excluded; when any question that might be construed to affect either "foreign policy" or "domestic" policy was barred; when these all inclusive bans had been set up, it would have appeared that the Senate was in no danger of having to veto projects for arbitration.

Yet two possibilities might exist: It was said that the English Government might propose to arbitrate whether or not an existing treaty continue in force; and Great Britain might raise the claims of her citizens who held many millions of bonds repudiated by our Southern States in the period after the civil war. Both these possibilities were, therefore, estopped as follows: "nor shall the question be submitted whether any treaty once existing continue in force; nor shall any claim against any state of the United States, alleged to be due to the Government of Great Britain, or to any subject thereof, be a subject matter of arbitration under this treaty. . . ."

Surely, after this, little chance for arbitration existed, but in case an occasion should still arise, the arbitration tribunal was enlarged, an article on suitable members for it in certain contingencies was struck out, the article providing a method of choosing the umpire in case of deadlock was eliminated, and the President was distinctly required to submit the

names of the American arbitrators to the Senate for confirmation. After ten additional amendments, the treaty
was eventually acceptable to the majority of the Senate.
But not to the minority, for on the final vote, May 5, 1897,
the sterile remnant of the treaty that remained failed of approval by a vote of 43 yeas to 26 nays. [2]

Reasons for the Rejection. The vote was preceded by a
debate in which Senator Mills of Texas, according to two
New York newspapers of May 6—the *Times* and the *Tribune*
—asserted that in its amended form it was still possible for
England to purchase Cuba or other American territory and
then insist upon arbitrating the consequent dispute with us.
He implored the Senate to protect the United States against
the proposed "alliance". Senator Hoar, of Massachusetts,
denied that territorial claims could be arbitrated as claimed.

The *Times* ascribed the defeat of the treaty by the narrow
margin of four votes to the circumstances that England was
a gold standard country and that the treaty had been negotiated by President Cleveland and Secretary Olney. With very
few exceptions the twenty-six Senators who voted against
the treaty were free silver men. Fourteen of the seventeen
states which they represented had been carried by Mr.
Bryan. Many of the twenty-six were rabid enemies of
Mr. Cleveland. Sixteen were classed as Democrats or
populists and ten as Republicans.

This view was concurred in by the Philadelphia *Press,*
which reported that of the Republicans voting against the
treaty all had been strong free silver advocates except Senators Quay and Penrose, of Pennsylvania, and Mason of
Illinois. Senator Frye, the oldest member of the Foreign
Relations Committee, expressed the opinion that the only
reason why the treaty was not ratified was because Great
Britain was a gold standard country and exhibited no
willingness to enter into any international agreement in re-

[2] *Senate Documents,* Vol. 14, 66th Cong., 1st Session, pp. 262–79.

gard to silver. The *Press* felt that as amended no real doubter could hesitate to accept it unless opposed to arbitration in any form. The large majority for it expressed the predominant sentiment of the country and its defeat cast a shade on the good name of the Republic. [3]

The *Tribune,* on the other hand, thought that there was little occasion for strong emotion over the failure of the treaty. The elemental passions of humanity were not likely ever to be outgrown and a general arbitration treaty was therefore likely to be observed by the European powers only so long as it suited their interests. And of course nobody was in danger from us. It would be superlatively silly, as well as false, to pretend that any nation on earth had cause to feel itself in danger from American aggression. It was for other nations rather than this one to give pledges of peace. There was no occasion for the most peaceable nation to "bind itself hand and foot" as the first draft of the treaty had done. "In its original shape it was, with one or two exceptions, antagonized by every Senator who had given the subject a minute's consideration. The amendments, carried finally and only after great difficulty through the Committee on Foreign Relations, were never designed to strengthen the lines upon which the original document was drafted, nor were they ever suspected of having been drawn in the interest of a more widely applied principle of arbitration. On the contrary they were solely intended to preserve with studied ostentation the shadow while sacrificing the substance of the instrument." [4]

The correspondent of the London *Times* wrote that Chairman Davis, Mr. Lodge and other Republicans had used all their influence first to wreck the treaty and then to ratify the wreck. He classed Mr. Davis as a jingo. Mr. Davis on his part attributed the defeat to England's attitudes toward

[3] Philadelphia *Press,* May 6, 1897.
[4] N. Y. *Tribune,* May 5, 1897.

the Greco-Turkish War, the Armenian massacres and the Transvaal.[5]

Criticism Evoked by the Defeat. After observing that the entire religious press and moral sentiment of the country had appealed to the Senate to ratify the treaty, *The Nation* felt constrained to record its conviction, on March 15, 1900, that "there is also, we cannot help seeing, a faction in the Senate which is against all treaties that make for peace. It wants the sores left open. It prefers to nurse old quarrels. Especially with Great Britain, it wants no settlement whatever of any outstanding dispute. If Lord Salisbury were to put his name to a treaty quieting, because conceding, every possible American demand on every possible subject, this faction in the Senate would be bitterly opposed to it. There are some Senators who would oppose any settlement of any kind with England, simply because it is a settlement. The more the friends of peace say in favor of a treaty, the more suspected and hated it becomes in the eyes of these professional stirrers-up of international strife." [6]

Reviewing the course of the preceding quarter of a century, Mr. H. L. Loomis stated, in *Harper's Weekly* for December 30, 1899, that no treaty of first importance had been entered into by the United States since the treaty of Washington in 1871. The most noteworthy treaty of the period had been the treaty with China recognizing our limitations on Chinese immigration. It had been insisted on by politicians of both parties so strongly that Senators who delighted in treaty obstruction were afraid of it. There had been extradition treaties ratified but these had been "struggled over with much waste of time and at much damage to the cause of justice." There had also been some commercial treaties, but besides the Behring Sea treaty the only important pacts had been the Fisheries Treaty, the Olney-

---

[5] New York *Times* and London *Times,* May 6, 1897.
[6] *The Nation,* March 15, 1900, Vol. 70, p. 199.

Pauncefote Treaty and the Treaty of Peace with Spain. The first two had been defeated and the last ratified only with great difficulty. [7]

Mr. A. Maurice Low, writing on "The oligarchy of the Senate" in the *North American Review*, of February, 1902, recalled the fear voiced by John Jay that two-thirds of the Senators would always oppress the remaining third, but felt, on the contrary, that it was always the one-third that oppressed the two-thirds and the Executive as well. A treaty now was "always sure to meet with political opposition, that is, of the party antagonistic to the President, or opposition originating in prejudice, self interest or ignorance." [8]

The effect upon our international position of the failure of our treaty making machinery to operate was plainly set forth by *The Nation,* on December 20, 1900, in summing up the record of the Senate, as follows:

"The United States is rapidly coming to be regarded by the other great Powers as a nation which is not able to make a treaty. We have been trying to conclude important international agreements during the past fifteen years, but have seen one after another of them go to wreck in the Senate. It is needless to enumerate the long and melancholy list. Whether the President was Cleveland or Harrison or McKinley, whether the negotiators were Democratic or Republican the power of the Senate to ratify treaties has been mainly exercised as to the Power to kill treaties. Three valuable conventions with Great Britain have been broken on the Senate's veto. The chief of State has made treaties with France and Germany, but the Senate has said with a sneer, 'They reckon ill who leave me out,' and has brought the whole work to the ground. With or without intention, we seem to the world to have stripped ourselves of a leading attribute of sovereignty—the power to make treaties.

[7] *Harper's Weekly*, December 30, 1899, Vol. 43, p. 1316.
[8] *North American Review*, Feb., 1902, Vol. 174, p. 241.

"That the result is badly to impair our national prestige admits of no question. Already foreign writers on government and international relations are beginning to say that it is absolutely worth no country's while to attempt to make a treaty with the United States. The President may be conciliatory, the Secretary of State may be willing to agree, but there is always the intractable Senate to say us nay; so what is the use? This is a most humiliating thing to be truthfully said of a great nation. It leaves us in a contemptible position.

"In a newly hatched and loudly cackling 'world-power', the inability to make a treaty is little short of ludicrous. To be a world power means at least to meet other powerful nations on equal terms. It is, indeed, an essential function of world powers to make agreements with each other for their reciprocal advantage and for the peace of the world. But here we are, thrusting ourselves into the company of the great Powers, and at the same time confessing that we cannot bear ourselves as a great Power should." [9]

THE HAY TREATIES

With the Senate developing a habit of rejecting treaties the lot of no Secretary of State could be conspicuously easy. An experienced politician who was a clever manipulator of men and at the same time big enough to have a statesman's long view of the world and the future—such a person would have been the ideal man to attempt to pilot treaties through the Senate after 1897. A man with such a combination of aptitudes is no doubt seldom to be found. At any rate, Secretary John Hay, who held the post for seven years after 1897, did not have either the desire or the equipment to groom the Senators for a ratification and keep them smoothed out during the trial of a treaty. He was a statesman of real vision, both sane and liberal, but

[9] *The Nation*, Dec. 20, 1900, Vol. 71, p. 481.

he had little acquaintance with Congressmen and would not court them. [10]

Secretary Hay's Attitude Toward the Senate. His first experience with the Senate, too, gave him a settled dislike of that body which grew into active resentment as he saw his handiwork repeatedly rejected. On March 7, 1900, he wrote to Joseph H. Choate in connection with the first Hay-Pauncefote Canal treaty, and others: "We have a clear majority, I think, in favor of all of them, but as the Fathers, in their wisdom saw fit to ordain that the kickers should rule forever, the chances are always two to one against any government measure passing. [11] Later, to Samuel Mather, he was sure that "There will always be 34 per cent of the Senate on the blackguard side of every question." [12]

The fact that some of his feelings on the subject became current did not improve his position with the Senate and he undoubtedly allowed his aversion to the tendencies in the Senate to carry him too far. He was so reluctant to go before the Committee on Foreign Relations, though invited, that the Senators had some reason to feel that they had to grope in the dark and inform themselves as best they could. [13] From Hay's point of view the treaties no doubt

[10] W. R. Thayer, *The Life of John Hay,* Boston, 1915, Vol. 2, p. 269.
[11] Ibid., 225.
[12] Ibid., 254.
[13] Cullom, *Fifty Years of Public Service,* 365.
When the first Hay-Pauncefote treaty passed the Senate with an amendment eliminating the pledge not to fortify the canal, Hay resigned, though McKinley would not accept his resignation. His biographer thought the Senate wiser than Hay on the point (Thayer, 225 ff.) as most of us would agree—unless it does develop that a couple of airplanes make a first class navy.
The second Hay-Pauncefote treaty, which was silent on the matter of fortifications, was ratified without amendment according to Senator Cullom, "after a good deal of effort."
Of the Hay-Buneau-Varilla treaty with Panama, Mr. Cullom says: "After nearly a month and a half of debate in executive session, devoted to its consideration, the treaty was finally ratified without amendment." The time was necessary to eliminate certain minor amendments inserted by the Foreign Relations Committee, of which he was a member. (pp. 381, 385).

spoke for themselves and no elaborate Senate inquisition was necessary to find something wrong with them.

The First Hague Conference an Impetus to Arbitration. In any case, the movement in favor of arbitration received a new stimulus in the Convention for the Pacific Settlement of International Disputes concluded at The Hague July 29, 1899, largely through American influence.   Within five years thirty-three arbitration treaties were signed among the powers and the state department did not wish to be too far distanced in pursuing its own policy. [14]   It accordingly took the treaty of October 14, 1903, between England and France, as a model for a group of American treaties.   This convention provided for the settlement of a strictly limited class of disputes by arbitration.   Only questions of a legal nature or relating to the interpretation of treaties were to be submitted, upon the failure of diplomacy; all questions affecting the vital interests, independence, or honor of the two contracting states, or the interests of third parties, were expressly excluded.   The reference to arbitration was, furthermore, not to be automatic; in each case a special agreement, or *compromis,* was to be concluded "defining clearly the matter in dispute, the scope of the powers of the arbitrators, the periods to be fixed for the formation of the Arbitral Tribunal and the several stages of the procedure." [15]

The Limited Scope of the Proposed Treaties.   The only point gained in fact was that the nations bound themselves to make such agreements for the settlement of the relatively unimportant disputes.   It was a step, however, and on the strength of it, Mr. Hay, instructed by President Roosevelt, sent out a circular letter to the signatories of the Hague Convention reciting the long standing position of the United States on arbitration and inviting the signature at Washing-

[14] W. F. Johnson, *America's Foreign Relations,* II, 364.
[15] *Foreign Relations of the United States.* Washington, 1904, p. 9.

ton of treaties similar to the Franco-British Convention. [16]
As a result of this note such a treaty was signed with
France, November 1, 1904, and others soon after with
Germany, Great Britain, Portugal and Switzerland. Mexico,
Italy and Russia were ready to sign when the first group was
transmitted to the Senate in 1904. [17]

Amended in the Senate. That body, however, had just
heard of the financial protectorate which President Roosevelt
had established over the Dominican Republic, without consulting the Senate, and even without its knowledge. This
incident is said to have determined the Senate to insist on
oversight of the compromis.[18]   The Senate felt also that if
even such disputes were henceforth simply sent by the President to The Hague the prestige of the Senate in foreign
affairs would be decidedly diminished.[19] For these reasons
and others, it therefore substituted the word "treaty" for
"agreement" in the conventions, thus insuring that every
proposal to arbitrate would come directly before it.[20]

Dropped by the Administration. Secretary Hay's opinion
of this slight but comprehensive change in the treaties was
expressed in his famous statement that "a treaty entering the
Senate is like a bull going into the arena: no one can say
just how or when the final blow will fall—but one thing is
certain—it will never leave the arena alive." [21]

Mr. Roosevelt's feelings, too, were about as strong. Agreements defining the scope and procedure of an arbitration
had been made by the Executive alone no less than fifteen
times in the preceding thirty years and the Administration

[16] Ibid., 8.
[17] Johnson, *America's Foreign Relations,* II, 364-66.
[18] Ibid.
[19] Fish, *American Diplomacy,* 474.
[20] Southern Senators were for the change as a means of preventing the
repudiated bonds from coming up.   There was also a current controversy with Canada over the Alaskan boundary and a lack of agreement
with England over the Clayton-Bulwer Canal treaty.   J. W. Foster,
"Prospects of Arbitration With England," *The Independent,* December
24, 1903, Vol. 55, p. 3025.
[21] Thayer, *Life of John Hay,* II, 393.

naturally expected the continuance of the practice.[22] Roosevelt wrote to his friend Senator Lodge, before the amendment was made, that it made shams of the treaties and that "we had better abandon the whole business rather than give the impression of trickiness and insincerity which would be produced by solemnly promulgating a sham. The amendment, in effect, is to make any one of these so-called arbitration treaties solemnly enact that there shall be another arbitration treaty whenever the two governments decide that there shall be one. Of course it is mere nonsense to have a treaty which does nothing but say, what there is no power of enforcing, that whenever we choose there shall be another arbitration treaty. We could have these further special arbitration treaties in special cases whenever desired just exactly as well if there were no general arbitration treaty at all. Now, as far as I am concerned, I wish either to take part in something that means something, or else not have any part in it at all." [23]

Defense of the Senate's Stand. The Senate defended itself by pointing to the fact that before the President began to make the *compromis* alone it had ratified thirty-seven special arbitration treaties without amendment, six with amendments, and had rejected but one.   Mr. Roosevelt evidently felt that this forbearance on the part of the Senate was back in the days gone by and did not operate to make the amended treaties mean anything, for when the Senate proposed the amendment to the treaties over his protest he dropped them.[24]

The Senate was supported by many, under the circumstances, in the stand which it took. Yet whatever reason the Executive may have given the Senate for defending its prerogatives, it does not seem open to doubt that the amend-

[22] Johnson, *America's Foreign Relations,* II, 365.
[23] *Selections From the Correspondence of Theodore Roosevelt and Henry Cabot Lodge,* N. Y., 1925, Vol. II, p. iii.
[24] Johnson, *America's Foreign Relations,* II, 366.

ment practically nullified the treaties as Hay and Roosevelt contended.

Effect on the Cause of Arbitration. Furthermore, it is doubtful if the treaties would have been accepted by the Powers with the proposed amendment, for "the very purpose of the original treaty was to bind the respective countries to submit questions to arbitration without further recourse to the treaty-making power." In the view of other countries, the formulation of the *compromis,* however important it may be, is a question of procedure. The amendment was therefore objectionable from this standpoint, for it compelled a foreign power to negotiate a treaty when by its constitutional practice no formal treaty was necessary.[25]

Certainly the final effect was again to negate our efforts to associate ourselves with other peoples for keeping the peace.

The Outlook of March 4, 1905, concluded that "the Senate has done what it could to stop the wheels of Government. It has done what it could to stop the progress of the civilized world toward the substitution of judicial process for war as a means of settling international disputes. It has for the time being absolutely prohibited the United States from having any share in that beneficent movement." [26]

THE ROOT TREATIES

Lamentable as the impasse was for the cause of arbitration there could be no denying that in the United States the Senate is a part of the treaty-making power and that the coöperation of both the President and Senate is necessary to bind the United States internationally. No one recognized this fact more than Elihu Root, who succeeded John Hay as Secretary of State in 1905, and put his constructive mind to the task of evolving a compromise that would make some

[25] Editorial, *The American Journal of International Law,* 1908, Vol. II, p. 388.
[26] *The Outlook,* March 4, 1905, Vol. 79, p. 516.

kind of arbitration treaty possible.   He succeeded by the
simple expedient of inducing President Roosevelt to agree
to send the *compromis* of each arbitration to the Senate
for approval, before it was signed, and by inducing the
latter body to forego its insistence that a treaty be concluded
in each case.   This was a compromise in which the Senate
got the substance of its contention; it got the recognition it
demanded and the power to block any proposed arbitration,
but the difficulty above considered of compelling the foreign
nation to conclude a treaty where its practice called for none
was eliminated.   The clause accomplishing this purpose stated
that "it is understood that on the part of the United States
such special agreements will be made by the President of
the United States by and with the advice and consent of the
Senate, and on the part of France they will be subject to the
procedure required by the constitutional laws of France." [27]

Until each government had agreed to the *compromis* according to its own procedure neither was bound.   Probably
the admission of the Senate to the framing of the special
agreement lessened the likelihood of cases being submitted,
but the expedient did secure the quick approval of the Treaty
of February 10, 1908, with France,[28] and by 1910 twenty-
two such treaties to which we were a party had come into
force.   Needless to say they all covered only questions of a
legal nature or relating to the interpretation of treaties and
excluded any questions affecting the vital interests, independence, or honor of the parties, and matters affecting third
states.[29]

THE TAFT-KNOX TREATIES OF 1911

President Taft felt that the time had come to drop these
all-excluding phrases and commit ourselves to the arbitration of serious and weighty disputes.   He, therefore, nego-

[27] *The Outlook,* March 4, 1905, Vol. 79, p. 516.
[28] The Senate kept it only nine days.
[29] Johnson, *America's Foreign Relations,* II, 370, 450.

tiated treaties with England and France to supersede the Root-Roosevelt treaties of 1908, and made them one of the two chief measures of his administration.[30] In the new conventions, signed at the White House on August 2, 1911, all differences which were "justiciable in their nature by reason of being susceptible of decision by the application of the principles of law or equity" should be submitted to the Permanent Court of Arbitration, or to some other arbitral tribunal, under the special agreement to be concluded in each case by and with the advice and consent of the Senate, as in the Root treaties.[31]

Article II of the treaties provided for the creation, at any time, of a special Joint High Commission of Inquiry to be composed of three of the nationals of each of the parties, or of other persons if agreed upon by an exchange of notes. This commission was to make a careful investigation of any question referred to it, whether of the kind described in Article I or not, for the purpose of elucidating the facts, defining the issues and making such recommendations and conclusions as it might deem appropriate. If when a request for a Commission of Inquiry was made by one party the other desired to continue diplomatic discussion for another year, it could do so before the creation of the commission. The purpose of such a body was to provide a further means of composing the dispute without referring it to arbitration. The reports of the commission were not to be regarded as decisions of the questions or matters considered, either of the facts or of the law, and should in no way have the character of an arbitral award.

If, however, the two parties were unable to agree in the last analysis that a dispute should go to arbitration under Article I, that question should, by the terms of Article III, be submitted to the Joint High Commission and if all, or all

[30] *Current Literature, October,* 1911, Vol. 51, p. 350.
[31] For the text of the treaties see *The American Journal of International Law,* Sup. to Vol. 5, 1911, pp. 253–57.

but one, of the members agreed that the difference was within the scope of Article I it was to be sent on to arbitration under the terms of the treaty, that is, a *compromis* should be drawn up, with Senate approval, providing for the selection of arbitrators, defining their powers, and stating the questions that they should pass upon.

Popularity of the Treaties. The popularity of the treaties was far greater than might have been expected. When Mr. Taft announced his purpose to negotiate a treaty with England under which all questions thereafter arising would be open to arbitration, the response was unprecedented on both sides of the ocean. "In England ratification meetings were held all over the kingdom, culminating in a great meeting in the historic Guildhall of London in which Mr. Asquith for the government and Mr. Balfour for the opposition pledged the acceptance of united England to Mr. Taft's invitation. In the United States the press supported the proposal with such unanimity, and the country as a whole signified its approval so clearly, that the administration advised the peace societies to keep quiet as it anticipated the ready approval of the treaties in the Senate. A little later, when opposition developed, one of them in a short time secured resolutions endorsing the treaties from two hundred chambers of commerce, representing cities containing twenty million people." [32]

Opposed by Roosevelt. But the Administration in measuring the opinion favorable to a real step in arbitration had left out of account the influence which one or two determined opponents might have on the Senate. It did not know that on June 12th, before the treaties were concluded, Mr. Roosevelt had written to Senator Lodge: "I have been thinking a good deal over the arbitration treaty . . . The more I have thought over it the more reluctant I am from the standpoint of your good name in the future that you should sanction an

[32] *The Independent,* August 31, 1911, Vol. 71, pp. 461–2.

act of maudlin folly when there is not a thing of any kind to be gained from it." Then, after listing half a dozen questions that we would refuse to arbitrate if any one asked us, he had closed with the suggestion that "all that is necessary to do is to state in the preamble that the two nations always agree to recognize one another's honor, integrity and international interests and with this understanding, agree to arbitrate whatever questions may come up between them." [33]

The Lodge Report: Unconstitutional. On August 11, a week after the treaties had been sent to the Senate, Mr. Lodge submitted the majority report of the Senate Foreign Relations Committee condemning the treaties in two respects. First: that they were unconstitutional; they provided that the Joint High Commission of Inquiry might decide in certain contingencies whether a question was justiciable and therefore arbitrable. This would never do; no question of the arbitrability of a dispute could ever be decided without a vote of the Senate. The Committee believed "that it would be a violation of the Constitution of the United States to confer upon an outside commission powers which, under the Constitution devolve upon the Senate." [34]

In the opinion of the *Independent*, of August 31, 1911, the argument that the Senate's prerogatives were infringed and therefore the treaties were unconstitutional was mere pettifogging quibble. Senator Lodge knew better than that, as did all his colleagues who voted with him.[35] It quoted, however, an exhaustive list of instances in which power to determine similar questions had been delegated. *The Outlook* likewise quoted many instances of delegation by

[33] *Selections from the Correspondence of Theodore Roosevelt and Henry Cabot Lodge*, N. Y., 1925, Vol. II, p. 404. On August 14 and 22 he wrote to Mr. Lodge congratulating him upon his stand on the treaties and promising to back him up heartily. He had written to Captain Mahan asking him to write a piece and would write one himself in the *Outlook* (p. 406).
[34] *The Outlook*, Sept. 2, 1911, Vol. 99, p. 3.
[35] *The Independent*, Aug. 31, 1911, Vol. 71, p. 492.

Congress of the power to determine when a law general in its provisions should be applied. It was willing to take the judgment of President Taft, Secretary Knox and Senator Root on the question of constitutionality, but pointed out that it did not take the professional mind of a lawyer to understand the issue. The power of the President and the Senate to refer any and all questions to arbitration was undoubted; it had been exercised too often to be called into question. If the treaties had provided outright for the arbitration of all questions no one could question the right of the Senate to confirm the treaty. The only question raised by the majority report was whether in case exceptions were made the Senate must past on each case as it arose, in order to determine whether it came within the specified exceptions. [36]

. This, however, did not satisfy Mr. Roosevelt. In his promised article in *The Outlook,* on September 9, 1911, he thought it would be quite proper to delegate to the Joint High Commission many subordinate functions, "but the high, the supreme function of deciding whether a question is of such vital importance to the country that it is or is not arbitrable, cannot with propriety be delegated to any outsider by either the President or the Senate. They are elected to perform exactly the vital duties implied in such decisions. If a President, after consulting with his Constitutional advisers, the Senate, could not make up his own mind about such a vital question, and had to have it made up for him by outsiders . . ." it would merely be proof that he was not fit to be President. He therefore heartily supported the Lodge Amendment striking out the clause providing for opinions on arbitrability by the Joint High Commission. He found it "difficult to characterize this provision truthfully without seeming to be offensive. Merely to speak of it as silly comes far short of saying what should be said." [37]

[36] *The Outlook,* Sept. 16, 1911, Vol. 99, p. 106.
[37] *The Outlook,* September 9, 1911, Vol. 99, p. 69.

War Treaties, not Peace. But the charge of unconstitutionality was not the most serious which the Lodge report had made against the treaties. In it Mr. Lodge had discovered, as he was to discover again on a much more fateful occasion, that the treaties were not peace pacts at all, but breeders of war instead. Immigration, "our territorial integrity, the right of each State, and of the United States to their territory might be forced before a joint commission." We might be flooded with Asiatics or actually dispossessed of house and home. To be sure, on the day of his report, before the fatal Article III could endanger our liberties, "no nation on earth would think of raising these questions with the United States. . . . But if we accept this treaty with the third clause of Article III included, we invite other nations to raise these very questions and to endeavor to force them before an arbitral tribunal. Such an invitation would be a breeder of war and not of peace, and would rouse a series of disputes, now happily and entirely at rest, into malign and dangerous activity." [38]

To *The Independent,* again, the doctrine that the peace treaties were disguised war treaties was enough to make even the injudicious grieve, [39] but it was a most serious matter to Mr. Roosevelt. Some great military power might attempt, directly or indirectly, to get possession of the Island of St. Thomas in the Caribbean, or Magdalena Bay on the Pacific Coast of Mexico, and an arbitral court might "very probably decide against us." Maybe such treaties would "bind us to arbitrate the Monroe Doctrine, the Platt Amendment with Cuba, the payment of state bonds to European bond-holders, the question whether various European countries are entitled to the same concessions that Canada is to receive under the reciprocity agreement, the right of other foreign nations to interfere at Panama. . . ."

[38] Ibid., 62.
[39] *The Independent,* Aug. 31, 1911, Vol. 71, p. 492.

Honesty Required Exceptions. The treaty, in fact, was not straightforward, charged Mr. Roosevelt, and "no moral movement is ever permanently helped by hypocrisy." When everybody knew there were some things we would not arbitrate the only proper course to follow was "to say in honest fashion that there are certain questions which this nation will not arbitrate at the dictation of an outside body." Moreover, there was the dangerous word "justiciable." What did it mean? Nobody could tell now, so what chance would there be of defining it after a dispute became acute? [40]

This was also one of the chief indictments of Senator Lodge in his long speech in the March session, "one of the most forcible speeches of his career," which was, said *Current Literature,* aside from politics, doubtless the most potent force in the emasculation of the treaty. [41]   And not only could he not define justiciable, but he could find no meaning for the phrase "claim of right" and outside the English speaking world they would never understand what we meant by "equity."

Menaces Now Dead Would Come to Life. But the Senator had plenty of other indictments against the new features of the treaties. He was, of course, speaking for their ratification all the time; he really wanted to make but one little, though highly important, amendment. Yet the risks were very unequal; all the questions we had ever arbitrated had been "without exception" American questions. It would be so in the future; European and Eastern questions would never come up. But, (in addition to the list of dangers enumerated by Mr. Roosevelt), we were placing at the mercy of a special court such questions as whether a foreign nation should be allowed to purchase the Galapagos Islands from Ecuador or the Island of Curacao from Holland, the question of our title to the Panama Canal, or the tolls we

[40] *The Outlook,* Sept. 9, 1911, Vol. 99, p. 68.
[41] *Current Literature,* April, 1912, Vol. 52, p. 376.

should fix for ships passing through it. We were tempting and inviting other nations "to raise these perilous and vital questions, which now slumber peacefully in a sleep which should know no waking." [42]

The Minority Report. The initial blasts against the treaties had caused the Editor of *Current Literature* to remark in October, that the "full and swift current of public sentiment which started to flow with such power when the arbitration treaties were announced" had encountered obstacles. He placed considerable confidence, however, in Mr. Root's long observed tendency to try to find a way out. In presenting the minority report to the Senate, for himself, Senator Cullom and Senator Burton, Mr. Root had felt, with Lodge and Roosevelt, "that there are some questions of national policy and conduct which no nation can submit to the decision of anyone else. . . . The undoubted purpose of the first article of these treaties is to exclude such questions from arbitration as non-justiciable. If there is a danger of misunderstanding as to whether such questions are indeed effectively excluded by the terms of the first article, such a danger of course should be prevented." To allay doubts and fears on the score he did not think it necessary to tamper with the vital machinery of the treaties; it would only be necessary to insert in the resolution of consent to ratification the following clause: "The Senate advises and consents to the ratification of the said treaty with the understanding, to be made a part of such ratification, that the treaty does not authorize the submission to arbitration of any question which depends upon or involves the maintenance of the traditional attitude of the United States concerning American questions, or other purely governmental policy." [43]

---

[42] Ibid., The utterances of the two seem to indicate that they were particularly opposed to any proposals to arbitrate Panama questions.

[43] *Current Literature*, Oct., 1911, Vol. 51, p. 352. Secretary Knox argued forcibly in an address at Cincinnati, November 8, 1911, that no right of the Senate was abridged and urged ratification, saying: "I respectfully urge the early action of the Senate thereon, not merely as a

Amendments Adopted.   The opponents of the treaties were too determined upon amputation, however, to permit them to escape with a mild reservation.   After the portentous dangers lurking in them had been held up to the public for six months, the ax fell, on March 7, 1912, and eliminated clause 3 of Article III, empowering a Joint High Commission to determine whether a dispute was arbitrable under the terms of the treaty.   The vote was close, being 42 to 40 in favor of elimination.   Then a combination of Democrats and Insurgent Republicans took control of the situation and rapidly read into the preamble a refusal to arbitrate any question which affected the admission of aliens into the United States or to its educational institutions, any question of defaulted state bonds, of the Monroe Doctrine, of the territorial integrity of any State or of the United States, or any other purely governmental policy.   Then, no one having further amendments to offer, the Senate consented to ratification with only three dissenting votes. [44]   Control of the Senate Foreign Relations Committee had been sufficient to deny a preponderant public sentiment in favor of another step in arbitration.

---

matter of policy, but as a duty to mankind. The importance and moral influence of the ratification of such a treaty can hardly be over-estimated in the cause of advancing civilization. It may well engage the best thought of the statesmen and people of every country, and I cannot but consider it fortunate that it was reserved to the United States to have the leadership in so grand a work." *American Journal of International Law,* 1912, Vol. 6, p. 177.

[44] *American Journal of International Law,* 1912, Vol. 6, p. 460. In addition to striking out clause 3 of Article III, the amendments further *"Provided,* That the Senate advises and consents to the ratification of the said treaty with the understanding to be made part of such ratification, that the treaty does not authorize the submission to arbitration of any question which affects the admission of aliens into the United States, or the admission of aliens to the educational institutions of the several States, or the territorial integrity of the several states or of the United States, or concerning the question of the alleged indebtedness or monied obligation of any State of the United States, or any question which depends upon or involves the maintenance of the traditional attitude of the United States concerning American questions, commonly described as the Monroe Doctrine, or other purely governmental policy."

Continued Public Interest.   Even after the publication of Senator Lodge's report and Mr. Roosevelt's editorials the newspaper opposition to the treaties had been negligible. The Boston *Herald* asserted that if the fear of loss of a little prestige is to prevail in the Senate in that case "it should convince the country that it needs not a new treaty but a new Senate." The Philadelphia *Ledger* was certain, too, that the Senate's prerogatives were adequately protected.   "The President", said the Los Angeles *Times,* "will have the backing of the whole country in his fight to cancel the paltry and preposterous action of the Senate committee and to maintain the original vigor of the treaties."   The Denver *Republican* was certain that "a great mistake, a most unfortunate retrograde movement," would be made if the Senate failed to approve the treaties.   The Baltimore *Sun* felt that the rejection of the treaties or their material amendment would be "an international misfortune," and the Chicago *Tribune* concluded that the American people "desire the ratification of the treaties and are surprised that any Senator should oppose them."

The New York *Post* was not blind to an element of risk in making the treaties, for the most carefully drawn treaty could not "take a bond of fate or foresee everything in the future," but war also had its hazards.   Surely enlightened and human public men would hazard something for peace. The Richmond *Times-Dispatch* and the New York *Times* were heartily for the pacts and the Baltimore *American* was willing to give up a part of the Monroe Doctrine rather than lose the treaties, while papers as far apart as the New York *World* and the San Francisco *Chronicle* united in testifying to the popular support of them.   The *World* believed that practically the entire nation had set its heart on the treaties, and the *Chronicle* felt that "The people of the United States are more nearly unanimous in their determination that all disputes with foreign nations shall be submitted to arbitration than they have been on any other question of public policy since the foundation of the Republic." [45]

Interpretations of the Result. But there was politics to be played. The people, even if angry, could not discipline the Senate in less than two elections and they could be depended upon, in the pressure of events, to forget long before then. "The trail of politics is over it all" declared the Independent New York *Post,* adding that it would be impossible to show that the defeat of the treaties was not due to a desire to take prestige from President Taft. The Chicago *Record Herald,* also Independent, was equally convinced that it may be "asserted with confidence that partisanship, peanut politics, opposition to the President, the desire to withhold from him something that might give him strength and prestige were factors in the deplorable and humiliating outcome." Recalling that the important clause eliminated had been originally suggested by Mr. Bryan it thought we should never hear explained why the Bryan Senators voted against it. In order further to fix the personal responsibility, the Springfield *Republican,* Independent, observed that since the balance of power rested with the Insurgent Republicans who were "inspired to take a strangle hold on the treaties by Theodore Roosevelt," he would be "held accountable in history for what he has done to influence the Senate's evil action."

The Democratic papers, too, used even stronger terms in characterizing the action of the Senate. "As demagogy," said the New York *American,* "it was cheap; as statesmanship it was contemptible," to which the Cleveland *Plain Dealer* added, "the most notable feature of the performance of the United States Senate is that in putting up its little barbed wire fence it has seized upon excuses even more paltry than those advanced by the loudest jingoes and most illogical special pleaders," and the New York *World* concluded that after cutting away the principle which gave life

[45] *Current Literature,* Oct., 1911, Vol. 51, p. 353–4.

and vitality to the treaties the Senate only added "insult to injury by ratifying the remains as if life were left in them." [46]

Dropped by the President. Confronted by the action of the Senate, President Taft simply said "We shall have to begin all over again" and dropped the treaties. Some thought that he should have ratified them, even as amended. The Joint High Commission was left, it was argued; it might still do invaluable work in investigation and conciliation, and in time the excised function might be restored to it. So much appeared to be true, but the months of protest against the scope of the treaty culminating in the flock of amendments sponsored by Senators Chamberlain and Bacon had done worse execution still. The Senators had excluded so much from arbitration that acceptance of their conditions would have left us in a less advanced position rather than a step ahead. Aspects of the admission of aliens to the country and to our schools, territorial questions and the repudiated state bonds—aspects of any of these matters might not be arbitrable, but other phases of them would and should be. Nothing is so settled in the history of arbitration, and in our own practice, as the arbitrability of boundary disputes and pecuniary claims. Many minor issues involving the construction of treaties or the admission and treatment of aliens might also come up which would be highly arbitrable. [47] If we fail to consider, then, the ground excluded by "American questions", "Monroe Doctrine" and "other purely governmental policy" so much territory had been marked off as non-arbitrable that the scope of admittedly arbitrable questions would have been more limited after the treaty than before, and its purpose therefore wholly defeated.

[46] *Current Literature.* April, 1912, Vol. 52, pp. 375-6. *Literary Digest,* March 16, 1912, Vol. 44, p. 521.
[47] See W. C. Dennis in *The Amer. Jour. of Int'l. Law,* 1912, Vol. VI, pp. 624–26. Also the text of the amendments.

The Danger to Domestic Security in the Taft Treaties

But surely, the cautious minded citizen will say, all of this frenzy of opposition to the treaties could not have been based on partisan and personal hostility alone; surely the gentlemen must have had some fear of the consequences, if the treaties passed as proposed.

Perhaps they were really afraid that some unpleasant question might be raised. Let us see, therefore, just how easy it would have been to bring our cherished policies into jeopardy under these treaties. Both Germany and Japan were said to be favorable to signing such pacts with us, if the English and French treaties were ratified. Let us suppose, then, that after signing such a treaty with us Japan contested our right to exclude Japanese immigrants. What would have been the consequence? The treaty tells exactly. After diplomatic negotiations had broken down it would have been Japan's privilege to ask for the creation of a Joint High Commission of Inquiry. That is the only step she could possibly have taken under the treaty. Such a Commission would then have been appointed consisting of three Japanese and three Americans.

These are the men whom Mr. Roosevelt persistently referred to as "outsiders," assuming that as soon as the American members were appointed they would be completely out from the control of the American Government, and perchance wholly oblivious to our interests. Nothing of the sort was implied about the Japanese members. Such a selection of commissioners, of course, was all but beyond the bounds of possibility. Any American Government would be most careful to name only men about whose ability not only to weigh evidence impartially but to conserve basic American interests there could be no question. It is true that the treaties permitted the governments to appoint foreigners if they wished, and in technical but relatively unimportant cases either government might desire to appoint a foreign expert, but such an appointment in a major controversy would have been wholly unlikely.

If for any reason, however, the American Government did not wish to submit even to inquiry it could have postponed the creation of the Joint High Commission for one year for the purpose of continuing diplomatic exchanges.

Commissioners Confirmed by the Senate. At the end of that time, if the Japanese still persisted, the Joint High Commission would have been appointed and would have proceeded to try to agree upon the essential facts in the controversy, define the issues and make such recommendations or conclusions as it could agree upon. Mr. Taft was willing to concede Senate confirmation of the American commissioners, thus giving the Senate positive assurance that the men would not be too judicially minded, but, however appointed, it is most unlikely that in a case of such gravity the American representatives would have been wholly out of touch with the American Government; that they would be in frequent communication with the State Department and under its control was much more probable. Yet even if they acted wholly independently, we could surely have rested assured that the American members would join in no analysis of the dispute that did not give us fair play.

In any event, the report would not have been a binding decision either as to the facts or on the law and would in no way have had the character of an award.

But in seeking our national downfall by this route we will assume that the Joint Commission did submit a report distinctly favorable to the Japanese side of the case, and that the judgment of the country was so clearly opposed to arbitration that our government refused to arbitrate. Then, and only then, could the Japanese government submit to the Joint Commission the question as to whether the controversy was justiciable, i. e., arbitrable. In order to achieve calamity even now, it is necessary again to suppose that two of the American members on the commission agreed with the Japanese members that the question should go to arbitration.

Senate Approval of the "Compromis" Required. A report of the Joint Commission decreeing arbitration in those circumstances could have come only if the government appointing them was woefully inefficient indeed. But having supposed everything else let us allow even that and suppose further that it proceeded to draw up with the Japanese a *compromis* for arbitration. This agreement would have had to be approved by two-thirds of the Senate before there could be arbitration, and if everybody else having failed the Senators, they too sat weakly in their seats and voted "yea," then an arbitration of the case would have been under way.

Even then if the arbitrators paid any attention at all to the clear rule of international law that immigration is basically a domestic question, we would still have been saved, and the Japanese Government made ridiculous. If, on the other hand, we refused to proceed with arbitration and war resulted, arbitration would indeed have failed, to say the least. But, unless one must assume the most unprincipled conspiracy on the part of the Japanese Government, such as it has never indulged in, is it likely that after so much discussion around a common council table, and so many waiting periods in between, that war would finally ensue? It hardly seems conceivable that such a result would follow, yet the insistent asking of the question, "If we do not mean to arbitrate immigration and a dozen other subjects why not frankly and honestly say so in the treaties?" had much to do with their defeat. This is the type of question which in its mere statement seems to carry its own plain answer, and if asked industriously enough, it is the kind of question that is capable of swinging large numbers of people into an incorrect position. The reply is not so easy to give and can never be made often enough. In the case under consideration, however, the answer is not occult to anyone who has studied the treaties.

What the Taft Treaties Actually did. The older Root treaties put the main presumption against arbitration. Nothing which might be construed by either party as touching their "vital interests" or "honor" was pledged for arbitration. They offered every inducement to refuse arbitration and made it most probable that only minor matters would be arbitrated.

This was not to their discredit because we had to start with small beginnings. Neither did the Taft treaties by any means reverse the real situation. They did not provide at all that every dispute should hereafter be arbitrated. They took no single question from the list of matters generally regarded as non-arbitrable. What they did do was to set up a presumption in favor of arbitration. The burden of proof was no longer to be wholly on those favoring arbitration; those opposing arbitration had to share it and show why the matter was not justiciable. It is true that this word could not be given an all-inclusive definition, but it offered no such possibilities for evading discussion of the difficulty across a council table as the all-exclusive phrases "vital interests" and "honor" did. The step actually taken in the Taft treaties was not a great one, but it did put the presumption on the right side—with the hearty approval of the people of three nations.

It is well to face the truth, of course, that when we do pledge ourselves to general arbitration as a method of settling our disputes, there will be times when we will chafe at having our hand stayed, yet no arbitration treaty will ever take away the elemental right of self defense, or reduce us to impotence in the face of sustained assaults on our rights such as finally brought us to war with Germany in 1917.

The Importance of the Treaties. The real importance of the treaties, of course, did not lie in their efficacy between the United States, England and France. Their great value lay in the fact that they were intended to serve as models for series of treaties between the United States and other powers and between the European signatories and their potential enemies. There were high hopes in England that some real insurance against the sudden outbreak of war in Europe might grow out of them. That enough of them would have developed to have averted the catastrophe of 1914, if the treaties had not been vitiated in the Senate, is more than we can say. If a cooling period could have been secured, the storm would have been averted, though it would have taken strong influences indeed to have altered Austria-Hungary's disastrous course in that year.

Be that as it may, the Senate was not to be moved by the powerful possibilities in the idea; it was more concerned with personal and party politics, and with conjuring up this or that spectre of advantage that particular nations might try to take if we should conclude similar treaties with them later on. Very well, your "hard headed" Americans will say, that was good business—exactly what the Senate is there for. But it was not good business even; no business man ever became great by refusing to risk small losses in the hope of great gain.

Moreover, the immediate purpose of the treaty, according to a leading authority on Anglo-American relations, was to prevent the combination of the English and Japanese navies against us, under the Anglo-Japanese Alliance, in case we should have an outbreak of war with Japan. Any insurance against such an eventuality was a very practical matter. [48]

---

[48] W. F. Hall, *From Empire to Commonwealth*, N. Y., 1928, p. 470. Mr. Root, among other Senators, pointed out to the Senate the wide

How Is National Honor Vindicated?   Still, says the voice of caution, at best the treaties left a presumption that questions involving even our honor might be arbitrated, and of course we could never consent to that.   This assumption was so widely broadcast in the assaults on the treaties that President Taft's good humored analysis of the defense of honor before the National Geographic Society, in December, 1911, appears to have gained little currency.

In that address he met squarely the issue of arbitrating disputes involving honor, as follows: "Now I am asked, would you arbitrate a question of national honor? Would you submit to arbitration your personal honor? I have no hesitation in answering that exactly as it is put: I would much prefer to submit to a board of arbitration, composed of intelligent jurists of impartial mind, the question whether our national honor has been attacked and if so what the reparation of the injuring nation ought to be, than I would to go to war about it.

"What would war settle? If we wiped our enemy off the map, it would settle the fact that we were the stronger nation, and if we were wiped off the map it would settle the fact that they were—and that is all it would settle!" [49] One could illustrate the operation of this principle from more than one angle out of the results of the Great War. Honor was certainly variously upheld in that struggle. But certainly the state which insisted on precipitating the War to avenge a supposed assault on its honor, and to protect its

---

importance of the Senate's decision, saying: "It is not so much that I think these treaties will lead to arbitration of questions between this country and Great Britain and France, which would not otherwise be arbitrated, that I want them ratified; it is because of the moral effect upon mankind of the Government of the United States taking what is believed to be a step forward as compared with the moral effect of the Government of the United States refusing what is believed to be a step forward will make for the education of mankind along the lines of civilization or the retardation of their progress along these lines." *Congressional Record.* Vol., 48, Part 3, p. 3050.
[49] *National Geographic Magazine*, December, 1911, Vol. 22, p. 1166-7.

vital interests, has reason to contemplate the result. That
state indeed is gone. The remnant of it around Vienna,
eking out a precarious existence and partaking of international charity, must have cause, when it thinks of the great
Empire it lost, to wonder just how national honor is best
vindicated.

Can We Agree to Arbitrate Any Kind of Disputes?
Men once embarked in a controversy often forget the
motives which animated them at the start. Arguments
originally evolved only as missiles of combat come to sound
well to the authors, and on repetition even to be believed.
Afterwards they are handy weapons for similar or even
different purposes. We shall doubtless have future im-
passioned defenses of the Senate's refusal to permit arbitration on the legal ground of preserving its constitutional
patrimony. It is well therefore to note Mr. Taft's clear
statement of the legal issue made five years after the defeat
of the treaties of 1911. "The turning point," he said, "was
whether the Senate had the power to agree that all questions
of a certain description should be submitted to arbitration
and to leave to the tribunal of arbitration the question of
jurisdiction under it, that is, the issue whether a future
controversy involved questions within the class. Learned
senators contended that this would be an invalid delegation
of the function of the Senate to a tribunal of arbitration.
It would not be a delegation of the authority of the Senate
any more than it would be a delegation of the authority of
the President, because the Senate's function is no more
sacred, and no more necessary to the making of a treaty,
than is the function which the President performs. I confess I have never been able to appreciate the force of the
negative argument by the Senate in regard to this matter.
The question of the jurisdiction of a tribunal to hear a
particular question and to decide whether the question
comes within the class of questions over which the treaty

gives them jurisdiction is a question of the construction of a treaty, and the construction of a treaty is one of the commonest issues between nations submitted to arbitration. The agreement to abide a judgment as to jurisdiction in future is no more a delegation of control over foreign affairs than is an agreement to abide a judgment of an existing controversy in respect to such relations. The narrow view that the Senate has taken in this matter is inconsistent with any arbitration at all, and it excludes all useful treaties of arbitration in advance of the occurrence of the quarrel to be arbitrated. It destroys all hope of an international court for the settlement of international disputes." [50]

THE BRYAN COMMISSION OF INQUIRY TREATIES

President Taft's conclusion that the Senate blocked the way to the extension of arbitration held true up to 1928. His elimination from the Presidency, however, to which much of the opposition to the treaties of 1911 had been directed, was followed rather unexpectedly by an important step toward the peaceful settlement of international disputes. The war on Mr. Taft, and on his in other respects not conspicuously progressive Administration, brought into power for the first time in many years a Democratic Administration which also controlled both the Senate and the House. It also brought another President and Secretary of State who were devoted to the cause of peace.

The Secretary, Mr. W. J. Bryan, had proposed as early as 1906 that, instead of fighting at once, nations involved in a dispute submit the quarrel to inquiry and wait a bit. There was nothing complicated about the idea. In fact it was so simple and so reasonable that it was hard to inveigh against it and predict the alienation of Caribbean or Central American territories thereunder. It could be ridiculed as a

[50] Taft, *The Presidency*, 102-4.

too simple substitute for the unpreventable use of war as an instrument of policy, but that treatment of the idea made it difficult to assemble the fears of calamity against it.

The Senate Consulted. Mr. Bryan, moreover, not desiring to meet the fate of his predecessors, laid his proposition before the Senate Foreign Relations Committee, on April 23, 1913, shortly after his inauguration, and it was understood that it would approve of any treaties negotiated along lines agreed upon. On April 26, therefore, Mr. Bryan, with the encouragement of President Wilson, submitted the proposal to all the nations represented by diplomatic officers at Washington [51] and threw himself into the task of furthering the plan with a zeal which brought charges that he neglected his other duties for this one project. He was rewarded by receiving the acceptance in principle of twenty-nine governments within six months. The text of the first treaty signed, that with Salvador on August 7, 1913, was understood to have been at once submitted to the Senate Foreign Relations Committee and approved by it, before others were concluded. [52] The work of securing signatures then proceeded and by July 24, 1914, twenty-one powers had concluded the desired treaties and thirteen others were in process of negotiation. On that date twenty were submitted to the Senate. [53]

Consent Given. The outbreak of the Great War a few days later might have killed the treaties, but it appears to have aided them instead. It certainly demonstrated the utility of a cooling off period if one could be secured. All the belligerents maintained that they were sincerely desirous of peace and fighting only in self defence, yet it had proved impossible to secure just a little more time for con-

---

[51] *Amer. Jour. of Int'l Law.* July, 1913, Vol. 7, p. 566. It will be remembered that the Taft-Knox treaties also contemplated commissions of inquiry of more limited scope.

[52] Ibid., 1913, Vol. 7, p. 824.

[53] Ibid., 1914, Vol. 8, p. 567.

ference. The shock with which the thing had struck American opinion made it difficult to argue that the Bryan plan was not desirable. The prestige of the new Wilson Administration, also, was still undiminished. One held his conservatism a little in abeyance after the overthrow of 1912. The country had overwhelmingly indicated its desire for a progressive administration and under the force of Mr. Wilson's leadership Congress had been steadily engaged in the most astonishing output of legislation in fifty years. The momentum of that impulse was still powerful. Moreover, it was late summer and very warm in Washington when the treaties were brought to a vote in the Senate on August 13, 1914, and ratified with only slight changes.[54] A bare quorum of fifty Senators was present. Mr. Lodge, who called the treaties "fatuous" was absent. What the result would have been if all those who agreed with him had attended cannot be said. Under the two-thirds rule every vote against a treaty counts double.

Inquiry Only Provided.   Whatever the circumstances, however, the Senate deserves the credit of approving in this instance the Administration's effort to advance the peaceable settlement of disputes. The Bryan Treaties were not arbitration treaties; they gave no tribunal the power to render judgment on anything. They were to operate only when "previous arbitration treaties do not apply in their terms or are not applied in fact" and "when diplomatic methods of adjustment have failed." Arbitration was neither to be superseded nor brought about. The signatories simply agreed that when all other means had failed a dispute was to be referred to a permanent commission consisting of one representative of each country and three others who were to be citizens of neither.

The concession of a majority on the commission to non-

[54] D. P. Meyers, "America—Lost Leader in World Peace," *The Independent,* Jan. 21, 1928, Vol. 120, p. 57.

citizens was an important one, not likely to have been granted if the commission had had power to make decisions. The same can be said of the clause giving the commission the power to initiate an investigation if neither contracting party requested it. However initiated, the commission was to have a year, or longer on agreement, in which to make its report, after which both parties were free to proceed as they liked. Both, of course, agreed to furnish the commission "with all the means and facilities required for its investigation and report." The signatories thus bound themselves to nothing except that they would not "declare war or begin hostilities during such investigation and before the report is submitted." The advocates of perfect freedom to decide what we shall do in the event of future disputes appeared to retain the substance of the coveted right. Those who had no faith in treaties of any kind could dismiss the treaties as a mischievous gesture. The advocates of arbitration, on the other hand, could rest assured that few wars would be fought after a period of delay and investigation during which pacific opinion the world over would have time to make itself felt. If any declarations of war were made after the presentation of the committee's report they would be made in a strong cause indeed or by a country bent on running amuck.

Not Tested in The Great War. Two of the original twenty treaties, those with the Dominican Republic and with Panama, were not approved by the Senate. Others with France, Great Britain and Russia were ratified later in the year. [55] The Central Powers did not see fit to sign the treaties offered them. If they had done so, and the pacts had become effective, the course of later events might have been considerably modified. Their application might even have prevented the United States from intervening

---

[55] Texts of the treaties may be found in *The American Journal of International Law,* Vol. 8, p. 569 and Vol. 9, p. 495.

effectively in favor of the Allies.   Certainly the postponement of hostilities for a year after April, 1917, would have
had that result.   Yet the commission would have been under
no compulsion to take a year to report its findings; it might
have begun its work early in 1917, when the unrestricted
submarine warfare was opened, and under pressure have
presented its report in weeks instead of months.   It is not
to be supposed that such an inquiry could be used by any
nation as a cloak to cover persistent and increasing warfare
upon the lives and property of another people.   Nor is it to
be assumed that the device would operate to stop the spread
of any world war once in full swing.   It might do so, but
its real test, and the fairer one, would come as a means of
preventing the original hostilities.

Peace Legislation Also Requires Administration.   One of
the chief merits of the Bryan treaties was the mandatory
requirement that the permanent commissions of inquiry
should be appointed at once and vacancies thereafter filled
as they occurred.   The appointment of members was not
to be left to chance or to prejudiced action after a dispute had
become acute; they were to be always ready and organized
to tackle any emergency when all other agencies had failed.
This key provision lacked administration, however, to such
an extent that in 1927 of the twenty-one contracts still "in
force" but two were supplied with full commissions ready to
function as the treaties provided. [56]   This situation was
rapidly rectified by Secretary Kellogg in the latter part of
his term in the State Department.

THE KELLOGG TREATIES

Mr. Kellogg also succeeded in inducing the Senate to
approve a new series of arbitration treaties which omit the
old bar of all questions affecting "national honor" or "vital

[56] D. P. Meyers, "America—Lost Leader in World Peace," *The Independent*, January 21, 1928, Vol. 120, p. 58.

interests." This long delayed advance was made in the Kellogg-Briand Treaty of February 6, 1928, which replaced the Root Treaty due to expire in the same month. [57]

The new treaty, which is to be offered to other countries as a model replacing the Root treaties, opens with a preamble "reaffirming" the policy of submitting to impartial decision all "justiciable" questions and expressing a desire not only to demonstrate by their example "their condemnation of war as an instrument of national policy" but to hasten the time when the perfection of arrangements for the settlement of disputes "shall have eliminated forever the possibility of war among any of the Powers of the world." These statements need not be considered as binding, but it is of considerable value to have the Senate committed to the impartial decision of all justiciable disputes and "the perfection of international arrangements" for the settlement of all disputes.

Article I provides that any dispute "of whatever nature," when diplomacy has failed and recourse to adjudication by a competent tribunal is not had, shall be submitted for investigation and report to the Permanent International Commission constituted under the Bryan treaty of September 15, 1914. In other words, the Bryan treaty remains in force.

Article II says that all justiciable questions, i. e., susceptible of decision by the application of principles of law and equity, not otherwise decided, shall be submitted to arbitration under the Hague Convention of October 18, 1907, "or some other competent tribunal," which apparently permits reference to the World Court. The details of every arbitration must be decided, as of old, "in each case by special agreement, which special agreement shall provide for the organization of such tribunal if necessary, define its powers, state the question or questions at issue, and settle the terms of reference." The Root formula of requiring the

[57] Text, *United States Daily,* Feb. 9, 1928.

advice and consent of the Senate in the United States and leaving France to agree "in accordance with the constitutional laws of France" is retained.   In other words, again, the Root agreement is reaffirmed with the omission of the prohibitory exclusions, national honor and vital interest.

Article III substitutes instead four classes of disputes which can not be sent to arbitration.   It requires that "The provisions of this treaty shall not be invoked in respect to any dispute the subject matter of which (a) is within the domestic jurisdiction of either of the High Contracting Parties, (b) involves the interest of third parties, (c) depends upon or involves the maintenance of the traditional attitude of the United States concerning American questions, commonly described as the Monroe Doctrine, (d) depends upon or involves observance of the obligations of France in accordance with the covenant of the League of Nations.

Article IV substituted for a definite term the provision that the treaty should run in perpetuity until terminated by either party after one year's written notice.   This is probably a gain, though not certainly.   It balances the chance of a nation terminating the treaty in a period of growing irritation against the chance of a dispute arising after a term treaty has been allowed to lapse.

Ratified Without Change.   The treaty was submitted to the Senate at once and explained by Secretary Kellogg to the Foreign Affairs Committee on February 29, 1928.   The Committee at once pointed out that Article I and III were contradictory.   Article I said that all questions should be submitted for investigation and report under the Bryan Treaty; Article III said that the provisions of the treaty should not apply to four excepted classes of disputes.   The Committee, desiring not to weaken the Bryan Treaty, indicated its intention of approving in such a manner as to leave no doubt on this score. [58]   Mr. Kellogg therefore hastened

[58] N. Y. *World,* Feb. 29, 1928.

to exchange notes with the French in which both Governments declared that it had been and was their understanding that the Bryan Treaty was to remain in complete force. The French Government declared that the new treaty not only leaves the 1914 treaty unchanged, "but even envisages its application." With this assurance before it that Article III excluded the four classes of disputes from arbitration, but not from investigation, the Senate ratified the treaty without change, on March 6, and by unanimous vote. [59]

The event shows that the Senate Foreign Relations Committee can be helpful in perfecting an arbitration treaty. It also illustrates a method in which the desires of Senators may be met, especially in bi-lateral treaties, without the adoption of any changes in or reservations to the treaty. Probably, too, it indicates the advantage of having a Secretary of State who has been promoted from the Committee.

Progress. Much still remains to be done apparently before the Senate will agree in advance to arbitrate any kind of dispute whatever. It must still continue to decide, when a dispute has reached its highest point of tension, whether to arbitrate it or not. The grounds under which it may refuse to arbitrate at all, by Article III, are still broad, but the improvement in this direction is great, and the Bryan compulsory investigation principle is not only retained but promoted. More important still, a step in the right direction is not only not obstructed in the Senate; it is sympathetically promoted.

[59] N. Y. *Times,* March 7, 1928; *Congressional Record,* Vol. 69, No. 64, p. 4288.

CHAPTER VI

THE EARLIER TREATIES OF PEACE IN THE SENATE

WHEN the majority by which the Senate would approve treaties was being considered in the Constitutional Convention, some objected that it ought not to be made more difficult to conclude peace than to make war. A majority of the Senate (and House) could declare war, whereas two thirds of the Senate must concur in the peace. The fear of difficulty in concluding peace treaties was not shared by many, however, and aside from a close shave on the Jay Treaty, of 1794, no serious trouble over terms of peace developed for many years.

The Jay Treaty. The Jay Treaty, of course, was not technically a treaty of peace. It probably composed more questions growing out of the War for Independence, though, than the Peace of 1783, concluded before the creation of the Senate. Relations with Great Britain over the non-execution of the earlier treaty had nearly reached the breaking point, and if Jay's Treaty, negotiated to avert a renewed break, had failed, war would at least have been on the calendar of the day.

The bitter struggle throughout the country over the Jay Treaty is a matter of common knowledge. In the words of John Quincy Adams, that was "the severest trial which the character of Washington and the fortunes of our country have ever passed through. No period of the War of Independence, no other emergency of our history since its close, not even the ordeal of establishing the constitution . . .

has convulsed to its innermost fibers the political association of the North American people with such excruciating agonies as the consummation and fulfillment of this great national composition of the conflicting rights, interests, and pretensions of this country and Great Britain." [1]

The fight in the Senate was similarly acute. The opponents mustered exactly a third of the Senate against the treaty but they could not secure the additional vote necessary to defeat it. Later they joined in recommending ratification subject to the condition that a new article be added to the treaty suspending so much of the twelfth article as affected the trade between the United States and the British West Indies. [2]

The Peace of Ghent. Passions must have been considerably spent in the War of 1812 with Great Britain, for in spite of the fact that the treaty closing that conflict said not a word about a single one of the issues over which the war had been declared and fought, the searching of our vessels, impressment of seamen, blockade, indemnities, etc., it was approved by the Senate after brief consideration on three days without a dissenting vote. [3] The prospect of facing the great military and naval power of Great Britain generated in the Napoleonic Wars, and just released by Napoleon's first exile, probably had much to do with the unanimous approval of the "amazing anomaly" which the treaty was.

The Treaty of Guadalupe-Hidalgo. The treaty closing the War with Mexico, however, was a different matter. Mexico had been conquered and was at our mercy. In the proposed treaty of peace, signed February 2, 1848, she had agreed to cede us 600,000 square miles of land, in addition to quitting her claims to Texas, another 300,000 square miles. But Mexico had nearly 800,000 square miles left, and

[1] W. F. Johnson, *America's Foreign Relations,* Vol. I, 192.
[2] *Sen. Exec. Jour.,* Vol. I, p. 186.
[3] *Sen. Exec. Jour.,* Feb. 16, 1815, Vol. II, p. 620.

Senators wished to appropriate that also. [4] Certainly there was no reason to approve this treaty so quickly. At the least many amendments were in order. These began to be offered on March 2, 1848, and were considered continuously until March 10, when the treaty was approved with amendments by a poll of 38 to 14.[5] Three articles were eliminated entirely and two others amended, none of which changes affected the main provisions of the treaty. Proposed amendments ranging from a disavowal of so much annexation, offered by Mr. Crittenden, to a proposal of a boundary much farther south by Mr. Davis were voted down, as were motions to exclude slavery from the new territory and to eliminate the article protecting the rights of non-combatants in future war. The articles struck out dealt mainly with the validity of Mexican land grants and the rights of the Catholic Church under the new régime. In view of the fact that President Polk had recalled his negotiator and then accepted the treaty negotiated by him after receipt of his recall, the amendments adopted were not more numerous than might have been expected.

The Treaty of Paris. A much harder fight developed over the approval of the Treaty of Peace with Spain, negotiated at Paris, in 1898. This treaty was opposed by those who disapproved of the annexation of the Philippine Islands. The opposition was led by Senator Hoar of Massachusetts, Republican, who exerted his full strength to prevent what he thought was an unjust deprivation of liberty to the Philippine people. The Democratic minority also objected to it on the issue of imperialism. Consequently the fate of the treaty was in doubt even before it was signed. On December 7, 1898, three days before the signature, Senator Lodge wrote to Mr. Roosevelt: "We are going to have trouble over the Treaty. How serious I do not know,

[4] Johnson, *America's Foreign Relations,* I, 400.
[5] *Sen. Exec. Jour.,* Vol. VII, p. 340.

but I cannot think calmly of the rejection of this Treaty by a little more than one-third of the Senate. It would be a repudiation of the President and humiliation of the country in the eyes of the whole world, and would show we are unfit as a nation to enter into great questions of foreign policy. I cannot believe that the opposition which is of course composed of Southern Democrats can succeed." [6]

Mr. Roosevelt, too, could not think with patience of the idea of a treaty of peace being rejected by political opposition and the President back of it thus discredited. He replied, on December 12: "You seriously alarm me about the treaty matter. It seems impossible that men of ordinary patriotism can contemplate such an outrage upon the country." [7]

The treaty was referred to the Senate on January 4, 1899, and was strongly contested for a month. On January 14, Mr. Lodge wrote that "The fight that is being made on the Treaty is disheartening, and every day that it is delayed increases our difficulties in the Philippines and the danger of bloodshed. The Spaniards are filling the papers with false reports in the hope that the rejection of the Treaty will throw the Islands back to Spain and the attitude of American Senators is helping them. It is not very easy to bear." [8]

As the debate proceeded the prospects of the treaty appeared to become even worse. Mr. Roosevelt wrote to Mr. Lodge on January 26th: "I confess that I am utterly disheartened and cast down at the thought that the treaty is in such serious danger. It is difficult for me to speak with moderation of such men as Hoar. That our barbarian friends on the other side of the political fence should be against us is not to be wondered at or wholly to be regretted; although of course it must be *really* a matter of regret that any American should go wrong at a time like this. . . . This huge materialistic community is at bottom either wrong or half-hearted on the Philippine question. . . ." [9]

The opponents of the treaty evidently thought that the country might be aroused on the subject, for on January 24, a motion for public debate was made but defeated. The following day unanimous consent for a vote on February 6 was obtained and on that day approval of the treaty was voted, 57 to 27, with two votes to spare. [10] Mr. Lodge expressed his relief in a letter of February 9 telling about the final vote in which he said: "Until the fight was over I did not realize what a strain it had been, but for half an hour after the vote was announced I felt exactly as if I had been struggling on the side of a mountain and as if there was not an ounce more of exertion left in any muscle of my body. . . . The line of opposition stood absolutely firm, to my great astonishment. I thought the news from Manila [of a fight with the Filipinos] would have shattered it, but it did not, marvelous as it may seem. It was the closest, hardest fight I have ever known, and probably we shall not see another in our time in which there was so much at stake." [11]

How much harder Mr. Lodge was to fight, twenty years later, against a peace treaty which committed us to a still wider participation in world affairs he little knew.

[9] Ibid., 389.
[10] *Sen. Exec. Jour.*, Vol. 31, p. 1234.
[11] *Selections From the Correspondence of Theodore Roosevelt and Henry Cabot Lodge*, 391-2. The following amendment, voted on the same day, was defeated 53 to 30, more than a third of the Senators voting for it: "The United States, desiring that the people of the archipelago shall be enabled to establish a form of free government suitable to their condition and securing the rights of life, liberty and property and the preservation of order and equal rights therein, assumes for the time being and to the end aforesaid the control of the archipelago so far as such control shall be needful for the purposes above stated . . . ." *Sen. Exec. Jour.*, Vol. 31, p. 1283.

Senator Hoar, however, was convinced that the lines of opposition had never been drawn tightly enough. He wrote, in 1903, that "the acquisition of a dependency to be held in subjection by the United States, the overthrow of the great doctrine that governments rest on consent of the governed; that all the painful consequences which have attended the war for the subjugation of that distant people, would have been avoided if the Democratic opposition had been sincere. . . The Democratic party, as a party, never meant business in this matter. I do not deny that many Democrats—I dare say a majority of the Democrats —were as earnestly and seriously opposed to the acquisition of the Philippine Islands as I was myself. But they never wielded their party strength in opposition to it." [12]

They were systematically urged not to do so by their leader, W. J. Bryan, who came to Washington at the height of the contest to urge his followers to support the treaty, end the war and let the future of the Philippines be settled in the campaign of 1900, then close at hand. Mr. Hoar was repeatedly told by Senators who refused to take Mr. Bryan's advice that he urged upon them that the Democrats must have the issue for the coming campaign. They could not hope to win a victory on the free silver and other issues of 1896 under improved business conditions after they had been defeated on them in a time of depression. [13]

Although besought by some of his political associates to allow the Senate to settle the matter, Mr. Bryan remained, and it became impossible to defeat the treaty. Seventeen of his followers including seven Populists, Silver-

---

[12] Geo. F. Hoar, *Autobiography of Seventy Years*, N. Y., 1903, Vol. II, pp. 321–2. Senator Bacon had even pledged the support of the minority to any measures necessary to suppress the Philippine insurrection, and his colleagues had sat without protest. Senator Hoar thought that they feared the fate of the Federalists who had opposed the War of 1812 and of the Democrats who opposed the War for the Union in 1861.
[13] Ibid.

ites and Independents, voted for the treaty, giving it the necessary two-thirds majority. These votes transferred would have given a majority against the treaty, even though only three Republicans voted against it. [14]

Whether the majority of the Bryan followers voted for the treaty in fear of the consequences of defeating it or because they believed it on the whole a good treaty, there seems to be no doubt that the two-thirds majority was provided to give Mr. Bryan a campaign issue. The treaty was not saved through desire to keep from humiliating a Republican President, or the country itself, but to provide a means of defeating that same President and his party. Probably Mr. Bryan's well known pacific tendencies played a large part in his action, but the mainspring of it seems to have been the belief that his opponents were presenting him with an issue on which he could win.

[14] Ibid.

CHAPTER VII

THE STRUGGLE OVER THE LEAGUE OF NATIONS

TWENTY years after 1898 another peace treaty was to be made, a treaty closing the greatest war in history and determining the general course of events for many years to come. Again a prolonged contest took place in the Senate over its terms and again Mr. Bryan came to Washington as the final test of strength approached to urge his friends in the Senate to defer to the opposition and ratify the treaty. [1] But this time the conflict of aims and purposes was too deep-seated to yield and Mr. Bryan was no longer the peerless leader of old. Moreover there was for months a wide difference of opinion in both parties as to what policy would best promote the party fortunes in the approaching election.

The Development of the League Proposal. The Russo-Japanese War seems to have been the impetus which called forth, in the years after 1905, a series of plans for world organization to keep the peace. It was the first combat on a large scale which had used the weapons of twentieth century warfare and its revelations had stimulated many people to active pursuit of some means of stopping the progressive development of destruction which was evidently under way. Of the Americans who participated in this movement in the early years the most notable were President Roosevelt and Mr. Andrew Carnegie. The latter proposed a plan for world federation and sponsored a great peace conference in New York in 1907. [2]

[1] New York *Times*, March 17, 18, 1929.
[2] *The Independent*, June 5, 1916, Vol. 86, p. 358.

Mr. Roosevelt, after mediating the Russo-Japanese War and playing an almost equally important rôle in the settlement of the first Moroccan crisis, came to the settled conclusion that "it would be a master stroke if those great powers honestly bent on peace would form a League of Peace, not only to keep peace among themselves, but to prevent, by force if necessary, its being broken by others." He was certain that "the ruler or statesman who should bring about such a combination would have earned his place in history for all time." [3] The development of the Great War confirmed and deepened this impression in Mr. Roosevelt and in a host of others. "What is needed in international matters," he concluded in 1915, "is to create a judge and then put police power back of the judge." [4] "A world league for the peace of righteousness" was the solution and if this was utopian then it was either "Utopia or Hell." [5]

This feeling was so general after the Great War broke out that a League to Enforce Peace was formed on June 15, 1915, in Independence Hall, Philadelphia, with Ex-President W. H. Taft at its head. Its purpose appeared so inherently reasonable that it soon had branches in every part of the United States and in less than a year it obtained the adhesion of the leaders of both political parties. Senator Lodge, for example, in addition to the many distinguished Republicans who headed the league, pledged his support at a great meeting in Washington on May 27, 1916, saying that putting force behind international peace might not solve the problem, "but if we cannot solve it in that way it can be solved in no other," and "not failure, but low aim, is crime." [6]

At the same session President Wilson stated his belief that the American people would wish their Government to favor

[3] Ibid., May 12, 1910, Vol. 68, pp. 1027–8. From his Nobel Peace Prize Lecture delivered at Christiania, Norway.
[4] Theodore Roosevelt, *America and the World War*, N. Y., 1915, p. 789.
[5] *The Independent*, Jan. 4, 1915, Vol. 81, p. 13.
[6] H. C. Lodge, *The Senate and the League of Nations*, N. Y., 1925, pp. 131-2.

at the close of the war a universal association of nations organized "to prevent any war begun either contrary to treaty covenants or without warning and full submission of the causes to the opinion of the world." [7]

Agreement that some such step was necessary and imperative was general in 1916. Unfortunately, a break occurred between Senator Lodge and President Wilson over certain charges made by Mr. Lodge which appears to have left them in a state of opposition that was seldom relaxed thereafter. [8] At any rate when the President addressed Congress on January 22, 1917, in advocacy of a League of Nations to administer the peace, the Senator replied in a long speech expressing grave fears about the proposal to enforce peace. It would probably necessitate our contributing 500,000 troops to an international police force and submitting to its being inspected by the league and ordered out by them, maybe on the vote of a majority composed of the little nations. [9]

Within a month the German submarine campaign brought our entry into the Great War in which the President called us to fight not merely for our rights upon the sea but for democracy, for the rights and liberties of small nations and. for "such a concert of free peoples as shall bring peace and safety to all nations and make the world itself free."

This appeal was renewed in his message to the Russian people of May 26, 1917, and, caught up by the leaders of public opinion, was carried incessantly to every part of the country. It was to be a war for something more than the vindication of our maritime rights.

The President himself, early in 1918, crowned his Fourteen Points with an association of nations "for the purpose of affording mutual guarantees of political independence and

---

[7] Albert Shaw, *Messages and Papers of Woodrow Wilson*, N. Y., 1924, Vol. I, p. 275.
[8] David Lawrence, *The True Story of Woodrow Wilson*, N. Y., 1924, pp. 145-7; Lodge, *The Senate and the League of Nations*, pp. 36-7.
[9] Lodge, *The Senate and the League of Nations*, 270-96.

territorial integrity to great and small states alike," and again on February 11, 1918, pledged before Congress that having set our hand to the task of creating a new international order we would not turn back before achieving it.

The war went on through the crucial spring of 1918 and just before the tide of battle turned, Mr. Wilson, in summing up the allied war aims on July 4, called again for such an organization of the peace as would secure it in the future. All our objectives in the war could be put into a single sentence: "All that we seek is the reign of law based upon the consent of the governed and sustained by the organized opinion of mankind."

Three months later when the collapse of the Central Powers was clearly under way he went to New York, on September 27, to state as deliberately as he could what the victory should bring. Declaring that the major issue of the war was the question: "Shall the assertion of right be haphazard and by casual alliance, or shall there be a common concert to oblige the observance of common rights?", he held the constitution of a League of Nations to be "in a sense the most important part of the peace settlement itself." [10]

THE PROGRAM CHALLENGED IN THE SENATE

Dissent from the high aims of the war had been almost negligible up to this time, but as the Congressional campaign of 1918 approached its close Mr. Roosevelt telegraphed to Senator Lodge and others, on October 25, that the President's Fourteen Points were "thoroughly mischievous" and urged the Senate to declare against them in their entirety. [11] The President replied the next day with his famous request to the voters to return a Democratic Congress, an appeal

[10] See Shaw, *Messages and Papers of Woodrow Wilson*, for the statements quoted.
[11] Lawrence, *The True Story of Woodrow Wilson*, 236.

which he had, however, long considered advisable. A few days later the Republicans carried the Senatorial elections in five states by narrow majorities and won a majority of two in the Senate, including the votes of Senator La Follette, who was practically outlawed from the party, and Senator Newberry, whose seat was challenged from the first and later made untenable.

Notwithstanding the fact that the armistice had been expressly concluded on the basis of the Fourteen Points and the President's subsequent addresses, Mr. Roosevelt declared, on November 27, as the President prepared to go to the Peace Conference, that "Mr. Wilson and his Fourteen Points and his four supplementary points and his five complementary points and all his utterances every which way have ceased to have any shadow of right to be accepted as expressive of the will of the American people." [12]

If the election had indeed invalidated the President's peace program the powers then gathering for the Peace Conference would have to seek a new basis for the peace.

Postponement Urged. Assuming in full whatever authority the election had given them the Republican leaders set out to block specifically the cardinal aim of the accepted program—the immediate creation of a League to Enforce Peace. On December 3, Senator Knox offered a resolution in the Senate which narrowed our war aims down to the vindication of our rights on the sea and the removal of the German menace and declared that any project for a league of nations should be postponed for separate consideration "by all the nations if and when at some future time general conferences on those subjects might be deemed useful." [13] He urged this program of postponement at length in a speech of December 18.

[12] David Houston, *Eight Years With Wilson's Cabinet,* Vol. I, pp. 359-60.
[13] *Congressional Record,* Vol. 57, Pt. 1, p. 23.

On December 21, after conference with Mr. Roosevelt, Senator Lodge openly warned the Allies that the Senate had a way of rejecting treaties and that if "extraneous provisions wholly needless for a peace with Germany" were unwisely added, such provisions "would surely be stricken out or amended, no matter how many signatures might be appended to the treaty." [14]

Meanwhile, the President had proceeded to Paris without taking any Senators or close associates of Republican Senators with him, and had announced on arrival that he considered the foundation of a League of Nations to be the first and foremost task of the conference.

In adhering to his purpose the President carried with him only the lukewarm support of many members of his party who had assumed strong positions against the expansion of our foreign power and influence in the Spanish War period. On the other hand, he was backed by a large section of the Republican Party to whom his efforts were but timely and logical extensions of the foreign policy of the last three Republican Administrations. Senator Porter J. McCumber, of North Dakota, was an outstanding leader of this wing. On January 7, 1919, he replied to speeches made against the immediate formation of the League, saying that "the time to present and adopt the restrictive or preventive measures is now, and not some indefinite time in the future—is today, when the awful horrors and consequences of war are apparent to every heart—and not when those horrors are forgotten and only the military glamour and glory remain to influence the sentiments of humanity." History must not repeat itself over and over again.

To those who raised the cry of "entangling alliances" he asked: "How can you in one breath approve the alliance to make war to save the world and in the next breath condemn an alliance to save the world by the prevention of any savage

[14] Ibid., 724 ff.

or brutal war which might threaten it?" It would not do to say one day that war was wrong and the next that such wrong could not be checked.[15]

Senator Sterling, of South Dakota, on January 13, granted that the President was wholly within his right in retaining full control over the negotiations, but saw no "acute necessity" for a league of nations. Indeed it was not feasible to give the Peace Conference that task. A congress assembled especially for the purpose would require "many months, more probably years" to accomplish the result. Good will and not force was the only sure guarantee of peace anyway.[16] On the other hand, Senator Myers, of Montana, was for using plenty of force in breaking up Germany, hanging the Kaiser and collecting indemnities. He agreed, however, that it would take a year or longer to create a league. That could wait.[17]

The next day Senator France, of Maryland, offered a resolution proposing that after the conclusion of peace the President call an all-American conference. After it had deliberated, he should then call a world conference which should attempt to deal with all the known economic and social causes of war as listed under nine heads. When this millennial work had been accomplished then the formation of a league of nations was to be considered.[18]

Direct Attack Opened. After the presentation of this resolution Senator Borah, of Idaho, delivered a direct assault on the idea of a league. It was based on force and therefore more destructive of human justice, liberty and progress than Prussianism itself. Any kind of internationalism was an evil force contemplating "world domination and the utter destruction of the national spirit everywhere." He prayed that we be spared the day when we should have "no defenders

---

[15] *Congressional Record,* Vol. 57, Pt. 2, pp. 1084-88.
[16] Ibid., pp. 1314–18.
[17] Ibid., 1319-22.
[18] Ibid., 1383.

save the gathered scum of the nations organized into a conglomerate international police force, ordered hither and thither by the most heterogeneous and irresponsible body or court that ever confused or confounded the natural instincts and noble passions of a people."

Senator Williams, of Mississippi, replied with equal conviction that all would be compelled ultimately to see the hand of God himself in the movement.[19]

The League Covenant Framed at the Peace Conference. While the proposal was being assailed in the Senate, President Wilson took the cause to the peoples of Europe in a series of speeches delivered in the three principal allied countries. He was countered by Premier Clemenceau who defended the old way of attempting to preserve peace by alliances and a balance of power. A determined drive in the early days of the Conference to proceed with a division of the conquests almost pushed the league idea far into the background but the President eventually succeeded in securing the appointment of a commission to frame a league constitution.[20]

Unexpectedly appointing himself to the League of Nations Commission and becoming its chairman, the President held night sessions with it, beginning February 3, until he saw a draft of a league covenant accepted by the Conference ten days later. The result was of course hardly the artistic product which some of the proposed conferences contemplating a year's deliberation might have produced. The Commission had to concentrate its intensive debates on the essential issue of the degree of security which the league was to give its members against aggressive war.

The disagreement on this point was acute throughout, the French and the other Continental nations backing a plan

[19] *Congressional Record,* Vol. 57, Pt. 2, pp. 1387-88.
[20] Ray Stannard Baker, *Woodrow Wilson and the World Settlement,* N. Y., 1922, Vol. I, pp. 357-78.

which would create a military super-state equipped with power to compel peace. This draft bristled with sanctions of every kind—legal, economic and military. The countries which had the horrors of invasion burned into their minds omitted nothing that would quickly suppress an invader. The Americans and English recognized throughout that a guarantee of security was the first essential, but felt that it would not do to go farther than mutually to guarantee "to respect and preserve as against external invasion the territorial integrity and existing independence of all members of the League." [21]

This pledge seemed painfully inadequate to the nations which had suffered most from war throughout the history of Europe and on whom its scars rarely healed, but the same mutual promise was to become a juggernaut indeed to the Senators in Washington, depriving the United States of its sacred liberty to go to war when as and if it wished.

Not Acceptable to Senate Leaders. Within twenty-four hours after the publication of the Covenant leading Republican Senators declared that it appeared to destroy the Monroe Doctrine and surrender America's independence.[22] The President's request that he be allowed to appear before the Foreign Relations Committee of Congress before debate in that body began therefore fell on unsympathetic ears, particularly when he proposed to land at Boston and make a speech or two on the subject before reporting to them. The ordinary rule of debate that the affirmative first explain its case did not appear to be applicable.

Senator Poindexter, of Washington, accordingly opened the attack on February 19, comparing the proposed League to the dreaded Soviet Government of Russia and labeling it as the most entangling and permanent alliance conceivable. It would compel the United States to "participate in the wars

[21] Ibid.
[22] N. Y. *Times,* February 15, 1919.

and controversies of every other nation and assume any burdensome mandate over distant territory that might be assigned to it. It didn't except any subjects from arbitration and it even surrendered to other nations the power "to regulate commerce with foreign nations." [23]

Senator Borah hailed it as the greatest triumph for English diplomacy in three centuries and Senator Reed, Democrat, of Missouri, expatiated on the British domination of the earth which was set up. He excoriated the entire Covenant, finding unbelievable things in almost every article. We would be told, for example, that "You shall have an army of a certain size" or "vessels of a certain number" and we could not exceed such numbers "without going to Europe and asking the gracious permission of eight gentlemen, six of whom probably cannot speak our language, and who have likely never set foot upon our shores!" Then an "international smelling committee" would be around to inspect our industries adaptable to warlike purposes. We could not even aid an Irish or Canadian rebellion and we should have to fight anybody who did.[24]

Senator Lewis, of Illinois, replied on February 23, that if the Council could so dictate our defenses it could destroy British naval supremacy and its members would have plenty of incentive to do so. The votes of the British Dominions, instead of being a danger to us would be in our support on any question of immigration which the League didn't have power to regulate anyway. As for its main purpose the very existence of the mutual guarantee in Article 10 would prevent most wars.[25]

When the President reached Boston on the same day he found two groups of his friends awaiting him, one to counsel a simple explanation of the League and the other to urge a fighting speech accepting the challenge of his opponents.

[23] *Congressional Record,* Vol. 57, Pt. 4, p. 3748.
[24] Ibid., pp. 4026–33.
[25] Ibid., 4125-35.

Each group was satisfied with one half of his speech. He explained the covenant simply in the first half and declared in the latter half that his fighting blood was stirred. He had no doubt where the American people stood on the issue.

Immoral and Dangerous. Senator Cummins, of Iowa, speaking on February 26, thought a development of internationalism inevitable. He had no doubt, either, that there was among the American people "a universal and passionate desire to do something, to enter into some compact to prevent war with all its deadly and destructive consequences." Yet the Covenant would not do; it contained more bad than good. Article 10 prohibited desirable change to such an extent that when he read it he thought that "nothing could surpass it in repugnance to good morals and to the civilization of the world," but when he contemplated the possibility of our being compelled by the League to take a mandate over the Turkish dominions his mind filled with more amazement than it had ever held before. But he was hardly less astounded when he pictured the possibilities of Japanese emigration being forced on us under Article 15.[26]

The President's conference with the Foreign Relations Committees, on February 26, did not change the minds of any of the Republican members. Probably its most important incident was the President's statement that he did not think the Covenant could be much amended owing to the difficulty of securing the concurrence of the other nations.

A War Breeder. Two days later Senator Lodge questioned the Covenant as thoroughly and minutely as could be desired. At the close of the speech he concluded that "this machinery would not promote the peace of the world, but would have a directly opposite effect." His main effort, however, was to counsel that every item should be investigated with the utmost thoroughness and weighed with the

---

[26] *Congressional Record,* Vol. 57, Part 5, pp. 4309-16. Senators Owen and Hitchcock spoke in defense of the Covenant on February 26 and 27.

greatest care. All that he asked was consideration, time and thought.

He could not refrain from pointing out the absurdity of the effort to preserve the peace "by a world constitution hastily constructed in a few weeks in Paris in the midst of the excitement of a war not yet ended." He did not say that agreements might not be made among the nations which stand for ordered freedom and civilization, which would do much to secure and preserve the peace of the world, but no such agreement had "yet been presented to us." [27]

On the same day Senator Lenroot, of Wisconsin, made a straightforward plea for amendment. He approved the general plan as proposed and hoped to be able to vote for it. Among other things he thought that the action of the Council under Article 10 should be clearly and purely advisory, that the holding of a mandate should depend throughout upon the pleasure of the legislature of the responsible country and that members should be allowed to withdraw from the League after ten years.[28]

Abandonment Demanded. Senator Knox's attack, on March 1, was massive and complete. Defining and assuming the League to be a super-state he presented it as striking down the precepts of our constitution, destroying our sovereignty and threatening national independence. "Why, then, this plan to strangle and crush us?" What was the hurry? War was farther away than it had been for centuries. Let us have an end of this, he demanded.[29]

Some minutes later the League was presented by Senator Sherman, of Illinois, as "a Pandora's box of evil to empty upon the American people the aggregated calamities of the world." It was an oligarchy that would "embargo our com-

[27] *Congressional Record,* Vol. 57, Pt. 5, pp. 4520-28.
[28] Ibid., 4569-72.
[29] *Congressional Record,* Vol. 57, Pt. 5, pp. 4687-94. The Knox speech was echoed the same day by an Anti-Wilson Democrat, Senator Hardwick of Georgia, and Senator Gore, Democrat of Oklahoma presented some amendments desired by Mr. Bryan.

merce, close our exchanges, destroy our credits, leave our merchandise rotting on our piers, shut the Isthmian Canal, order Congress to declare war, levy taxes, appropriate money, raise and support armies and navies . . ." It was "the death knell of the American Republic . . . a fantastic idealism, a polyglot philanthropy as vain in the realms of world philosophy and morals as it is impossible in peaceable execution." [30]

At the conclusion of this speech Senator McCumber took the floor lest the impression go out that the Republican Party as a whole was opposed to any league of nations. The critics of the League ignored its purposes even in assailing it. Article 10 he regarded as the very foundation stone of the structure. He challenged any Senator to give a clearer and more concise declaration of an agreement to preserve peace. Altogether one must be led far afield indeed by his prejudices to conclude that we were compelled to submit our domestic affairs to every nation in the world which questioned any of our internal policies. The Covenant could not be condemned on scattered phrases. Honesty was needed in the discussion.[31]

Senator McCumber's protest, however, did not prevent the following declaration from being read into the Record by Senator Lodge on the last day of the session, March 4, 1919. It was signed by thirty-seven Republican Senators and Senators-elect and read:

> Resolved by the Senate of the United States in the discharge of its constitutional duty of advice in regard to treaties, that it is the sense of the Senate that while it is their sincere desire that the nations of the world should unite to promote peace and general disarmament, the constitution of the league of nations in the form now proposed to the peace conference should not be accepted by the United States, and be it
>
> Resolved further, that it is the sense of the Senate that

[30] Ibid., 4864-69.
[31] Ibid., 4872-82.

the negotiations on the part of the United States should immediately be directed to the utmost expedition of the urgent business of negotiating peace terms with Germany satisfactory to the United States and the nations with whom the United States is associated in the war against the German Government, and that the proposal for a league of nations to insure the peace of the world should be then taken up for careful and serious consideration.

More than a third of the Senators thus endorsed with their signatures the demand of their leaders that the peace conference ignore Mr. Wilson and go ahead with the peace making according to the old methods. When all the settlements had been made and everybody was either satisfied with what had been obtained or bitter over what he had lost, when the President no longer had any restraint on the conflicting interests of the nations, when the negotiators were exhausted by their labors and the peoples had lost something of their poignant realization of the need for peace protection, when the old order had been fully entrenched again, "the proposal for a league of nations to insure the permanent peace of the world should be then taken up for careful and serious consideration."

To be sure the way was left open for the possible acceptance of the covenant if amended, and this enabled some of the Senators who wanted the League to sign it who otherwise would not have, but the leaders of the group were further embittered when the Peace Conference eventually proceeded on the assumption that an amended covenant would be accepted.[32]

On the evening of the same day that the Round Robin was published the President accepted the challenge in a speech in New York City, as he departed for Europe again, saying that when the treaty came back gentlemen on this

[32] See the later chapters of: Lodge, *The Senate and the League of Nations.*

side would find the covenant "not only in it, but so many threads of the treaty tied to the covenant that you cannot dissect the covenant from the treaty without destroying the whole vital structure."

This plain statement has been widely regarded as unwise, in view of the undoubted power of the Round Robin group to defeat the treaty as they had threatened. Perhaps it was a mistake. Undoubtedly it deeply offended the Senate leaders who sought to block the President's course. Still, his later success, without specifically restating his purpose to go on, would have maddened them quite as effectively. The words of his defiance gave them phrases to quote as proof of his colossal stubbornness, but the forceful insistence of Ex-President Taft, who spoke just before Mr. Wilson from the same platform, that it would be the President's duty to insert the Covenant in the treaty as indispensable to the peace sought did not arouse similar condemnation, though it probably led directly to the President's statement.

The Covenant Retained and Amended

Mr. Taft's strong support on that occasion must have worked powerfully, too, to convince the European leaders that the President would prevail. Such conviction was needed, for during the President's absence the League had fallen into the background. The British Conservatives had rebelled almost as violently as their American contemporaries and many of the leaders of the Continental nations were quite willing to make the peace by old familiar methods, as the American Senate Republicans demanded. Even despite the warning in the President's New York address the League was generally considered dead when Mr. Wilson landed in France again on March 14.[33]

It was something of a shock therefore to read his state-

[33] Baker, *Woodrow Wilson and the World Settlement,* I, 291-309.

ment of the 15th that "the decision made at the Peace Conference at its plenary session, January 25, 1919, to the effect that the establishment of a League of Nations should be an integral part of the Treaty of Peace, is of final force and that there is no basis whatever for the reports that a change in this decision was contemplated."

This again was plain speaking, and it produced wrathful eruptions in Conservative quarters on both sides of the ocean, but there did not seem to be any immediate way of upsetting the decision, especially since the Allies had not been able to find any formulæ aside from the League which would solve many of the knotty problems.

So the Conference returned to the League and the President took up the task, among many others, of amending the Covenant to satisfy its American critics. He was under no illusions as to the possibility of satisfying a section of his opponents in the Senate. "No matter what I do," he had said during the return voyage, "they will continue the attack." But the urgent requests of the Taft wing of the Republican Party for revision, continued by cable, and the advice of his own party leaders left him no choice but to attempt to meet enough of the objections to secure ratification in the Senate. He was sure to alarm the French and their allies at each suggestion of weakening the Covenant, and his position in the Conference would be considerably weakened by the necessity of asking for concessions, but he must attempt to secure the changes most generally demanded regardless.

Two of the desired amendments were secured with comparatively little opposition. One inserted the phrase "and who are willing to accept it" into the description in Article 22 of those to whom mandates should be intrusted; the other attempted to quiet the fear of interference with immigration and the tariff by adding to Article 15 a clause saying: "If the dispute between the parties is claimed by one of them and is found by the Council to arise out of a matter which by international law is solely within the domestic jurisdiction of that party, the Council shall so report and shall make no recommendation as to its settlement."

The amendment permitting withdrawal after two years produced more acrimonious debate, but the bitterest fight came over the exclusion of the Monroe Doctrine from the jurisdiction of the League. The French, with their security ever in mind, feared that it would lead to the abstention of the United States from European affairs in a crisis, a fear which was increased by the original attachment of the reservation to Article 10. The President on his part had taken the principle of Article 10 from the Monroe Doctrine itself and believed that in extending the principle to the world he was safeguarding the Monroe Doctrine as it could be in no other way. The necessity of forcing its specific recognition by the powers therefore seemed to him a work of supererogation. Nevertheless, he put it through at the close of the last session of the League Commission after a two day struggle as gruelling as any he had during the Conference.[34]

Agreement Withheld. The revised Covenant was published on April 28. Early on the 29th Senator Lodge and Senator Curtis, of Kansas, as majority leaders, sent the following telegram to all Republican Senators:

> "We suggest that Republican Senators reserve final expression of opinion respecting the amended league covenant until the latest draft has been carefully studied and until there has been an opportunity for conference."

This was supplemented by a press statement from Mr. Lodge saying that of course further amendment would be necessary.

The suggestion that the changes secured by the President should not be received as satisfactory was accepted by all

[34] Seymour and House, *What Really Happened at Paris*, N. Y., 1921, pp. 416-17.

the Senators addressed except Senator McNary, of Oregon, who announced that he would support the Covenant as adopted. "In my opinion," he said, "the Covenant has been amended to meet all the legitimate objections raised against it." [35]

On May 19, Congress met in special session to enact the appropriation bills, a result of the Republican filibuster of March 3 and 4 designed to compel a special session. On May 20, Senator Johnson offered an unprecedented resolution calling upon the Secretary of State to transmit the unfinished treaty to the Senate. The Senators were anxious to begin work on it, though not in secret session as usual. Mr. Lodge served notice, on the 23rd, that the document would be treated with "pitiless publicity." The Covenant had been made "much worse than it was before." [36]

Article 21, reserving the Monroe Doctrine, said that:

"Nothing in the covenant shall be deemed to affect the validity of international engagements, such as treaties of arbitration or regional understandings, like the Monroe Doctrine, for securing the maintenance of peace."

But no! cried Senator Lodge on June 6, it was never an international engagement and is not an international understanding! It is ours! "It is all ours; and now it is carried into this league of nations. It is already interpreted by England, although it is wholly our affair, and it is to be determined in future by the League of Nations."

The Foreign Relations Committee Packed. Meanwhile the Senate Foreign Relations Committee had been packed with new members known to be wholly or largely opposed to the Covenant.[37]

[35] New York *Times*, April 30, 1919.
[36] *Congressional Record*, Vol. 58, Pt. 1, pp. 63, 161.
[37] Ibid., pp. 791-2, Senator Hitchcock; Philadelphia *Public Ledger*, April 20, Mr. Taft.

On June 9, Senator Borah forced a copy of the unsigned treaty which a Chicago newspaper furnished him into the Record.

The next day Senator Knox essayed one more drive on the Peace Conference, giving final notice that the Covenant should be cut out of the Treaty. His resolution bluntly gave "notice of the limits of the present obligations against the United States in which the Senate of the United States is now prepared to acquiesce. . . ." [38]

It is difficult to believe that Senator Knox seriously hoped that the Conference would surrender at this late date, though some Senators believed a new round robin might accomplish the desired result. The resolution did give Mr. Knox the opportunity to plead for time to consider the Covenant. Time to deliberate, time to weigh was what was needed. The Senators doubted that the country was with them, but they did believe that given enough time, sufficient racial, partisan and other feeling could be aroused to make it safe to emasculate the treaty.

What Was The Great Menace?   The anti-leaguers had first pictured the League as dominated by the kings; then it had been the British; a little later Senator Reed had proved that we were likely to fall under the sway of the Negroes and other colored peoples; now Senator Sherman pointed to the Pope as likely to control the League. Were not 24 of the 40 Christian nations in the League "spiritually dominated by the Vatican?" No broad field of prejudice was left uncultivated; nor were any smaller areas of racial antipathy overlooked. [39]

By June 21, however, it became evident that the latest Knox resolution could not be passed. Mr. Lodge therefore published a letter from Mr. Root advising that the defects of the Covenant be dealt with in a qualifying resolution of

[38] *Congressional Record*, Vol. 58, Pt. 1, p. 894.
[39] Ibid., Vol. 58, Pt. 2, pp. 1435-44.

ratification. Very shortly thereafter, on June 28, the Germans signed the Treaty and the President was quoted as opposed to amendments for the reason that the adoption of that practice would lead to hopeless negotiation and delay. This announcement served completely to unify the Senate Republicans behind the program of amendment by reservation. None could be found who doubted that there must be reservations.[40]

THE TREATY BEFORE THE SENATE

After receiving a welcome in New York, on July 9, which was apparently as warm as he could desire, the President laid the Treaty before the Senate the next day. Senator Swanson, of Virginia, gave what normally would have been the opening speech on the treaty on July 14. He stressed the deterrent power of Article 10, and its defensive value to us, but maintained that its authority was moral, not legal.

The next day the Shantung settlement was brought to the fore as the iniquitous surrender of a great Chinese province to Japan, the Democrats replying that only property rights had been given and that Japan would keep her promise to hand political control to China.

Senator Colt, Republican, of Rhode Island, spoke for the League on July 17. He could see no super-state in the Covenant; it was rather an association of free nations. It asked no surrender of true nationalism when it substituted a reign of law for the reign of force.[41] Senator Pomerene, of Ohio, then defended the constitutionality of the league and replied at length to objections against it. Senator McNary, of Oregon, continued the defense on July 22, holding that Article 10 was a moral bond, but the pillar section of the Covenant. The demand for amendments and reservations, he thought, came without proper regard for the results that

---

[40] New York *Times,* June 29, 1919.
[41] *Congressional Record,* Vol. 58, Pt. 3, pp. 2721-2.

would follow. Senator Johnson, of South Dakota, also could not see anything in Article 10 that was dangerous. Senator Moses, of New Hampshire, could see little that was good in the entire treaty.

Senator Beckham, of Kentucky, granting sincerity and patriotism to all, asked the Senate to consider what would have happened if the alarms and fears of Patrick Henry and James Monroe about the Constitution had prevailed— fears which were never realized in practice. He was followed by Senator McKellar, of Tennessee, who delivered a counter attack quite in the style of the opponents of the treaty. The proposal of Senator Knox that the United States would consult with the nations whenever trouble arose and, "the necessity arising in the future, carry out the same complete accord and cooperation with our chief cobelligerents for the defense of civilization," he characterized as an agreement that Europe could stir up all the wars she wanted to and we would be the policeman to stop them. With no machinery to keep the peace provided, it would take 5,000,000 American soldiers on guard in Europe all the time to keep order, and the greatest navy on earth. Mr. McKellar would outdo the alarmists.[42]

The Effect of Reservations Discussed. After a speech in defence of the Shantung settlement by Senator Robinson, of Arkansas, on July 24, Senator Lenroot, of Wisconsin, spoke for reservations. He argued that since the Fourteen Points had not been fully complied with we were under no obligation to accept the Treaty as signed by the President. There was disagreement about the interpretation of Article 10 and two or three others, therefore reservations would have to be adopted to remove the doubts. Each reservation, held Senator Pittman, of Nevada, on the same day would have to be accepted by the treaty ratifying power in every state signatory to the treaty. Moreover, our exceptions

[42] *Congressional Record*, Vol. 58, Pt. 3, pp. 2995-3000, 3022-32.

would not stand alone; other disappointed powers would press for the things they had not obtained and the Senate would have to accept their counter-reservations, distasteful though some of them would be, if it got its own. Either deadlock or interminable renegotiation would ensue. It was better to reject the Treaty than to reopen contention.

Senator Borah agreed at once that all reservations would have to be agreed to by all signatories and granted that legally Congress would retain, without any reservations, its right to declare war. He was "not interested in any form of interpretations or amendments or reservations." It was "either fundamentally right to enter this enterprise or fundamentally wrong." He thought it was wrong because it entangled us in European affairs and lessened our independence, but if it was fundamentally right he would not waste his time with reference to the details concerning it. No one but the Divine Power could, without experience, perfect a thing out of mind.[43]

Was Article 10 Oppressive? Mr. Borah spoke immediately after Senator Smith, of Arizona, who attacked the critics professing to be for *a* league but not *this* one. Why all the hypercritical interpretation of the terms of the covenant, he asked? The Monroe Doctrine was just as much a promise to make war as Article 10 was. It would be a silly threat if it wasn't, yet no one had attacked it as unconstitutional or complained that Congress was deprived of its freedom of action under it. Moreover, our treaty with Panama bound us *legally* to maintain the independence of a foreign state. Yet the great mass of busy Americans were being disturbed by the oft repeated charge that the covenant must be defeated or qualified because it violated the palladium of their liberties. The impression was being created that all burdens fell on us alone, whereas every member of the League was mutually responsible.

[43] *Congressoinal Record*, Vol. 58, Pt. 3, pp. 3141-45.

Senator Walsh, of Montana, on July 28, emphasized the persistent ignoring of the phrase "as against external aggression" in Article 10. He denied the assumption that the right of revolution was infringed and challenged anyone to show where armed force for the freeing of Ireland or Shantung was to come from. History afforded so few examples of states unselfishly intervening in behalf of rebels fighting for freedom that our intervention in Cuba had been proclaimed as absolutely unique in that respect, and yet we came out of the war with Porto Rico and the Philippines.

Article 10 was the soul and spirit of the Covenant, said Mr. Walsh. That was why those who wished to defeat the whole plan desired to emasculate it. They said American boys would have to fight in this or that hypothetical war, forgetting to say that if this was so boys from every other quarter of the globe would have to go too. Senators lost sight of the deterrent effect of the article even while extolling the Monroe Doctrine. How had the Doctrine preserved peace except by the promise to punish aggression? There were only two ways to maintain peace—either by agreements such as this or by actually establishing an international police force equal to the job.

Senator Williams then applied the doctrine of the free and untrammelled choice to the units within a state. Suppose each citizen or each state in the union said "I am my own sovereign, responsible to nobody but God, and at the right time I will do the right thing, and I want to be free to say when I shall do it and where I shall do it and how I shall do it." Could you get civilization within the nation this way?

Was War Inevitable? The assumption that it was human nature to fight and you could not change human nature was a stupid, barbarous utterance, said Mr. Williams, as if human nature had not changed from the day our ancestors drank mead out of the skulls of their enemies. Human beings were fallible—so was the United States and so was the League—but why gaze so intently at the specks on the rising sun of the Covenant that you failed to see that sun itself? [44]

Another Democratic Senator, Mr. Thomas, of Colorado, delivered a long considered speech the next day in which he held that morality was static and human nature unchanging. Internationalism would be a menace if racial instincts didn't make it unattainable.

He was followed by the venerable Senator Nelson, Republican, of Minnesota, who thought the entangling alliance argument came entirely too late. He favored some reservations because doubt and controversy had arisen but he had not "groped around to find objections to defeat the treaty" for he was imbued with the faith that fundamentally the general purpose of the League was sound and fully warranted.

Senator Ransdall, of Louisiana, then reviewed the progressively rising costs and destructiveness of war and Senator Owen linked the Monroe Doctrine and the Covenant together as common in purpose and as mutually strengthening each other. [45]

But all the arguments made in the Senate did not advance ratification. Republican Senators had been generally pledged to a policy of reservations or rejection, with the understanding that reservations would be thus insured, and the President was not ready to accept reservations, though Mr. Taft was by this time convinced that the Treaty could not be ratified without them. [46]

Committee Investigations. By the end of July the Senate Foreign Relations Committee had finished formally reading the Treaty line by line. The Committee then proceeded to hold a series of hearings at which all the available Americans of importance who had been attached to the American

[44] *Congressional Record,* Vol. 58, Pt. 4, pp. 3230-35.
[45] Ibid., 3404-10.
[46] New York *Tribune,* July 24 and 27, 1919.

Peace Commission were examined. These gentlemen, together with written replies from the President, convinced the Committee that they were not to have access to any detailed records of the Peace Conference that indicated how the many disputed points had been settled there. They got an opinion from Mr. Lansing that the President need not have yielded on Shantung, but the early hearings were not very productive. So, after they had examined everybody who might enlighten them, except Colonel House who was still in Paris, they decided to question the President himself publicly, if he would consent. He agreed, and, on August 19, the session was held in the White House while a group of stenographers relayed the proceedings to a large gathering of newspaper men in the basement.

The conference lasted three and a half hours with the discussion covering a wide range of subjects, but turning generally around the obligations in Article 10. The President maintained throughout that the guaranty was moral, not legal. A legal obligation specifically bound you to do a particular thing under penalty. Such an obligation could not exist between sovereign states. A moral obligation was indeed superior to a legal obligation and even more binding, but it always involved the right to exercise judgment and decide whether under the circumstances the obligation applied and called for action. This discretion remained in Congress and could not be taken away.

The results were much as usual. "A careful canvass of the committee on the return of the Senators to their offices showed an absolutely unchanged alignment. The President did not convince any Senators who are opposed to the league or treaty, or any of those who want reservations. But, on the other hand, he inspired with more enthusiasm, apparently, those who favored ratification without change." [47]

A few days later the Committee voted, 9 to 8, to amend

[47] New York *Tribune*, August 20, 1919.

the Treaty directly to put Japan out of Shantung. On the same day, August 23, it adopted 50 amendments designed to remove the American members from nearly all of the commissions set up to enforce the Treaty.

Then in answer to the President's plea for a report on the Treaty it opened "the American Conference" and proceeded to hear the grievances of every group of people disappointed at the Peace Conference who cared to appear before it. The Egyptians led off, followed by the Irish, Lithuanians, Latvians, Esthonians, Negro Americans, Hungarians, Albanians, Jugo Slavs, and Italians. Many of the delegations were self-appointed, but the Committee listened gravely and sympathetically to their troubles, as if it could do something about them. Most of them were American citizens and voters. No suspicion of hyphenation was lodged against them.

As this program got well under way the President made his final decision, at the close of August, to appeal in person to the people of the West who had elected him.

Attack Continued. In the meantime, the speech making had continued in the Senate. Senator Fall, of New Mexico, reminded the Senate that this idea of a millenium was rather old and protested that if we joined the League we would not only destroy the government of our fathers, but, commit a "crime against the nations of the earth, against civilization itself. . . ." Senator Sterling, on the 4th, suggested that the clause requiring the fulfillment of obligations before withdrawal would make departure from the League impossible. Senator Watson, of Indiana, attacked Japan's record at length. Senator Kellogg, defended the constitutionality of League membership, at the same time pleading for reservations.

On August 12th, Senator Lodge delivered his first prepared attack after the submission of the Treaty. He began with the preamble of the Covenant. "Brave words, indeed!" Then he discovered that Article 3 actually gave the league the right to interfere in the internal conflicts of its members—to "deal with" any matter affecting the peace of the world. He could see no distinction whatever between legal and moral obligations in connection with Article 10. We might well have to help Japan whip China in Shantung. And if King Hussein of Hedjaz, then attacked by the Bedouins, appealed to us for aid we would be bound to send American troops to Arabia. There would be no escape except by breach of faith. And there was no doubt whatever in his mind that other nations might order American ships and troops to any part of the world. This must not be. It must be made perfectly clear that not even a corporal's guard could ever be ordered anywhere except by the constitutional authorities of the United States.[48]

Senator Nugent, Democrat, of Idaho, speaking on August 25, knew of no reason why a distinction should be drawn between the "sovereign right" of a nation to plunder its weaker neighbors and the "right" of an individual to do so. Moreover, whatever sovereign rights we lost would be lost by the other members also, so we would be in the same relative position. The "sovereign right" to declare war exactly when it pleased us had been given up already in the twenty-eight Bryan peace treaties ratified by the Senate.

But Senator Townshend, of Michigan, could see little but danger in the Covenant. The other members of the League were all more or less insolvent. If trouble occurred, our Government would have to settle it "even though a majority of its men are sacrificed and its whole treasure is exhausted. . . . If we engage ourselves with all the Bolshevist, monarchical, revolutionary, territory-grabbing nations of the Old World, we will not only be unable to help them but we may destroy ourselves."[49]

[48] *Congressional Record*, Vol. 58, Pt. 4, pp. 3778-84.
[49] *Congressional Record*, Vol. 58, Pt. 5, pp. 4453-55.

Senator Knox closed the August debates by declaring himself opposed to the whole treaty. He had held a conference of irreconcilable Senators on August 21, a week before the President finally announced his decision to go before the country, at which plans were made for a speaking tour of Senators in the West designed to bring about the complete defeat of the League.[50]

The President Appealed to the West. The President set out from Washington on September 3 to attempt to stir sufficient public opinion to bring about an early ratification of the Treaty as signed. Travelling 8000 miles in three weeks, he delivered forty-four speeches and participated in a dozen great parades before suffering a breakdown in Kansas from which he never recovered. Meeting with apparent apathy at the start, his receptions increased in warmth as he swung out through Missouri, Iowa, and Minnesota to the Northwest, and down the Pacific Coast to Southern California. He lacked half a dozen speeches of completing his itinerary on the return journey.

In his appeals he maintained that the critics viewed only details and ignored the scope and purposes of the plan. The important thing was to try to insure some time for cooling and conference before resorting to war. The alternative was armaments, and alliances again—with the inevitable result. The peace could never be organized unless all the great powers joined in one unity. It could never be done without the United States and it was our glorious destiny to lead in this greatest of enterprises. We could ask for no special privileges for ourselves. We had fought for a new deal and we would not turn back.

The Committee Reported. After the President's trip was well started the Senate Foreign Relations Committee brought in its report, on September 10. The Committee defended itself against charges of delay. The demand for haste

[50] Ibid., 4493-4501; New York *Tribune,* August 22, 1919.

had been largely artificial, though aided by the "unthinking outcry of many excellent people." The Committee had been delayed through inability to get information.

There need be no difficulty about securing agreement to the fifty-odd amendments proposed. The Peace Conference was still in Paris and would be more usefully employed in considering them than in "trying to force upon the United States the control of Armenia, Anatolia and Constantinople through the medium of a large American army." Securing the consent of Germany need not present great difficulty either. The journey from Berlin to Paris was "within the power of a moderate amount of human endurance." Germany need not be consulted about the League anyway.

None need worry about the Allies accepting our terms, "for without us their league is a wreck and all their gains from a victorious peace are imperilled." [51]

Mr. Bullitt Testified. Two days later the Committee heard the testimony of Mr. W. C. Bullitt, who had resigned from the staff of the American Peace Commission because he felt that his efforts and views had not received proper support. Mr. Bullitt quoted Secretary Lansing as saying that the league would be entirely useless and that if the Senate and the American people could really understand what the treaty let them in for it unquestionably would be defeated. He had some hope that Senator Knox would understand the Treaty and instruct the country in its real meaning.[52]

More damaging opinions to the cause of the league could hardly have been released at that particular time.

While the President and the Committee were paying their best respects to the league idea the oratory proceeded in the Senate. Senator Hitchcock on September 3, reviewed the utterances of a number of Senators who had demanded uncon-

[51] *Congressional Record,* Vol. 58, Part 5, pp. 5112-14.
[52] *Senate Documents,* 66th Congress, First Session, Vol. 10, pp. 1161-1291.

ditional surrender by Germany a year before. Now, he said, the same men were proposing a separate and unconditional peace. Senator Poindexter, on the 8th, dwelt upon the huge sums and forces it would take to police Turkey and asked how then should we perform our "obligations" in Mexico?

The Necessity for Reservations Stressed and Denied. Senator Spencer, of Missouri, maintained, on the same day, that the issue was not between acceptance or rejection. He demonstrated the need of reservations by asking if Japan couldn't buy Magdalena Bay from Mexico and be protected in possession of it by Article 10.

On September 10, Senator Kenyon, of Iowa, made a strong plea for reservations. Mr. Kenyon had refrained from speaking on the treaty until the Committee had reported it to the Senate, "feeling it better to wait until the matter was before the Senate." Few Senators had been so restrained. Nor had any been unable to decide at a given moment whether the Covenant was too strong or too weak until Senator Harding, of Ohio, apparently found himself in that predicament on September 11, though he inclined toward the super-state interpretation. Senator Jones, of New Mexico, analyzing the Covenant with reference to the charges of super-government, on the 15th, could find no basis for "the spectre of an overreaching power destined to destroy American institutions and make vassals of American citizens." Reservations he thought likely to nullify the whole scheme.

After the formal reading of the treaty began in the Senate, on September 16, to be continued until October 20, Senator Overman, of North Carolina, reviewed our war aims as voiced by the President, traced their universal acceptance and asked if they could all be reversed. But Senator Thomas adhered to the view that the burden of suppressing distant wars must fall on us because we only still possessed the sinews of war.

Senator Wadsworth, on the 19th, solemnly contended that

the operation of the economic boycott would probably lead to the internment of several hundred thousand Greek aliens living in the United States in the event that Greece attacked Bulgaria. Senator New, of Indiana, on the 25th, ridiculed the idea that the League would prevent war. It was quixotic, a mirage, comparable to believing that a potato carried in the pocket would prevent rheumatism.

But Senator Nelson thought the Committee proposed a dishonorable abandonment of the new nations we had helped to create, and Senator Smith, of Maryland, could see no justification whatever for dissipating the strength of the Covenant by reservations that would weaken or cancel the reciprocal obligations set up.[53]

Amendments Defeated. Notwithstanding the general assumption that the issue was between outright ratification and approval with reservations, the entire month of October was consumed in efforts directly to amend the Treaty.

The Fall amendments, taking us out of the commissions for executing the Treaty were defeated first, 38 for to 58 against. Further oratory then brought the Shantung amendments to a like fate, some 18 of the moderate Republicans uniting with the Democrats. This left the Johnson amendment, designed to give the United States as many votes as the British Empire, as the only hope of direct amendment, but it was lost by a narrow vote on October 27. Voting on the amendments continued up to November 6, but none received a majority.[54]

Reservations Adopted. Attention then turned to the reservations which the mild reservationists by this time had agreed to support. To keep them in line the tone of the reservations was softened somewhat and they were rapidly adopted. A

[53] *Congressional Record,* Vol. 58, Pt. 6, pp. 5622-25; pp. 5902-3.
[54] *Congressional Record,* Vol. 58, Pt. 8, pp. 7680, 7683, 7692, 7992, 7969.

preamble requiring the written assent of three of the principal associated powers was approved on November 7, 48 to 40. The first reservation passed 50 to 35 the same day and the crucial one on Article 10, on the 8th, by the same majority, 11 Senators not voting. Nine others were adopted on the 15th under cloture by votes averaging 53 to 40.[55]

Having seen the reservations adopted by their votes the bitter-enders then voted with the Democrats against them and ratification was refused by a poll of 55 nays to 39 yeas on November 19. Unconditional ratification was then rejected, seven Democrats voting against it and only one Republican, McCumber, for it.[56]

As the final vote neared, the League to Enforce Peace gave up the fight against treaty changes and urged Senators to vote for the Lodge reservations. Its leaders had apparently decided that the Lodge resolution offered the best terms the Republicans would grant.[57] The President, however, sent a final word to his Democratic supporters giving his opinion that the Lodge terms meant nullification of the Treaty and advising their rejection.

Compromise Attempted. The Democrats in complying with the President's request apparently believed that after a complete deadlock had been established by the two votes upon ratification a set of compromise reservations acceptable to both sides would be worked out. This hope proved vain at the close of the session, but the demand for a compromise was so strong in the country that an unofficial conciliation committee was constituted after the holidays consisting of two Republican regulars, Senators Lodge and New, two middle grounders, Kellog and Lenroot, and five Democrats. The irreconcilables were not directly represented, but at the

[55] Ibid., Vol. 58, Pt. 8, pp. 8068, 8074, 8139, 8437; Pt. 9, pp. 8560–70, 8730, 8741.
[56] *Congressional Record,* Vol. 58, Pt. 9, pp. 8786, 8803.
[57] Ibid., Vol. 58, Pt. 9, p. 8773.

crucial moment, when the group seemed about to agree on a reservation to Article 10, Senators Lodge and New went into conference with them and progress ceased.

The President, on the other hand, remained opposed to altering the Treaty and was so convinced that the country thought likewise that he wrote the Jackson Day diners, on January 8, urging a great and solemn referendum on the subject in the coming election. "We cannot rewrite this treaty," he said. "We must take it without changes which alter its meaning, or leave it, and then, after the rest of the world has signed it, we must face the unthinkable task of making another and separate kind of treaty with Germany."[58]

This prospect did not appal the Republican leaders, nor did the idea of an appeal to the people arouse enthusiasm among the Democratic chiefs. They had already had too much evidence of the hostility of the Irish, German and Italian voters to the League and toward its maker. Other great leaders, too, urged submission to the Lodge program. Mr. Bryan counselled acceptance strongly, and Lord Grey, after a period as British Ambassador here, advised likewise.

He had found a real conservative feeling for the traditional policy of isolation, and he thought the curbs on the President's freedom of action set up in the reservations reasonable. Both the necessity for the reservations and their hampering effect upon the League would in all probability disappear in practice. This would even be true of the dispute over the British Dominion votes. The important thing was to start the League in good spirit.[59]

The President himself, writing to Senator Hitchcock, agreed to accept his reservations a few days before the publication of Lord Grey's views. He maintained that he had "never seen the slightest reason to doubt the good faith of our associates in the war nor ever had the slightest reason

[58] Shaw, *Messages and Papers of Woodrow Wilson,* II, 1163.
[59] London *Times,* January 31, 1920.

to fear that any nation would seek to enlarge our obligations under the Covenant of the League of Nations, or seek to commit us to lines of action which, under our constitution, only the Congress of the United States can in the last analysis decide." He ventured to suggest that the President be allowed to exercise his veto upon withdrawal from the League and thus require a two-thirds vote of Congress to accomplish that important step, but he would accept the Hitchcock reservations as they stood.

The Treaty Rejected. Some two weeks later the Treaty was reconsidered in the Senate, on February 9, and reported back the next day with the reservations rejected in November. Debate, resumed on February 16, continued another month before the final failure to ratify on March 19, 1920. On this date approval with the Lodge reservations revised and stiffened received a substantial majority, 49 to 35, composed of some 30 Republicans and 20 Northern Democrats. The Southern Democrats and a dozen Republican bitter-enders made up the minority. After this final failure the Treaty was returned to the President and a resolution for a separate peace with Germany introduced.

The Peace Conference had been five months in drawing up the Treaty of Versailles. It was finally rejected in the Senate eight months after it was submitted for approval, a year after the Republican Senators had declared in the Round Robin that the League would not do, and sixteen months after they had begun their campaign to postpone it.

CHAPTER VIII

THE SENATE RESERVATIONS TO THE TREATY OF VERSAILLES

THE reservations over which there was such a complete failure to agree are still likely to seem necessary or superfluous according to the political or temperamental viewpoint of the reader. That they became politically necessary to the ratification of the treaty cannot be questioned.

What their effect would have been cannot perhaps now be determined. Some of the League's best friends in the United States have come to believe that they would have hampered our membership in the League little, if at all, and this conclusion is shared by the leaders of the irreconcilable group. Others continue to regard them as nullifying any membership that might have been granted us under them.

Whether we would have been admitted to the League under the terms laid down by the Senate can similarly never be known. The desire for our adherence was then so strong that all but a few of them would doubtless have been accepted by the powers without question. The preamble to the proposed resolution of ratification as finally adopted provided that the assent of the signatories was to be assumed unless they objected prior to the deposit of ratifications. As interpreted by Senator Lodge, the preamble required "the assent of every signatory to the treaty" and if objection were made the United States stayed out until the contested reservations were accepted.[1] The reader may form his own conclusion

[1] See *Congressional Record,* Vol. 59, Pt. 5, pp. 45–99, for the reservations in their final form. The preamble read:

as to whether all of the 15 reservations would have been accepted by each of the 28 signatories to the treaty.

The first reservation dealt with withdrawal, as follows:

1. The United States so understands and construes Article 1 that in case of notice of withdrawal from the League of Nations, as provided in said article, the United States shall be the sole judge as to whether all its international obligations and all its obligations under the said Covenant have been fulfilled and notice of withdrawal by the United States may be given by a concurrent resolution of the Congress of the United States.

This declaration made it certain that in case the United States became uncomfortable in the League no technical objections should impede her exit. The fear of such a predicament was peculiar to the American objectors to the League and, in spite of their long emphasis upon the necessity of a clear path to the rear, no other country, European or American, acquired their apprehensions. Very probably, however, the powers would have granted the right of the strongest nation in the world to be nervous if she chose.

The President's principal stated objection to the reservation was that it gave to Congress the right to take us out of the League by a concurrent resolution, that is, by a bare majority vote and without his consent. Undoubtedly both the President and the Senate exaggerated the probability of

---

"*Resolved* (two-thirds of the Senators present concurring therein), That the Senate advise and consent to the ratification of the treaty of peace with Germany concluded at Versailles on the 28th day of June, 1919, subject to the following reservations and understandings which are hereby made a part and condition of this resolution of ratification, which ratification is not to take effect or bind the United States until the said reservations and understandings adopted by the Senate have been accepted as a part and a condition of this resolution of ratification by the Allied and Associated Powers, and a failure on the part of the Allied and Associated Powers to make objection to said reservations and understandings prior to the deposit of ratification by the United States shall be taken as a full and final acceptance of such reservations and understandings by said powers."

a Republican Congress wanting to remove us from the League against the opposition of a Democratic President.

Article 10.   The second and most bitterly contested reservation disavowed any obligation to be bound by Article 10, and other parts of the Covenant, unless a future Congress should assume the obligation at the time.   It said:

> 2. The United States assumes no obligation to preserve the territorial integrity or political independence of any other country by the employment of its military or naval forces, its resources, or any form of economic discrimination, or to interfere in any way in controversies between nations, including all controversies relating to territorial integrity or political independence, whether members of the League or not, under the provisions of Article 10, or to employ the military or naval forces of the United States, under any article of the treaty for any purpose, unless in any particular case the Congress, which, under the Constitution, has the sole power to declare war or authorize the employment of the military or naval forces of the United States shall, in the exercise of full liberty of action by act or joint resolution so provide.

According to one faction this statement was vitally necessary to preserve our liberty and fully safeguarded it; to another it destroyed the effectiveness of our membership in the League completely; to a third group it was a superfluous and ungracious assertion of a right of Congress known to everyone; to still others it was a futile recital, totally inadequate to save us from the destruction that was sure to come with League membership.   If one is not clear as to the wisdom and necessity of the declaration he need only add the often made distinction between legal and moral obligations to complete his uncertainty. [2]

[2] Reflection upon the fact that none of the other American republics were impressed with the Senate's fears on this score enough to adopt them will furnish one basis for judging the seriousness of the dangers guarded against.

Mandates and Domestic Affairs. The third reservation provided that no mandate over any of the conquered territories should be accepted by the United States without action of Congress, a statement which was, again, needless or urgently required according to the attitude held toward the Presidency and especially toward the President of the time. It would be a rash President indeed who would attempt to assume on his own authority such a responsibility for the country, one that he could hardly maintain long without action of Congress.

Number four warned the League away from interference with our domestic affairs or with any concerns that were even partly domestic. The delicate subjects, immigration and the tariff, were of course reserved and "all other domestic questions" oblivious of the fact that many domestic questions have international aspects that must be dealt with. The League was not even to come telling us how to suppress our white slave and opium traffics. We would do our own suppressing. It was a brave Senator indeed who refused to proclaim in 1920 that we would manage our own affairs. The other nations flocking into the League did not, however, feel it necessary to make similar declarations.

The American reservation read:

4. The United States reserves to itself exclusively the right to decide what questions are within its domestic jurisdiction and declares that all domestic and political questions relating wholly or in part to its internal affairs, including immigration, labor, coastwise traffic, the tariff, commerce, the suppression of traffic in women and children and in opium and other dangerous drugs, and all other domestic questions, are solely within the jurisdiction of the United States and are not under this treaty to be submitted in any way either to arbitration or to the consideration of the Council or of the Assembly of the League of Nations, or any agency thereof, or to the decision or recommendation of any other Power.

The Monroe Doctrine. The Senate's reassertion of the inviolability—and ambiguity—of the Monroe Doctrine might also have been allowed to pass at that time. It would not have been an occasion for surprise, however, if some Latin American country had felt it a good opportunity to disavow our hegemony over this hemisphere and to maintain that since the assertion of the Doctrine's validity in the amended Covenant did not appear to be sufficient it was time to have some definition of the Doctrine and some limitation of our pretensions under it. The fifth reservation informed the members of the League that:

> 5. The United States will not submit to arbitration or to inquiry by the Assembly or by the Council of the League of Nations, provided for in said treaty of peace, any questions which in the judgment of the United States depend upon or relate to its long-established policy, commonly known as the Monroe doctrine; said doctrine is to be interpreted by the United States alone and is hereby declared to be wholly outside the jurisdiction of said League of Nations and entirely unaffected by any provision contained in the said treaty of peace with Germany.

Shantung. The long attack upon the Shantung settlement and upon Japan's motives came to an end with the adoption of the comparatively mild statement that "The United States withholds its assent to Articles 156, 157, and 158, and reserves full liberty of action with respect to any controversy which may arise under said articles."

Whether the Japanese Government of the day would have been tolerant enough and strong enough to have assented to our entry into the League under this condition can never be known. What we can be sure of is that the United States was not the only country which had political and nationalistic groups clamoring that the country's "rights" and "interests" be upheld. The pride of the Japanese people had been deeply hurt by the rejection of their racial equality declaration by the Peace Conference and this feeling had not been allayed by the sustained effort of the American Senators to hold up their succession to the German property in China as an example of the gross immoralities perpetrated in the treaty. Political necessity, if nothing more, may well have led the Japanese Government to refuse to assent to this reservation.

The Lesser Reservations. The seventh reservation was designed to prevent any American from serving either officially or unofficially upon any body set up by the Treaty or the League unless authorized by Congress to do so. The eighth claimed for that body a right to overrule the Reparations Commission in certain contingencies. The ninth informed the League that Congress would have to pass upon any of its expenses attributed to us. Two of these declarations may have been easily overlooked by the powers, but the principal Allies would have had cause to hesitate before giving our Congress a veto over one of the most important powers of the Reparations Commission. [3]

The tenth proviso sought to make sure that the ancient right of self defense was not abolished and that Congress might approve any arms reduction, while the eleventh quieted the professed fears of Senators that the economic

[3] The seventh, eighth and ninth reservations were:

7. No person is or shall be authorized to represent the United States, nor shall any citizen of the United States be eligible, as a member of any body or agency established or authorized by said treaty of peace with Germany, except pursuant to an act of the Congress of the United States providing for his appointment and defining his powers and duties.

8. The United States understands that the Reparation Commission will regulate or interfere with exports from the United States to Germany, or from Germany to the United States, only when the United States by act or joint resolution of Congress approves such regulation or interference.

9. The United States shall not be obligated to contribute to any expenses of the League of Nations or of the Secretariat, or of any commission or committee, or conference, or other agency, organized under the League of Nations or under the treaty or for the purpose of carrying out the treaty provisions, unless and until an appropriation of funds available for such expenses shall have been made by the Congress of the United States, Provided, That the foregoing limitation shall not apply to the United States' proportionate share of the office force and salary of the Secretary General.

boycott applied to a covenant breaking state might be extended to its citizens living in other countries. No possibility, however remote, of future tyranny by the League was being overlooked by the reservationists and no opportunity to stoutly defend the rights of Americans was passed by. Thus the twelfth reservation dealing with two articles of the treaty which provided for the liquidation of debts between citizens of the signatory states forbade the construction of these articles into anything "otherwise illegal or in contravention of the rights of citizens of the United States." [4]

The thirteenth clause of the proposed resolution of ratification looked with suspicion on the International Labor Organization and proclaimed once more the right of Congress to regulate our coming and going in the League. It said:

> The United States withholds its assent to Part XIII (Articles 387 to 427, inclusive) unless Congress by act or joint resolution shall hereafter make provision for representation in the organization established by said Part XIII, and in such event the participation of the United States will be governed and conditioned by the provisions of such act or joint resolution.

[4] The text of these reservations is as follows:

10. No plan for the limitation of armaments proposed by the council of the League of Nations under the provisions of Article 8 shall be held as binding the United States until the same shall have been accepted by Congress, and the United States reserves the right to increase whenever the United States is threatened with invasion or engaged in war.

11. The United States reserves the right to permit, in its discretion, the nationals of a covenant-breaking state, as defined in Article 16 of the Covenant of the League of Nations, residing within the United States, or in countries other than that violating said Article 16, to continue their commercial, financial and personal relations with the nationals of the United States.

12. Nothing in Articles 296, 297 or in any of the annexes thereto, or in any other article, section or annex of the treaty of peace with Germany, shall, as against citizens of the United States, be taken to mean any confirmation, ratification or approval of any act otherwise illegal or in contravention of the rights of citizens of the United States.

The Votes of the British Dominions. The sustained campaign to convince sections of the American people that the League would be controlled by Great Britain ended in the declaration that:

> Until Part I, being the Covenant of the League of Nations, shall be so amended as to provide that the United States shall be entitled to cast a number of votes equal to that which any member of the League and its self-governing dominions, colonies, or parts of empire, in the aggregate shall be entitled to cast, the United States assumes no obligation to be bound by any election, decision, report or finding of the Council or Assembly in which any member of the League and its self-governing dominions, colonies or parts of empire in the aggregate have cast more than one vote.
>
> The United States assumes no obligation to be bound by any decision, report or finding of the Council or the Assembly arising out of any dispute between the United States and any member of the League if such member, or any self-governing dominion, colony, empire or part of empire united with it politically has voted.

The result was that we put it up to the countries who are most like us in language and customs, in blood and in religion, and whose international problems are most akin to ours, either to have any action of the League in which they participated open to question and disavowal on our part or to give us a representation which would upset the principle of the equality of states—the only basis upon which there was a chance of building the League. It might be true enough that every member of the League would in practice wield influence in proportion to its power and resources, but the smallest states prized their formal equality in the family of nations. The action of the American Senate might be due solely to internal politics. Nevertheless, the developing nationalities within the British Empire could hardly be expected to sink back to a lower status at our request nor the powerful Allies to allow us multiple votes without increasing their own.

The chaos due to follow such a scramble for power and place was of no consequence to the Senators. Nor were they concerned over the probable rejection of this condition to our entry into the League. People as proud as our own were expected to acquiesce. The advent of the British Dominions to nationhood, which their membership in the Peace Conference and in the League had announced, had been cordially accepted by the other nations and contested by none, no matter how alien to them in culture and institutions the new states thus recognized might be. It remained for leaders of the country most akin to them to preach a supposed domination that aroused nobody else.

Self Determination for Ireland. The reservationists would have stopped here, content to have matched the President's Fourteen Points with an equal number of their own creation. Just when the structure was complete, however, the Senate, growing by what it fed upon, got out of hand and added a fifteenth "reservation" which would have either increased the number of British Dominion votes in the League or have created a wholly independent nation out of the territory of an ally.

The Irish reservation said:

15. In consenting to the ratification of the treaty with Germany the United States adheres to the principle of self-determination and to the resolution of sympathy with the aspirations of the Irish people for a government of their own choice adopted by the Senate June 6, 1919, and declares that when such government is attained by Ireland, a consummation it is hoped is at hand, it should promptly be admitted as a member of the League of Nations.

Even the Senators who had been so long engaged in "perfecting" the League and making it safe for American membership were non-plussed by this extension of the doctrine of avoiding entanglements and minding one's own business. They could picture their own feeling if the British House of Commons had passed a similar resolution in behalf of the Philippine Islands, and they appreciated the likelihood of this final expression of the Senate's solicitude passing without challenge.

The reservation program had reached its logical conclusion. Decreeing that if one of the reservations should be rejected by a single power the United States would remain out of the League, the Senate had repeatedly proclaimed its suspicion of the prospective members of the League collectively and ended by requiring the assent of several of the recent allies of the United States to terms or statements reflecting upon their conduct so strongly that their consent even by silence would be practically impossible.

CHAPTER IX

WHILE the Senate was failing to ratify the Treaty, the other nations had continued to join the League. The Allied Powers, some of whom had not been very enthusiastic about originating the institution, went in as a matter of course. The smaller countries of Europe that had maintained their neutrality throughout the War and that had most to lose by being entangled in a "war breeder" entered unanimously. The countries of Latin America, with one or two exceptions, joined without reservation or demur. Their constitutions also gave the Congress the right to declare war, yet after all the warnings that issued from Washington not one of them showed any alarm about the possible loss of that right. Neither did they take fright over the spectre of their boys having to fight and die on the other side of the world to police troubled areas and keep the peace which all agreed to maintain. Even Canada, which had suffered far more in the War than the United States, refused to believe that the road to Geneva was the way of death.

The year and a half of campaigning against the League in the United States did not convince a single country abroad that the proposed league of peace was something that could be entered only guardedly and at peril. But, said the enemies of the President and of the League, the campaign succeeded marvelously in the United States. The "solemn referendum" that Mr. Wilson demanded repudiated him and his league by the tremendous majority of 7,000,000 votes.

That it was a vote against Mr. Wilson and his party none could deny, and that much of the Republican vote was anti-league by the time the campaign was over was correspondingly clear.   That other issues and feelings growing out of the war determined the attitude of multitudes of voters was as widely contended and the pro-League Republicans pointed out that they were among the majority.   Many had undoubtedly followed the lead of the thirty-one famous Republicans who had held up the Republican party as the best means of entering the League. [1]

An Association of Nations.   The Republican candidate, Senator Harding of Ohio, had made many speeches that could be interpreted as favoring entrance into the League, though his speeches declaring against the League had been more strongly worded. [2]   He had not spoken highly of "this league," but had often promised a real "association of nations."

What the new association of nations was to be like apparently was not defined until Dr. Jacob Gould Schurman, after a conference with the President-elect gave it as his opinion, on January 12, 1921, that the "association" would include: (1) codification of international law; (2) the establishment of a world court; (3) the organization of a world conference which would be able, in a spirit of conciliation, to arrange disputes among nations that are beyond the reach of codified international law; and (4) disarmament. [3]

Beginning with the last item in this program, the new administration succeeded handsomely in stopping the competition in dreadnought building at the Washington Arms Limitation Conference of 1921.   After this substantial

[1] New York *Times,* October 15, 1920.
[2] See his Des Moines and Marion Speeches, *Literary Digest,* October 23, 1920, Vol. 67, No. 4.
[3] New York *Times,* January 12, 1921.

success the next step in associating with the other nations did not readily appear.   The other peoples, it seemed, were desirous of trying out the existing league and not disposed to abandon it for another and better way.

A Senator in the President's Chair.   The Administration was embarrassed, too, by its origin.   Mr. Harding, a Senator, had not been one of the leading candidates for the Republican Presidential nomination in 1920, but the Senators in their fight upon the League had seized control of the party, and a month before the Republican National Convention gathered, a group of them had met and selected one of their number, Mr. Harding, as the candidate, although they waited until the convention had been properly deadlocked before imposing him on it. [4]

The platform which was adopted before the nomination, commended the Senate for its "courage and fidelity" and pledged the party to "fulfill our world obligations without sacrifice to our national independence."   Then, on the night of June 11, a group of Senators, including Lodge, who was Chairman of the Convention, Smoot, Watson, Wadsworth and New, met and arranged that Mr. Harding should have the nomination.   The next day his vote jumped suddenly from 65 to 692. [5]

The new President thus owed his nomination to his friends in the Senate and to the fight on the League. It was not easy, therefore, to take any steps toward the League, and no measures to replace it appeared practical.   It was accordingly declared to be dead and its existence ignored. [6]

Mr. Harding could probably have done little to bring the United States back into any kind of association with the nations of the world.   Knowing that he was expected to be

[4] D. S. Muzzey, *The United States of America,* Vol. II, pp. 762-3.
[5] Ibid.
[6] See Senator Harding, *Current History,* Dec. 1920, Vol. 13, p. 369. Also, Manley O. Hudson, "America's Role in the League of Nations," *American Political Science Review,* February, 1929, pp. 18–19.

the mouthpiece of the Senate he selected the strongest Secretary of State the party afforded, Mr. Charles E. Hughes, but none knew better than he the truth of the contemptuous remark of Senator Penrose, "It doesn't make any difference who is appointed Secretary of State." [7] The Senate was in the saddle so far as foreign affairs were concerned and the irreconcilable minority dominated the Senate. So Mr. Harding attempted to insure the approval of the treaties signed at the Washington Conference by reverting to the McKinley practice of appointing Senators as his negotiators. Mr. Lodge and Mr. Underwood sat on the Commission and advocated the treaties in the Senate. They were approved. [8]

After that there was inactivity for a year in joining with the powers to keep the peace while the League struggled to find a footing and perfected its machinery, including the long desired Permanent Court of International Justice—a World Court fully organized and ready at all times to decide international disputes.

THE HARDING ADVOCACY

But eventually, on February 24, 1923, the Senate was considerably surprised by the receipt of a message from the President which advised it that a World Court had been established at The Hague and that the Court was "organized

[7] New York *Times,* January 12, 1921. Mr. Hughes was the logical selection aside from the need for a strong man.

[8] It does not follow that these treaties would not have been otherwise approved, nor that the treaty of Versailles would have been readily ratified if Mr. Wilson had appointed his Senate opponents to the American Peace Commission.

There is a good deal of reason for believing, however, that the Four Power Treaty, upon which the success of the Washington Conference apparently depended, would have been in grave peril indeed if the Democratic leader had not exerted his full influence for it. Two thirds of the Democrats strongly opposed it as a backward step toward combinations of nations based upon the old balance of power principle. It was approved by the Senate with 5 votes to spare, 12 votes for it coming from the Democrats. A shift of less than half of these votes would have defeated the treaty. *Congressional Record,* Vol. 62, Pt. 5, pp. 4486-97.

and functioning." The implication was clear that the possibility of organizing a rival court which would be entirely independent of the League was as remote as that of organizing another league itself. The United States was already a competent suitor before the Court, the message continued, but that relation was "not sufficient for a nation long committed to the peaceful settlement of international controversies. Indeed our nation had a conspicuous place in the advocacy of such an agency of peace and international adjustment, and our deliberate public opinion of today is overwhelmingly in favor of our full participation and the attending obligations of maintenance and the furtherance of its prestige." [9]

Here was a shocking statement, indeed, from the viewpoint of the Senators who had always maintained that whatever sentiment had existed in the United States for "entanglements" with other nations designed to keep the peace was wholly manufactured. But were they daunted? Not they. They had resisted the demand that we should take our high place in the League, gradually wore it down and had finally overcome it by arousing counter feelings of infinite number and variety. Should they admit now that the country was still overwhelmingly in favor of doing something to acknowledge our responsibility for the peace? No indeed! The President and his Secretary of State might so admit and the country might pile up the most imposing evidence of demand for action that could be assembled, as it later did, but they would never admit that it was a genuine demand. To the bitter end they maintained that it was all an artificial clamor concocted by the "leaguists" and "pacifists" and Mr. Bok, who offered large prizes to anyone who would devise a feasible way for us to cooperate for peace and then get the Senate to approve it. It was all the work of such "propagandists."

[9] *Congressional Record,* Vol. 64, Pt. 5, p. 4498.

But, said the President in closing his message, "It is not a new problem of international relationship, it is wholly a question of accepting an established institution of high character, and making effective all the fine things which have been said by us in favor of such an agency of advanced civilization."

Was not this the unkindest cut of all? It even sounded like the rhetorical Mr. Wilson. Vice President Coolidge, and many others, had hailed the victory of 1920 as the "end of a period which has substituted words for things," [10] yet here we were already being reminded of the fine words which had been said in favor of machinery to settle disputes without war. Such an unpleasant reminder might have been expected from the stubborn, impractical Mr. Wilson, but wasn't it a bit too much from the sane and amiable Mr. Harding, himself a former Senator and near-irreconcilable?

Reservations Proposed. There was comfort, though, for the aggrieved Senators in the fact that there were reservations that disavowed again the hated League—and which might be added to in the last analysis. The reservations proposed by Mr. Hughes read:

1. That such adhesion shall not be taken to involve any legal relation on the part of the United States to the League of Nations or the assumption of any obligations by the United States under the Covenant of the League of Nations constituting Part I of the Treaty of Versailles.

2. That the United States shall be permitted to participate, through representatives designated for the purpose and upon an equality with the other States, members respectively of the Council and Assembly of the League of Nations, in any and all proceedings of either the Council or the Assembly for the election of Judges or Deputy Judges of the Permanent Court of International Justice, or for the filling of vacancies.

[10] Muzzey, *The United States of America,* II, 768.

3. That the United States will pay a fair share of the expenses of the court as determined and appropriated from time to time by the Congress of the United States.

4. That the statute for the Permanent Court of International Justice adjoined to the protocol shall not be amended without the consent of the United States.[11]

Committed to the Irreconcilables. The proposal to adhere to the Court under these reservations was, of course, referred to the Foreign Relations Committee which was still dominated by the irreconcilables who had been placed upon it to insure the proper handling of the Wilson League. Prompt approval of joining a court created by the League was, therefore, hardly to be expected. Nor did it occur. The thing was branded at once as "a League court" with the assumption that that was enough to condemn it as far as the United States was concerned. Need anything more be said?

In the psychology of the day the implication was a powerful one, and if it wasn't powerful enough the bitter-enders were. They must somehow be placated. So most of the court proponents proceeded to argue exhaustively that it was not a League court at all. It was true that the League had been back of it, had fathered it, but it was now an independent entity, standing upon its own statute and independent of its creator. Thus Secretary Hoover, of the Commerce Department, argued before the National League of Women Voters' Convention in Des Moines, on April 11, 1923, that the connection with the League was remote.

The Smallest Possible Step. Joining the Court, he said, was the smallest possible step we could take. "The court," he continued, "is not the total solution of international cooperation for peace, for the great field of political action as distinguished from judicial action remains unsolved, but

[11] *Congressional Record,* Vol. 64, Pt. 5, p. 4500.

this step is sound and sure. It is the minimum possible step in eliminating the causes of war."

These two truths will stand much repetition still, for great as the value of our adhering to the Court would be as a sign of our willingness to cooperate in keeping the peace "the great field of political action," from which the more dangerous disputes come and in which they must long continue to be settled, remains (for us) unsolved. That is the major consideration which no amount of overlooking can remove. "The delicate machinery of social production and commerce cannot stand another shock like the World War," warned Mr. Hoover, "and there can be no confidence in the continuity of our civilization unless preventive safeguards can be established." [12]

The urgency of acting upon this warning will seem a little less acute as we recede from the Great War, but its basic soundness will stand out all the more clearly if the next Great War is allowed to happen. Imperial America may easily ignore such predictions of disaster as did Imperial Russia a few short years ago.

HELD IN COMMITTEE

The Lenroot Plan. Perhaps one should not talk too much about the major issue even yet. Certainly then the chief desire was to steer away from the political machinery which must cope with the bulk of serious disputes if major wars are to be averted. Therefore, Senator Lenroot introduced a resolution on December 10, 1923, proposing that all states accredited to the Dutch capital be permitted to join and that the Court be cut apart from the League. A new electoral scheme divided the powers into two groups. Group A, to be composed of the British Empire, France, the United States, Italy, Japan, Germany, and Brazil, would receive the power

[12] New York *Times,* April 12, 1923.

to vote for judges conferred on the Council of the League. Group B, to include all other states, would receive the powers conferred upon the League Assembly. The duties of the Secretary General of the League would go to the Registrar of the Court and the expenses would be paid outside the League. [13]

In this fashion did an American Senator propose, with an apparently straight face, that the forty-four charter members of the Court should separate it from the organization which had made it possible in order to conform to a section of American feeling, say the dominant section. To put it still more concretely, the nations were asked to fasten a label of "unclean" upon the League of Nations, to which they all belonged and from which they hoped for security and peace, in order to soothe the sensibilities of the dozen American Senators who had done all that lay within their power to keep the League from being created in the first place and who had at the last succeeded in preventing American participation in it.

A Court But Not This One. It may well be doubted that this resolution represented the views of Senator Lenroot, but it did represent the desires of Senator Lodge and Senator Borah. Mr. Borah had explained in a New York address on March 19, 1923, that he was strongly for *a* court, but not this one. His objections to the existing court were: (a) That it was unable to enforce its decisions, and (b) that it was subject to the manipulative tactics of European politicians. The "manipulative tactics" of American politicians were not referred to, but the Senator lauded the compulsory jurisdiction that Mr. Root had proposed for the Court and believed the United States should adhere if this jurisdiction could be given to it. To establish a court which would have far reaching influence and whose decisions would eventually become binding it would be necessary to pattern it after the

[13] *Congressional Record,* Vol. 65, Pt. 1, p. 151.

Supreme Court of the United States—but no armies and navies back of it, only public opinion. [14]

Mr. Lodge was equally in favor of *a* world court, but it must be a true one, as he explained in a letter to his constituents published a few days after the introduction of the Lenroot resolution. "I am thoroughly in favor of a World Court," he said, "but I desire that it should be a true World Court and not involved in any way with the League of Nations." The easiest way to get the true court would be to take the old Hague Court of Arbitration and make it permanent. He was distinctly "not in favor of adhering to the protocol unless reservations could be made which would separate the court from the League and make it a genuine World Court." [15]

Approval Urged by President Coolidge. Mr. Lodge's committee did not find ten month's sufficient time to act upon the proposal. Nor did it find time after President Coolidge had urged its favorable consideration in his message of December 3, 1923, saying: "As I wish to see a court established, and as the proposal presents the only practical plan on which many nations have ever agreed, though it may not meet every desire, I therefore commend it to the favorable consideration of the Senate (applause) with the proposed reservation clearly indicating our refusal to adhere to the League of Nations." [16]

The Committee continued to be very busy, Mr. Lodge explained in the Senate on April 4. They had had great difficulty in getting a quorum. Four of the members were

[14] New York *Times,* March 20, 1923.
[15] New York *Times,* December 14, 1923.
[16] *Congressional Record,* Vol. 65, Part 1, p. 96. The League was further disposed of as follows: "The incident, so far as we are concerned, is closed. The League exists as a foreign agency. We hope it will be helpful. But the United States sees no reason to limit its own freedom and independence of action by joining it. (Applause) We shall do well to recognize this basic fact in all national affairs and govern ourselves accordingly."

often kept away by the investigations. [17] He admitted, however, that no measure had been withheld from consideration
or action for this reason. [18]

Later in the month, when the session neared its close and
a strong demand arose for some action on the Court proposal, Mr. Lodge replied to the League of Nations Non-
Partisan Association that the press of business in the Committee was great. He had never seen so many treaties taken
up in a single session in his life. "As to the Permanent
Court of International Justice established by the League, it
has seemed to the Committee one of those that did not require
immediate action, because we now have fifty individual arbitration treaties with other countries. . . . The United States
was also a signatory of the Hague Convention establishing
a Permanent Court of Arbitration." [19]

A Hearing Eventually Held. A little matter of fourteen
months delay was perhaps not to be complained of, especially
when a sub-committee hearing was finally scheduled to be
held at once. At this hearing, on April 30, a score of
prominent men and women plead for consideration. Among
them former Attorney General Wickersham urged that
"we cannot decently urge the creation of such a court
as this upon the rest of the world through a long series of
years and then repudiate the court when they consent to it,
unless we offer some adequate reason."

At the same hearing, Bishop Brent, chief chaplain of the
A.E.F., scored Senator Lodge's excuse for delay—that it
was "caused entirely by the fact that there were other matters which seemed to the committee to require more immediate action, although the point has never been made in the
committee."

---

[17] Investigations into the conduct of the Departments of the Interior,
Navy and Justice, under the administrations of Secretaries Fall, Denby
and Daugherty, commonly called the Oil Investigations.
[18] *Congressional Record*, Vol. 65, Pt. 6, p. 5554.
[19] New York *Times*, April 28, 1924.

"In other words," said Bishop Brent, "a measure originally considered so important as to call for wide publication by the chief leaders of the Administration . . . has been passed over for other proposals which, however important, are little known to the country at large. Senator Lodge in his apologies for inaction damns the court with faint praise." It puzzled the Bishop to know "why any measure of the origin and history of the one under consideration should be treated as it has been. Placed before the country by the party in power, endorsed by the opposition, it stands in peril of death from neglect on the part of its parent."

"Unless our Government," he added, "provides a moral substitute for war, as far as in it lies, a vast proportion of our citizenry are presently going to find themselves in the predicament of being opposed to war as an arbiter in international disputes, but without any provision being made for an adequate substitute of a peaceful and orderly character." [20]

Further appeals for action were made by a dozen leading citizens the next day, but no action was indicated. It appearing to be a favorable opportunity, however, for the Democrats to test the sincerity of the Republican advocacy, Senator Swanson introduced a resolution proposing to adhere to the Court under the Harding-Hughes terms. In a statement made later he said he had delayed introducing the resolution hoping that some Republican would. There was an impression that the Court proposal was a political gesture. If the Administration and Republican Senators now mani-

---

[20] New York *Times,* May 1, 1924. The compulsion of offering some moral substitute for the machinery of the League is one which the more conscientious of those responsible for its defeat have never ceased to feel. For a time it appeared that the Court could be offered as the substitute. Latterly the tendency seems to be to deny the efficacy of all machinery and preach a faith in the sufficiency of "outlawing" war that is even more mystical than the fondest dreams of the League enthusiasts.

fested no earnest intention to get action this would be proved. [21]

The Pepper Plan. The campaign of 1924 being imminent, some action on the part of the Republican majority did appear to be advisable, so, on May 22, Senator Pepper, of Pennsylvania, a member of the Foreign Relations Committee, brought out an elaborate plan for painlessly divorcing the Court from the League. The Lenroot resolution cutting the two apart without ceremony had not seemed to find favor, so a more scientific plan was now advanced. The resolution "expressing with greater precision the safeguards" of President Harding's message was lengthy and supported by two annexes. The second of these contained six substantive amendments to the Court statute and ten formal ones.

Briefly, the plan provided that the judges should be elected by a "council of signatories," composed of the five principal allied and associated powers named in the Treaty of Versailles together with others elected by the signatories, and an "assembly of signatories" containing representatives of all the members. These electoral bodies were to meet at the call of the Secretary General of the Permanent Court of Arbitration. [22]

The scheme seemed likely to cause the powers little actual inconvenience for apparently a motion in the Council and Assembly of the League would bring these electoral bodies into existence at a moment's notice, the delegates from the

---

[21] *Congressional Record*, Vol. 65, Pt. 8, p. 7904. New York *Times*, May 7, 1924. The restiveness of the pro-league Republicans was indicated by the recent speeches before the sub-committee, notably those of Mr. Everett Colby, a former State Senator from New Jersey. Referring to the recommendation of the 1920 campaign that the Republican Party was the way into the League, Mr. Colby said, on May 1: "The leaders of the Republican party made a statement at that time for the purpose of getting votes. They got my vote and the votes of thousands of others on faith, but so far as I know, nothing has been done up to this time." New York *Times*, May 2, 1924.
[22] *Congressional Record*, Vol. 65, Pt. 9, pp. 9157-8.

United States would step in and the election of judges proceed.

The merits of the plan were as clearly evident. The pure Americans could thus be relieved from the contamination which would come from sitting in those "political" bodies, the Assembly and Council. The great aim of maintaining the United States "wholly free from any legal relationship to the League of Nations" would be achieved.

And why should the nations of the world object? The inconvenience to them would be small indeed. Their representatives on the Council and the Assembly would not need to move out of their seats or lose a moment's time. To be sure, the general revision of the Court statute proposed by Mr. Pepper would involve a confession on their part that there was something that was sinister, or at least hardly respectable, in the relationship between the League and the Court. It would be necessary to admit that the political association in the League was fraught with danger and impropriety—that they had gravely erred in retaining the slightest connection with it when they created that potentially clean institution the World Court. But why should the nations of the earth mind this abasement when the men on the Foreign Relations Committee of the United States Senate, who had originally created these impressions, would be appeased? Did they not realize that these gentlemen could never recognize the League in any fashion, however indirect? [23]

[23] It may be protested that such moumental vanity could not really exist even among the anti-league members of the Foreign Relations Committee—that they did not seriously expect that their proposals would be accepted by the civilized world—they were merely under the political necessity of conforming to the great anti-league verdict of the people in the 1920 campaign. This may be granted in part, but even so, the same popular fear and dislike had been stirred to heat under the incessant activity of the men on that Committee who had dictated these new maneuvers to cleanse the Court of the League.

Otherwise it must be explained why the same aversion to and dislike of the League was not stirred in any other civilized country.

A Danger Discovered. About this time, too, the political isolationists began to make some headway in convincing the other Senators that possibly there might be something to lose by going into the Court. The council could ask the Court for advisory opinions on matters of law and might it not put the United States in an embarrassing position some time? Wasn't it reasonable to believe that the prodigiously rich and prosperous United States, standing aloof from world association and proposing to collect huge war debts from the impoverished countries of Europe, might find the Council asking questions of the Court which would be unpleasant to hear? Under the circumstances might it not even be asked why the repudiated bonds of certain states of the American Union should not be paid? It did not seem altogether unlikely.

Then there was also the always convenient matter of Japanese immigration, which has just been made acute by our passage of an immigration law providing for total exclusion of Japanese immigrants. A proud and sensitive people felt themselves unjustly discriminated against, and their Foreign Minister, M. Matsui, had stated that his Government contemplated asking the Court to pass in an advisory way on the action of the United States in abrogating the "gentlemen's agreement" respecting the immigration between the United States and Japan and substituting for it a statute forbidding the admission of Japanese laborers.

When the Committee heard this they agreed, on May 23, that an additional reservation must be added disclaiming all responsibility for advisory opinions. [24]

A Report Voted. The next day the Committee adopted the Pepper plan by a vote of 10 to 6, after the Swanson resolution, containing the Harding-Hughes terms, plus an advisory opinion reservation, had been rejected 10 to 8, and after Senator Lodge had withdrawn his still more elaborate

[24] New York *Times,* May 23, 24, 1924.

plan for revising the machinery of the League so as to divorce the Court from it absolutely. [25] Several Senators, however, voted for the Pepper Plan only to get the question before the Senate in some form, reserving the right to oppose it later.   The opponents of the Court on their part felt that the adoption of the report would enable them to appear to support Mr. Coolidge in the coming campaign. [26]

The Court in the Campaign of 1924. This was well, for the Republican National Convention of 1924, meeting in Cleveland a few days later, declared in its platform: "The Republican Party reaffirms its stand for agreement among the nations to prevent war and preserve peace. As an important step in this direction we endorse the Permanent Court of International Justice and favor the adherence of President Coolidge." [27]

The election which followed resulted in another sweeping Republican victory, President Coolidge receiving 4,000,000 votes more than his two opponents combined and 8,000,000 more than his Democratic opponent, Mr. John W. Davis. The Court issue did not figure as largely as the League had in 1920, but if the results in the earlier year was a repudiation of the League, the verdict of 1924 was an endorsement of the Court, particularly since the Democrats also favored it.

The election, however, did not lead to action toward entry into the Court. Mr. Lodge had died, but Mr. Borah reigned

[25] Senator Lodge's plan, as submitted to the Senate on May 8, 1924, contained 67 articles which nearly filled an ordinary page. He ignored the World Court entirely and called upon the President to summon a third Hague Conference to set up a new one on the basis of his plan. The machinery for electing the judges already in existence was closely copied, but the British Empire was restricted to one vote. The President was, of course, required to consult the Senate before submitting any case to the Court. *Senate Joint Resolution,* No. 122 (S. Doc. No. 107) 68th Congress, 1st Session. *Literary Digest,* May 24, 1924, Vol. 81, No. 8, p. 12.

[26] New York *Times,* May 25, 1924.

[27] *Current History,* July, 1924, Vol. 20, pp. 653-4. The remainder of the paragraph read: "This Government has definitely refused membership in the League of Nations and to assume the obligations under the Covenant of the League. On this we stand."

in his stead as chairman of the Foreign Relations Committee. He warned the committee, in January 1925, that if the World Court were forced upon the Senate it would interfere with all other legislation awaiting consideration, and made it clear that he would oppose all efforts to take up the question in that session of Congress. [28] He was successful in his opposition, and the session closed, March 4th, without the Court having been considered. [29]

Consideration Pressed by the President.   On the same day President Coolidge referred to the situation in his Inaugural Address as follows:

Where great principles are involved, where great movements are under way which promise much for the welfare of humanity by reason of the very fact that many other nations have given such movements their actual support, we ought not to withhold our own sanction because of any small and unessential difference, but only upon the ground of the most important and compelling fundamental reasons. We cannot barter away our independence or our sovereignty, but we ought to engage in no refinement of logic, no sophistries and no subterfuges to argue away the undoubted duty of this country by reason of the might of its numbers, the power of its resources and its position of leadership in the world, actively and comprehensively to signify its approval and to bear its full share of the responsibility of a candid and disinterested attempt at the establishment of a tribunal for the administration of even-handed justice between nation and nation.   The weight of our enormous influence must be cast upon the side of a reign not of force, but of law and trial, not by battle, but by reason.[30]

[28] New York *Times,* January 15, 1925.
[29] The Pepper plan was reached on the calendar on February 28, but quickly put aside and an effort of Senator King, of Utah, to secure consideration on March 4 was also blocked, New York *Times,* March 1 and 5.
[30] *Congressional Record,* Vol. 67, Pt. 1, p. 5.

This candid statement was intended as an exposition of our proper attitude toward the Court only, though it might have been applied equally well to our attitude toward the League itself. It led to the fixing of a date when the consideration of the Court would at last begin in the Senate. But the date was not to be immediate in the special session of the Senate which convened at once. It was fixed (on March 13, 1925) for December 17, 1925. Mr. Curtis, the Republican leader, proposed unanimous consent to take up a resolution of adherence on December 17. This being refused by Senator Dill, Democrat, of Washington, Senator Robinson, the Democratic leader, moved that the Swanson resolution be taken up on the December date, and the motion carried 78 to 2, Dill and Norbeck dissenting. [31]

The Reaction of the Country

Thus after the Committee had succeeded in delaying consideration for two full years, it was eventually agreed that the matter should come to debate after an additional delay of nine months.

The new interval was used by Senator Borah, at least, in earnest opposition to adherence. On May 11, he was explaining in Boston that he would have no objection to the League origin of the Court, if the League would only divorce it. The advisory opinion function made the Court a part of the League. There was nothing to prevent any kind of political question from being submitted to the Court in that manner and reservations to political treaties were utterly worthless. In June he was continuing the campaign; on September 15 advocating that Court and League be separated, and on December 1 that they be divorced.[32] One

---

[31] *Congressional Record,* Vol. 67, Pt. 1, p. 207.
[32] New York *Times,* May 12, June 30, September 15 and December 1, 1925.

need never despair of defeating a treaty in the Senate, no matter how strong the original sentiment for it.

Supported by the Great National Organization. The sentiment for the Court appeared to be as nearly unanimous as could be expected on any controversial question. Both political parties favored it, and the National House of Representatives had voted by the overwhelming count of 301 to 28 on March 3, 1925, for adherence. [33] The American Legion, the American Federation of Labor, the National Association of Manufacturers, the National Economic League, the National Republican Club and the United States Chamber of Commerce approved the step. [34] The American Bar Association voted for going in, as did the National League of Women Voters and the American Association of University Women, the General Federation of Women's Clubs, and the National Federation of Business and Professional Women's Clubs. [35]

Backed by the Churches. Religious bodies voting for entry included: the Presbyterian General Assembly, the National Council of Congregational Churches, the Federal Council of Churches of Christ, the World's Sunday School Association, the United Christian Endeavor Societies, the General Conference of the Methodist Episcopal Church, the Northern Baptist Convention, the House of Bishops of the Protestant Episcopal Church, [36] the Church Peace Union, the American Unitarian Association, the Synod of the Reformed Presbyterian Church, the General Conference of Friends, the International Convention of Disciples of Christ, the United Presbyterian Church of North America, the Uni-

---

[33] New York *Times*, March 4, 1925.
[34] *New York Times Index*, April-June, 1923, p. 310; July-September, 1923, p. 290; *Congressional Record*, Vol. 56, Pt. 3, p. 2357.
[35] *New York Times Index*, July-September, 1923, pp. 290-91; January-March, 1924, p. 296; July-September, 1925, p. 394.
[36] *New York Times Index*, April-June, 1923, p. 310; October-December, 1923, p. 309; April-June, 1924, p. 315; October-December, 1925, p. 315.

versalist General Convention, and scores of lesser religious bodies. [37]

Endorsed by Occupational Groups of Every Kind. Some fifteen state fraternal orders also passed pro-court resolutions in addition to many educational and racial associations and all of the great Jewish organizations. The most striking expressions of opinion, however, came from business and professional bodies. An extended list of those passing resolutions of adherence is given below to indicate the range of interest represented. [38]

Favored by Four-Fifths of the Press. A survey of the press taken by the American Foundation, an organization established to further the cause of the Court by Mr. Edward Bok, one of the most reputable of American journalists,

---

[37] New York *Times,* October 18, 1925; *Congressional Record,* Vol. 67, Pt. 3, p. 2498.

[38] The following list of business and professional organizations supporting the Court was compiled by the American Foundation and released on October 18, 1925: The United States Junior Chamber of Commerce, the Chamber of Commerce of the State of New York, The Bar Associations of Ohio, Texas, Wisconsin, Delaware and Colorado, the Commercial Law League of America, the Delaware and Minnesota State Federations of Labor, the Department of Delaware of the American Legion, the 78th Division United States Army, the American Manufacturers Association, the National Association of Credit Men, the Association of Credit Men of Missouri, The Eastern Soda Water Bottlers' Association, the Kansas Master Plumbers' Association, the Georgia-Florida Pecan Growers' Association, the National Retail Hardware Association, the National Pipe and Supplies Association, the Mississippi Travelers' Association, the Southern Interstate Coal Operators' Association, the Southern Retail Furniture Association, the Texas Retail Dry Goods Association, the Eastern Association of Dyers and Cleaners, the International Association of Machinists, the Southern Sash, Door and Millwork Manufacturers' Association, the Indiana Travelers' Protective Association, the Minnesota Implement Dealers' Association, the Commonwealth Club of California, the Funeral Directors' Association of Kentucky, the American Association of Wholesale Opticians, the Connecticut State Police Department, the Minnesota State Fire Department Association, the American Institute of Homeopathy, the New Mexico Medical Association, the Ohio Society of Osteopathic Physicians and Surgeons, the Montana Osteopathic Association, the Executive Committee of the American Association of Colleges of Pharmacy, the Ohio Dental Society, the Missouri Veterinary Medical Association, the California State Nurses' Association and the Delaware State Association of Graduate Nurses.

showed a striking agreement. Of 1,042 leading daily news-papers, 865, or 83 per cent, had expressed themselves as favoring adherence; 114 or 11 per cent were opposed and 62 or six per cent had taken no stand. The opposition in-cluded the twenty-two Hearst papers, the New York *Sun,* the Kansas City *Star,* the Chicago *Tribune* and the Washing-ton *Post.* This group in general opposed the step as a back door entry into the League, though a considerable number of the 114 opposed took that position on the ground that joining the Court was too small a step, merely a smoke screen to cover our failure to enter the League. [39]

Opposed by the Klan and Irish Organizations. The op-position mustered adverse votes in the Connecticut Assembly and the Wisconsin Senate and was considerably augmented by the Ku Klux Klan, which opposed the Court on grounds indicated by the following heading of an article in one of the organs of that order: "New World Court merely 'back door' into League of Nations, where America's interest would be outvoted ten to one, Government's immigration policy at stake, as Vatican would use World Court as tool for Romanizing America, and force Papist aliens into country. Clever scheme to embroil nation in old world troubles." [40]

This opposition, however, was by no means sufficient to give the Court the organized support of Catholic Americans. The Irish Catholic newspapers attacked it bitterly as some-thing dominated by England. (See footnote at the close of this chapter.)

The Meaning of Abstention. The case for the Court in public morals was well stated by Mr. John R. Quigg, Na-tional Commander of the American Legion, who said on Armistice Day, 1925: "Today is Armistice Day . . . It is also peace day, the day when we who came out of that conflict

[39] New York *Times,* December 13, 1925.
[40] Ibid., November 7, 1925.

unscathed should give an accounting of our efforts to keep
faith with the dead and bring into reality the ideal for which
they died—world peace." The American Legion was pledged
to a three-fold program, the first step of which was the immediate adherence by the United States to a permanent court
of international justice. The Legion, in the name of those
who could not speak for themselves, offered this program
of peace "in the belief that future generations may be spared
the cost, in blood and treasure, of a war so terrible that
civilization itself might not endure." [41]

Mr. Henry A. Stimson stated the broad issue as emphatically. Noting that forty-seven nations had joined the Court
and fifty-four the League, and reviewing the countries outside of both, he concluded: "Whatever may be thought of
others, we are by virtue of our size sure to be counted as
arrayed against those who are united in the organized effort to secure a permanent peace." In the light of this fact
and of the public opinion working for the Court he found it
hard to comprehend the constant assertion that the people are
opposed either to the Court or the League. [42]

THE SENATE DEBATE

As the time for open consideration of the question in the
Senate approached, mass meetings were held in scores of
cities,[43] and public interest was keen in the stand President
Coolidge would take in his Annual Message.

Advisory Opinions Upheld by the President. His attitude
was stated as clearly as either side could desire. After reviewing our part in laying the foundations for such a court
and explaining the reservations, he stressed the slight connection with the League and came to the chief point upon

[41] New York *Times,* November 12, 1925.
[42] New York *Times,* December 13, 1925.
[43] New York *Times,* December 6, 1925.

which the opposition had concentrated, the advisory opinion function of the Court, saying:

> It does not seem that the authority to give advisory
> opinions interferes with the independence of the court.
> Advisory opinions in and of themselves are not harmful, but
> may be used in such a way as to be very beneficial because
> they undertake to prevent injury rather than merely afford
> a remedy after the injury has been done. It is a principle
> that only implies that the court shall function when proper
> application is made to it. Deciding the question involved
> upon issues submitted for an advisory opinion does not
> differ materially from deciding the question involved upon
> issues submitted by contending parties. Up to the present
> time the court has given an advisory opinion when it judged
> it had jurisdiction and refused to give one when it judged
> it did not have jurisdiction. Nothing in the work of the
> court has yet been an indication that this is an impairment
> of its independence or that its practice differs materially
> from the giving of like opinions under the authority of the
> constitutions of several of our states.
>
> No provision of the statute seems to me to give this court
> any authority to be a political rather than a judicial court.
> We have brought cases in this country before courts which,
> when they have been adjudged to be political, have been
> thereby dismissed. It is not improbable that political ques-
> tions will be submitted to this court, but again up to the
> present time the court has refused to pass on political ques-
> tions and our support will undoubtedly have a tendency to
> strengthen it in that refusal.

Concession and Accommodation Necessary.   Then followed sound words of wisdom on the first requisite for international cooperation.

> If we are going to support any court, it would not be one
> that we have set up alone or which reflects only our ideals.
> Other nations have their customs and their institutions,

their thoughts and their methods of life. If a court is going to be international, its composition will have to yield to what is good in all these various elements. Neither will it be possible to support a court which is exactly perfect, or under which we assume absolutely no obligations. If we are seeking that opportunity, we might as well declare that we are opposed to supporting any court. If any agreement is made, it will be because it undertakes to set up a tribunal which can do more of the things these other nations wish to have done.

The same good common sense might be applied equally well to the major issue of our relation to the League, although Mr. Coolidge had no intention of doing so. Nor was he pleading for the League as the organization on which the real responsibility rests, presumably, when he said in conclusion: "Like all others engaged in the War, whatever we said as a matter of fact we joined an alliance, we became a military power, we impaired our independence. We have more at stake than any one else in avoiding a repetition of that calamity." [44]

A Fifth Reservation Added. The Seventeenth Day of December being reached the Senate took up the Swanson resolution and heard Mr. Swanson in support of it. To the original Hughes reservations he had added a fifth, on advisory opinions, saying:

5. That the United States shall be in no manner bound by any advisory opinion of the Permanent Court of International Justice not rendered pursuant to a request in which it, the United States, shall expressly join in accordance with the statute for the said court adjoined to the protocol of signature of the same to which the United States shall become signatory. [45]

[44] *Congressional Record,* Vol. 67, Pt. 1, p. 459.
[45] *Congressional Record,* Vol. 67, Pt. 1, p. 974. On December 18, Senator Lenroot exposed an anonymous "Catechism of the World

After having added this reservation to the list he defended the asking of advisory opinions as an old, established custom in many commonwealths.   It was done in Canada and in England, in Colombia and Panama, in Massachusetts, New Hampshire, Maine, Rhode Island, Tennessee, South Dakota, Colorado, Delaware, Alabama and Oklahoma. The American state constitutions and laws conferring the power in certain contingencies ranged in date all the way from 1784 to the present.

The Dangers of a League Court. Senator Borah spoke the following day on the relationship of Court and League and quoted from founders, leaders and friends of the League to prove that the Court was an integral part of the League system. Choosing the weakest point in the pro-court case first, he demonstrated so completely that it would be difficult to deny that it was a court dependent for its very existence on the League.

Proceeding then to the advisory opinion function he declared that Mr. Root and Judge Moore had originally opposed giving it to the Court and held that it could be invoked on any kind of question and rendered by a majority of the Court.[46]

Senator Walsh, of Montana, followed.   He was not troubled at all about the Court being an organ of the League. The general sanctions in the Covenant could be invoked to enforce the decisions of the old Hague Court of Arbitration, to which we belonged, just as easily as those of the World Court. So no new danger was incurred.[47]

On December 21, Mr. Walsh continued with a discussion of the Mosul case in which the opponents of the Court contended that Turkey, a non-member of the League, had

---

Court" which was being circulated in opposition to the Court, demonstrating that it contained statements which were complete misrepresentations. p. 1067.

[46] *Congressional Record*, Vol. 67, Pt. 1,   pp. 1067-75.

[47] Ibid., 1084-92.

been inveigled into it for the proposed settling of the Mosul dispute and then maneuvered out of her claim by the device of an advisory opinion. He quoted the proceedings in the case extensively to show that Turkey had not been haled before the Court without her consent. The process of giving an advisory opinion was much better safeguarded under the rules of the Court than in our own states. Here, opinions were arrived at without hearing arguments, a custom which might lead to hasty and ill considered action; before the Court, as Judge Moore had testified, a spectator would detect no difference between a proceeding for a judgment and a proceeding for an advisory opinion. Nor was it a valid criticism that no judgment was entered in the latter procedure. In nine cases out of ten decided by the Supreme Court of the United States no judgment was entered, the opinion of the Court sufficing.

The Monroe Doctrine Imperilled? The contention that the Monroe Doctrine might come before the Court was subject to similar reduction. If the United States were involved in the dispute we could not be forced before the Court without our consent. If, asked Mr. Walsh, other American nations wished to send their disputes with each other, or with European powers, to the Court, how were we going to stop them? Even in the Venezuela dispute the most that we had insisted upon was that there should be an arbitration; we did not attempt to say where or by whom. A dozen other cases, which he cited, proved that we had never presumed to say to the American republics that they could not submit their controversies to any tribunal not of our choosing. Concern over the Monroe Doctrine was not what agitated those who argued that we ought not to countenance the hearing of American disputes by old world judges; it was an increase in the prestige of the League of Nations which they feared.

The charge that the League had emasculated the Court by

refusing to give it compulsory jurisdiction was likewise without body. The simple truth was that the world was not yet ready to give compulsory jurisdiction to any court—and least of all the men who continually feared entanglement of some kind.[48]

A New Pepper Plan. Following Senator Walsh's address, Senator Pepper, of Pennsylvania, made the suggestions that were later to evolve into the amendment to reservation No. 5, which kept us out of the Court.

His suggestions were three in number, (1) that the United States declare its understanding that the present practice of the Court in giving no secret or confidential advice was to be permanent—we must state in no uncertain terms that we were adhering to a court, not a conclave; (2) we should pledge the other signatory powers to the principle that the policy laid down by the Court in the Eastern Karelia case of refusing to give an advisory opinion when one of the parties refused the jurisdiction of the Court was not to be reversed; and (3) instead of merely declaring that we would not be bound by any advisory opinion which we had not joined in submitting we should go further and require "that there shall be no advisory opinion on any matter directly affecting the United States unless the United States shall have consented that the court take jurisdiction." He thought that two-thirds of the Senate would take the view that the relationship between the League and the Court constituted no genuine obstacle to adherence, "if we can safeguard this subtle means of communication between the League and the Court which is represented by the advisory opinion jurisdiction." [49]

Are Such Precautions Not Wise? These suggestions taken together, form an excellent example of the kind of dangers the lawyers of the Senate feel compelled to ward off when

[48] *Congressional Record*, Vol. 67, Pt. 2, pp. 1236-45.
[49] *Congressional Record*, Vol. 67, Pt. 2, pp. 1245-6.

treaties are being considered. No one could deny that the proceedings of the Court should be public. That is the practice of the Court. What harm then in writing it into fundamental law that the Court shall never become a secret conclave? Isn't it a small and reasonable request to make? It is difficult to say no, though it may be asked in reply whether the precaution is really necessary. Will it not be time to combat sinister practices in the Court when they begin to occur? Is it worth while to question the integrity of the Court in this fashion when in all probability the rule of public proceedings is established for all time? Conceivably not, is the reply, but the rule was not established without some difficulty and it might be reversed. It will be best to make sure that it is permanent before we adhere. Afterwards we would be only one voice among many.

Again with the rule of consent to jurisdiction established in the Eastern Karelia case, the probability of that reasonable principle ever being upset would appear to the student at a distance to be small, and likely to become progressively smaller with the hardening of usage. But the Senators at grips with the problem had been informed on high authority that a minority of the Court still opposed the rule. Moreover, the Council had never recognized it. If then the Court should feel disposed to render an advisory opinion against the wishes of the United States it could do so by a majority vote. All that would be required, was repeated almost daily in the Senate, was that two judges should change their minds. When it was replied that the Court would be most unlikely to offend one of its great members, even though a non-League member, especially when it would be necessary to reverse a generally app...   d rule to do so, and that it would be time to bind the Court forever in this regard when the need arose, it was rejoined that it would be much more difficult then. In the view of many Senators now was the time to make sure. How could the Court, or any one, object to the fixing of the existing rule? To some it was wise simply because we were dealing with the Philistines. If they objected on the ground that it was not necessary that would certainly prove that it was.

Still again with Mr. Pepper's third point, which proved to be the most important of all, it would seem to the average layman sufficient to say that we would be bound by no advisory opinion which we had not joined in asking for, since that function of the Court had so far been conservatively and properly used. But when the Senators had thought of all the embarrassing questions that might conceivably be propounded to the Court for an advisory opinion without our consent they convinced themselves, and many others, that we had best not only refuse to be bound, but also to risk being embarrassed. And if you asked them if it was necessary to stir up everybody else's sensibilities now in order that your own might be insured against possible jars far into the future they would answer with the classic formula of the days of 1919: "It is no reply to say that these evils may not occur! It is only necessary to show that they can happen!"

By the time they were done it was easy to feel that to be a real American one must vote for preventing all the possibilities as well as the probabilities. And if one happened to have an adverse set of feelings about that "foreign agency," the League of Nations, why then of course all "subtle means of communication" with it had to be especially guarded against.

Two Retrospects. Senator Willis, Republican, of Ohio, quoted the Republican National platforms from 1904 to 1924, on January 4, 1926, together with the utterances of Republican statesmen to show how consistently strong the party attitude was in favoring the extension of judicial settlement for international disputes. His array of utterances seemed conclusive as did his exposé of the fallacy of delaying entrance into the Court until international law could be codified.[50]

An equally frank discussion of the issue was made on the following day by Senator Bruce, Democrat, of Maryland, in which he declared that the more readily the features of the League of Nations could be seen in the Harding-Hughes-Coolidge Court, the better he liked the child. He was for the Court with the League or without it; preferably with it, but cordially even without it.

He was not under the impression that the clock could be turned back, but our entry into the Court would "give to the rest of the world the definite assurance that our great influence as a nation would, thenceforth, at least as a member of this court, be exerted in behalf of world peace." That assurance could never again mean as much to other lands as it would have meant "during the crucifying period, immediately after our refusal to ratify the Covenant of the League of Nations, when the cry that came to us from across the Atlantic was little less agonizing than that of Mount Calvary, 'Lama Sabacthani, why hast thou forsaken me?'" Without attempting to apportion the blame for that refusal it was to him "a thought almost too painful for words that no matter under what circumstances, or to what extent, we may hereafter become a party to the present world concert for preserving world peace, we can never again hope by doing so to win the mighty guerdon of national honor and prestige that we would have won if we had promptly ratified the Covenant of the League of Nations with or without reservations."

A Warning. The great opportunity was gone, continued Senator Bruce, but accepting the Court would renew our connection with the nobler past. All that he asked was that the Court "be not so transformed by our reservations that the nations which are now members of that court will be un-

[50] *Congressional Record,* Vol. 67, Pt. 2, pp. 1417-27.

willing to admit us into it; and in weighing the possibility of this result, we should not forget that the other great civilized powers of the earth have lost to a considerable extent their eager desire that we should become a party to the international concert which they have so successfully established." [51] But this reasonable warning fell on deaf ears. The Senate went ahead with scarcely another single doubt voiced that the world would accept its terms when at last refined to hold in line all Senators who might complete the one-third of the Senate necessary to defeat the project.

"Equality" Demanded. Shortly after, on January 9, the opponents of the Court began to press the inadequacy of reservation number 5. It by no means put us on an equality with the other great powers, urged Senator Williams, of Missouri. They had seats on the Council and could by their single votes prevent not only the giving of an advisory opinion adverse to their interests, but the submission of the question itself. All advisory opinions came to the Court by way of the Council and a unanimous vote was required there. We would suffer in dignity, independence, and honor unless we asserted the right to bar advisory opinions as well as ignore them. [52]

The difficulties of obtaining the advantages of the new world concert without being in it thus became starkly apparent, but none of the last-stand Senators paused to bewail that condition.

Two Views of Political "Entanglement". They pressed the attack instead, saying that "ratification of the Treaty of Versailles would have been a detestable act, but it would not have been so instantly suggestive of ignominious furtiveness as is the present scheme to take the United States into an international alliance foot by foot, inch by inch, up the back way marked 'entrance for mandates and money lenders.' "

---

[51] *Congressional Record,* Vol. 67, Pt. 2, pp. 1497-81.
[52] Ibid., 1757.

Information about the negotiations preceding this proposal was demanded and time to study it.[53]

Contemplation of the responsibilities which rested upon the United States was equally in order, thought a middle ground Senator, who said: "If we want to live in a civilized world, I think it is high time we screwed our courage up to a point that will enable us to treat our neighbors in a civilized manner. We know that for the purposes of trade and the distribution of good and bad advice the earth today is no larger than was the District of Columbia 100 years ago. While trade may not follow the flag, we know that politics will follow trade as surely as noontide follows the dawn. With our goods in every port and our debits and credits in every court and counting house, we might as well try to keep the Mississippi River out of the Gulf of Mexico as to try to keep politics out of our foreign relations."

And suppose, he asked in conclusion, the League of Nations should prove to be of real and lasting assistance in the spread of sound economics and eugenics and the World Court should meet the expectations of its friends? If this should happen and Uncle Sam should officially decline to lend a helping hand or an encouraging word, he would pass from the limelight to a rear seat in the gallery, no longer the hero in a great play, but a prophet discredited abroad as well as at home.[54]

But, said Senator Borah, on January 14, "We are going into a court for all time. . . . Through all the sweep of the years we are to be there. Who knows what the situation will be ten years from now or twenty years from now with reference to electing judges in that tribunal of which we are to be a member? Who knows how strongly Great Britain will seek to control the court . . ?"

[53] Senator Shipstead of Minnesota, *Congressional Record,* Vol. 67, Pt. 2, p. 1958.
[54] Senator McLean, of Connecticut, Republican, *Congressional Record,* Vol. 67, Pt. 2, pp. 1971-2, January 13, 1926.

Would anyone contend, continued the Idaho Senator, that the leading nations on the Council would not determine the submission and form of advisory opinions? "Yet, notwithstanding we are not upon that Council and would have no voice in submitting such questions and no voice in framing them, the proposition is that we shall enter the court with Great Britain having seven votes to our one in the selection of judges." [55]

One might have thought that Senator Borah almost wished we were occupying our chair on the Council. Again, later, he complained that if the Court should decide to give an advisory opinion against us "we could not object, because we are not on the Council, and we could not shape the question, because we are not on the Council, and yet we would have all the influence and power and prestige of the Court thrown against us in our absence and notwithstanding our refusal to consent." [56]

Insofar as such a menace can be said to exist, the United States, by the testimony of the prince of isolationists, stands under it today, and we are trying to remove it by demanding that the members of the League give us the privileges of membership on the council without our assuming any of the responsibilities that go with such membership. Truly is it not a proud position into which the mightiest nation on the globe has drifted under the dominance of the Senate minority which fears for her to walk abroad among the peoples of the earth? [57]

[55] *Congressional Record*, Vol. 67, Pt. 2, p. 2037.
[56] Ibid., p. 2046.
[57] Senator Lenroot described the continuing tactics of 1919, as they were being echoed in 1926, on the same day. He had never known of greater opportunity for the expression of public opinion, yet the complaint was being made that time enough had not been had.
The first reservation, disclaiming any legal relation with the League, he deemed "absolutely unnecessary." He had no doubt that in framing it Secretary Hughes "had not forgotten what had occurred here previously" and that he foresaw what actually had happened. *Congressional Record*, Vol. 67, Pt. 2, p. 2045.

Other Reasons for Rejection. Yet to Senator Blease, of South Carolina, courage was to be shown by staying out. After explaining how he had been denied all federal patronage in his state during the War, he asked, on January 14, "Senators, why should we go into this thing? Are we afraid of anybody? Who are we afraid of? The international bankers that have their money invested abroad?" [58]

And Senator Fernald, of Maine, an irreconcilable, quoting Washington, Adams, Jefferson, Lincoln, Cleveland, Hale and Roosevelt, protested against our approaching a court composed of eleven judges, ten of whose names no American citizen could correctly pronounce. Of the eleven judges, just one was an American, and of the deputy judges "Not an American! Of the four not a single American!" [59]

Senator Brookhart, Republican, of Iowa, did not come to scoff and to detract. He regarded President Wilson's Fourteen Points as "a landmark in the history of the world, because upon its foundation principles must be built every future political structure for the peace of the world." His objection did not come from the connection of the Court with the League. It was more fundamental, because he did not regard a technical law court as the proper agent of "genuine cooperative economics." Because of the diverse degrees of civilization he thought arbitration courts best.[60]

Must We Not Have A Veto? On January 18, Senator Borah again pressed at length the objection that the power to call for advisory opinions created "a definite permanent association with a political institution." Should not the United States have at least the protection afforded by a provision that no advisory opinion shall be called for which concerns us without our consent? [61] Senator Moses, of New Hampshire, had shortly before held that there was no legal

[58] *Congressional Record*, Vol. 67, Pt. 2, p. 2048.
[59] Ibid., 2100-03.
[60] *Congressional Record*, Vol. 67, Pt. 2, p. 2118.
[61] Ibid., 2484-87.

obstacle to prevent the Council from submitting to the Court the competence of any of our debtors to pay the money owed us, or to render an opinion on immigration or our tariffs or Panama Canal tolls. [62]

Having small hope of preventing adherence if the question once came to a vote, the opposition played the old game anew, proposing that it was the part of wisdom at least to stiffen the reservations further. If they could be stiffened enough, rejection by the powers would result; if not, it could be said that our patrimony had been protected from the scheming foreigners.

Time for Discussion Desired. On January 19, Senator Blease made the orthodox move by offering a resolution, reciting that:

> Whereas the people of the United States have not had the opportunity to fully inform themselves as to the true meaning of the so-called World Court; and
>
> Whereas, there is no immediate necessity for the United States to pass any resolution in reference thereto; and
>
> Whereas it is but fair and just to give the people the right to express themselves thoroughly upon this subject; now, therefore, be it
>
> *Resolved,* that the date to vote upon the pending resolution and protocol of the World Court is hereby fixed for the 8th day of December, 1926.[63]

The strategy of the opposition had been apparent since the beginning of the session. It was merely 1919 over again— to continue the debate, pointing out dangers in the way and postponing a vote until enough Senators could be weaned away from support to encompass rejection.

The situation did appear almost hopeless in 1926 to some

[62] Ibid., 2191.
[63] *Congressional Record,* Vol. 67, Pt. 3, p. 2347.

of the band, but while there was delay there was hope. Senator Johnson, of California, gloomily recognized the situation in following Mr. Blease. "No words of any man, no power within these doors" could perhaps enable the Senate to escape from the foreordained situation. The Court was to be "put over" because of "a poisonous propaganda" that had been in vogue since 1920—a perfect "avalanche, a maelstrom of propaganda from New York City. . . poured forth in a constant and continuous flood." It had penetrated into every church, every women's organization, every quasi-public organization, even into "little children's schools." Propaganda had succeeded before, but none "more deceptive nor of worse duplicity." The "sinister force", one gathered from the Senator's philippic, was the desire to make money by trading and lending abroad. This would not have been so bad, of course, if the sordid traders had only relied wholly upon the big stick and the American marines to protect their investments.

Slipping into a Sea of Hate. He was against it because if it was as represented our entry would be a futile act, because the Hague machinery was good enough, and because it would finally take us into European political life and into the League itself. "We are going into the court because we are going to be taken into the League of Nations. It follows just as absolutely as night follows day. There can be no escape from it."

But could the Senators not see? "Oh, face the realities, you gentlemen here! Do you not realize what the situation is? No man comes out of Europe today but understands it and will tell it to you. No secret is expressed when I say however they may snarl at one another across the sea and however they may make faces at one another across their shadowy boundaries, there is a common feeling with them all, a feeling of jealousy, distrust, suspicion, and hostility to the United States of America."

That there was much truth in this picture of our standing abroad, all Senators would have been compelled to recognize, but Senator Johnson would have been the last to admit that the action of the Senate in 1919 had been in any considerable degree responsible for the "distrust, suspicion and hostility to the United States."

Instead, he explained the situation in terms of jealousy and resentment at our debt collection policy plus "many, many incidents." "You cannot deny it. Whenever a creditor presses his debtor it results." He had heard of debtors submitting themselves to the judgment of their creditors, but he had never yet known of a creditor who submitted himself to the judgment of his debtors.

If the Senator's thesis was right, that the demand for entry into the Court was motivated by the desire for gain, his attack was well placed, though it implied that the commercial and banking world really didn't know what it was doing.

The Utility of Reservations. He had little respect for reservations. "To join this court in the manner suggested, avoiding every question of consequence and asserting our aloofness whenever peace might be threatened by other countries would make us the poltroon among the nations of the earth." He could not give his acquiescence to reservations "except, in frankness, for the purpose ultimately by indirection of defeating that which I believe should be directly defeated."

The Senator was not too hopeful, but he recalled a day when some of the Senators present "sat upon an ex-parte committee for the purpose of preparing a reservation to Article X which should be put over, and under which we should enter the League of Nations." The task was almost completed when sixteen men—call them what you please, he cared not—"the job was perfected and we were right at the entrance of the League of Nations when those sixteen men called the thing off through the then leader of the Republican party in this Chamber." [64]

Mr. Johnson need not have been as despondent as he was. Reservations had served the purpose before, and they would again, so great is the power of sixteen determined men in the Senate to convince that body that if concessions are not granted the handful may be able to swing thirty-four votes against the treaty, whatever it is.

Results Were in Sight. That the objectors were on the right track in pressing for an extension of reservation No. 5 was indicated, after Mr. Johnson's speech, by Senator Heflin, of Alabama, replying to Senator Reed. A reservation offered by Senator Swanson would be adopted specifically providing that the Court should take no jurisdiction over any case in which the United States was "interested" unless our Government consented. He thought this addition unnecessary but he was going to vote for it. [65] And so, no doubt, would many other Senators.

Meanwhile, Senator Reed, of Missouri, observed that nine-tenths of the American people knew "substantially nothing" about the Court, and nobody had any authority to speak for even one-tenth of them. Neither, he indicated, was it possible for the American people to have an intelligent opinion on the matter. The problem was "so intricate as to require a study by the best lawyers of days and even weeks before the responsibility which we assume can be grasped and understood."

[64] *Congressional Record,* Vol. 67, Pt. 3, pp. 2349-55.
[65] Mr. Heflin had some views on propaganda too. The anti-court literature which Senator Johnson had described as "pitiable little circulations" Mr. Heflin had found to be "great big pamphlets" costing, he was sure, hundreds of thousands of dollars to print. The Capitol had been flooded with them. Who was back of this propaganda? The gun and ammunition makers and the battleship builders were the gentlemen back of it. Compared with their interest and activity was it so dreadful that Senators should get letters from little children asking them to vote for the Court? Some of them missed their fathers killed in France. Did they not have a right to appeal?

The People Needed Help.   How could the people, then, be expected to grasp the tremendous implications? It would seem that they would have to rely on some one to tell them about it. The trouble was they had listened to the wrong advocates—the international bankers, foreign investors and League advocates. But the Senators would now explain it to them, and any attempt to cut off the debate would "react most disastrously upon its authors and most unfortunately for the country."

Calling the names of the judges of the Court Mr. Reed asked how Senators would like to sit shivering in their chairs waiting for the decision on American questions of Dionisco Anzilotti, or Antonia Sanchez de Bustamente, or Vorozo Oda? This was the kind of exposition of the Court, evidently, that the lawyers of the opposition would like to give the people, if only they had time.

But there was more in Senator Reed's repertoire. There was Andrew Carnegie's plea for the reunion of the English speaking peoples, the international bankers, Mr. Bok, the seven votes of the British dominions, Mr. Reed's old tables showing that the colored races in the League vastly out-numbered the white, and pages of the names of League of Nations delegates and officials—all sounding most strange to good American ears.

Thus would the American people be enlightened on the inner workings of the Court, as they had been of the League in 1919, if only the debate could be prolonged indefinitely.

Madness.   After having spoken at length on January 19 and 20, Mr. Reed continued on the 21st, reading the tele-gram of the American Foundation, urging that the question be not sidetracked, explaining that it was a League court, and pointing out the terrors of the Geneva Protocol which had proposed a further stiffening of the League machinery to deal with aggression. We would "combine against our-selves if we shall recognize this power, the force of all the fifty-five nations that make up the League. This, sir, is madness. This, sir, I unhesitatingly say is disloyalty."

Quoting M. Benes on the Protocol, which had failed of approval and had never gone into force, he cried: "Tell me this is not a league of offense against the United States! Tell me that it does not exist!" [66]

But if the nations of the League had really come into combination against the United States would Mr. Reed have admitted any responsibility on his part for that state of affairs?

The Juggernaut Again. On January 22, Mr. Borah saw an evolution of the League away from all the ideals Mr. Wilson had for it into a "gigantic world military machine" such as Clemenceau had wanted. If it hadn't already become that it would. But he also never thought of suggesting that this colossus might be more easily controlled from within than opposed from the outside. Rather, he developed at length the argument that force could never be used to keep international peace without resulting in tyranny or war. He would abjure all force utterly—unless, of course, somebody started a war. [67]

Something to Fight For. Senator Pepper, following, disposed shortly of the danger of our being coerced by the League for failure to accept a decision of the Court. No sanctions could apply to the failure of any state to agree with an advisory opinion because no duty existed anywhere to conform to it. No case would be submitted by the United States except by voluntary act and we would never need to be coerced into acceptance of the decision. If war did result from the failure of a European state to accept a decision, at least the fight would be to vindicate the decision

[66] *Congressional Record,* Vol. 67, Pt. 3, pp. 2363-5, 2416, 2421-3, 2424-9, 2487-9, 2492-3. Senator Harreld, Republican, of Oklahoma, continued in opposition on the 21st speaking chiefly against the League.
[67] Ibid., 2555-61.

of a court, which would be better than a war based on no principle or sound determination of right. [68]

Why All Our Greatness?   The notable speech for the Court at the close of the debate was given by Senator Tyson, of Tennessee, who reviewed the antecedents of the creation of the League and the Court and asked what it was all for, saying:

> We of the United States of America say that we are the greatest Nation in the world; that we are the richest Nation in the world; that we have the greatest resources of any Nation in the world and that none of the nations of the world can come here and attack us; in fact, it is said that all the nations of the world might attack us at one time and they could not overcome us. I agree to every single one of those statements; and yet we are so afraid of ourselves, so afraid to take a chance, so afraid to do what even the smallest nations of the world have done, that it seems to me we have no reason to be so self satisfied; that we cannot feel any pride in being the greatest, the most powerful, the strongest nation, because we will not take any chance of getting hurt. Why all this greatness? Why all this wealth? Why all this strength? Is it the destiny of one so great to be so small? Has God blessed us with riches, empowered us with strength, and endowed us with greatness that we may be of all nations the least and the last to comprehend his blessing of "Peace on earth; good will to men?"[69]

Could a Vote Be Prevented?   The plan of the opposition was to take up time in the Court debate until there would hardly be time to pass a much desired tax reduction measure

---

[68] Ibid., 2567. Senator La Follete, Jr., spoke on the 22nd against the Court, the League and the Treaty of Versailles, particularly the latter. Senator Nye, a new Senator from North Dakota, also spoke against the Court on January 23, asking what the big rush was about and offering a resolution providing for a vote of the people on the subject after six months. pp. 2643 ff.

[69] *Congressional Record*, Vol. 67, Pt. 3, pp. 2637-43.

before the end of the short session. Then, if the Court
resolution could once be displaced, they would see that it
got no more consideration at the close of the session—and
for another year. The strategy seemed, too, to be working.
Conservative Senators like Mr. Smoot, of Utah, were already restive for the tax bill when Senator Reed introduced
a resolution calling on the Secretary of State to send down
the "original protocol of the so-called World Court," which
was, of course, deposited at The Hague or Geneva and not
available for circulation.

The majority did not surrender, however, for shortly
after the introduction of the Reed resolution a petition for
cloture signed by forty-eight Senators was presented.

The Fifth Reservation Expanded.   On January 23,
Senator Swanson introduced his amended reservation No.
5, which now said that the Court should not "without the
consent of the United States entertain any request for an
advisory opinion touching any dispute or question in which
the United States has or claims an interest." [70]

Senator Moses followed by offering the abandoned Pepper
Plan anew and Senator Overman, of North Carolina, presented a reservation barring the Court from considering
without consent "the question of the alleged indebtedness
or moneyed obligation of any state of the United States"
or of immigration or of the Monroe Doctrine. This reservation was to lie on the table only to be called up in case
the amended version of the 5th reservation failed. That
sweeping assertion of an American right to bar advisory
opinions was, then, evidently to receive the support of the
Southern Democrats because of the repudiated state bonds,
held by foreign citizens. [71]

[70] Ibid., 2656-7.
[71] The states which have repudiated bonds outstanding are: Alabama,
Arkansas, Florida, Georgia, Louisiana, Mississippi, North Carolina, and
South Carolina. The face amount of the bonds totals about $75,000,000 on
which some $300,000,000 of interest is due. With minor exceptions these
obligations were issued by the "carpet bag" governments set up after the

Bitter complaint then ensued from Senator Reed because debate was to be shut off. Various dates were suggested in February, but they were too soon. Mr. Reed suggested March 1, which would greatly improve the chances of side-tracking the measure. It would even be difficult to make closure effective in the last four days of the session.

Closure was adopted on January 25, however, by a vote of 68 to 26. [72]

The Stiffening of Reservation 5 Condemned. On January 26, Senator Gillett, Republican, of Massachusetts, contributed a noteworthy discussion of the proposed reservations. He thought the first reservation disclaiming any legal relation to the League or the Treaty was not necessary. He thought no representative of the United States would be contaminated by association with the other members of the electoral college and that our money would not become tainted by going through the treasury of the League.

He disapproved further of the addition to reservation

Civil War and the people of these states are determined not to honor them. The bonds were bought largely by citizens of Great Britain who feel themselves to be innocent investors deprived of their money without recourse. Their feelings on the subject have become even more acute of recent years since Great Britain has begun paying her huge war debt to us.

The charging off against the British debt of the comparatively small sum represented by these defaulted obligations, perhaps at a minor fraction of their possible value, would not only improve the feeling in England on the whole debt question; it would also remove the permanent objection of many Southern Senators to any arbitration treaty or any kind of judicial settlement of international disputes which might possibly call these debts into question.

For a full description of the repudiated bonds and further reasons justifying their settlement by the Federal Government see: C. P. Howland, "Our Repudiated State Debts," *Foreign Affairs,* April 1928, Vol. 6, pp. 395-407. Other discussions of the subject have been made by: J. F. Hume in the *North American Review,* December, 1884; Raymond Turner in *Current History,* January, 1926; and J. G. de R. Hamilton in the *Virginia Quarterly Review,* October, 1927.

[72] *Congressional Record,* Vol. 67, Pt. 3, p. 2679. Senator Bingham in the debate of that day subscribed to the statement of former Senator Platt, of Connecticut, that a "nation has no right to live to itself alone. To assert such a doctrine is to contend that selfishness is right. Selfishness in a nation is as much worse than selfishness in an individual as the nation is stronger and more influential than the individual." p. 2693.

No. 5. It seemed to him quite superfluous. Without the reservation he saw no reason to fear that any advisory opinion would be asked or given against our will that would affect the United States. He had originally preferred that the Court be given no power to render advisory opinions at all, but that jurisdiction had been given and experience had so far justified the experiment. The questions submitted by the Council had enhanced both its own reputation and that of the Court.

Moreover, the Court had established thoroughly proper practices—notice to interested parties, open hearings, and public decisions with refusal to render any opinion in the single case where a party had refused its jurisdiction. The probability of a reversal of these sound rules he regarded as remote indeed. The judges had pride in the Court; they would not lightly make a break with any great country. Even the Council would be most unlikely to invite certain loss of prestige for itself and the Court by asking for an advisory opinion which the earlier version of reservation 5 had served plain notice we would not recognize.

Altogether the contestants in the debate had exaggerated the consequences of adherence to the Court, both the dangers and the gains. On the latter side it was but a first step on the road to peace, and but a short step. The real goal was the acceptance of compulsory jurisdiction by all the nations, great and small.

In the meantime it was our duty to take the next step toward ending war, "to follow the lines which this generation has decided are the best, and then in the future let the next generation follow out its lines with the assurance that some time a method will be found which will end all war. [73]

The Resolution Adopted. Later in the same day the official reservations were adopted by nearly unanimous votes and the hostile reservations rejected by large majorities.

[73] *Congressional Record,* Vol. 67, Pt. 3, pp. 2747-49.

The Reed reservation to limit the British Empire to one vote in selecting judges was lost 73 to 20, the Moses declaration against the use of force to execute any decree of the court failed 69 to 22 and his proposal of the Pepper Plan was rejected 72 to 21.   The final vote on the resolution of adherence was 76 for to 17 against.   It was taken on January 27, 1926, almost three years from the time it was originally proposed by the President. [74]

The debate was closed by Senator Bruce in a one sentence speech in which he congratulated the Republican and Democratic members of the Senate as having done, under the leadership of our honored President, a great and memorable thing that would sensibly promote the cause of international justice and peace throughout the world.

---

[74] *Congressional Record,* Vol. 67, Pt. 3, pp. 2816, 2820. Senator Stephens of Mississippi declared on the final day of the debate that at no time within his recollection had stronger efforts to arouse prejudice and passion been made.   He divided the opponents of the Court into four classes: (a) Those believing in the policy of isolation, (b) Those moved by intense hatred of Woodrow Wilson, (c) Those blinded by prejudice against England, and (d) Those fearing a superstate controlled by a religious sect (Klan and Pope).   There had been assembled together more inharmony of thought, more discordant elements in ideas and beliefs than he had ever seen together before.   All Irish Catholic newspapers, for example, had bitterly denounced the Court as controlled by England, while the Klan organs were attacking it as dominated by the Pope. pp. 2799-2801.

CHAPTER X

THE resolution of adherence to the World Court, as finally adopted by the Senate, was carried in the press on January 28, 1926. To many who read it the chance of its having any practical result seemed remote indeed. To the cynical the Senate had ended in an empty gesture which would please the peace loving people of the country, without creating any serious probability of our actually joining the Court. To the hopeful the chance of the resolution being accepted by the other nations seemed as slim. The only sure gain an optimist could see was that the Senate had voted in some fashion to recognize the duties of membership in the family of nations.

Under the head "The Shift in Foreign Policy" the Springfield *Republican* (Mass.) said, on February 4, 1926:

Were it not for the determined opposition of an irreconcilable minority, which was finally rendered futile only by the application of the Senate's closure rule, the approval of the World Court resolution by a vote of 76 to 17 would not be significant of a perceptible shift in the policy of the United States. The reservations are so drastic in restraining America's utilization of the court in any conceivable international controversy that enthusiasm over the outcome is wholly beyond our emotional range of feeling and expression.

All that can be said with realistic fidelity to the facts is that the Senate, rather than the United States government, has extended a very cool and reluctant quasi-recognition to the permanent court of international justice. The court can never be appealed to without the approval of two-thirds of the senators in each specific case. Even now adherence to the court cannot be completed unless 48 other nations agree in diplomatic notes to all the conditions which the Senate has imposed on the transactions. The Senate becomes virtually the whole government in the future regulation of this phase of our foreign relations. The Senate sulkily gives a distant nod of recognition to the court, but under its breath it swears in the future to ignore its existence.

"Mainly a Gesture". Under the caption "Mainly a Gesture" the Des Moines *Register* similarly concluded, on January *29*, 1926:

The *Register* hopes we shall not be suspected of undue pessimism when we suggest that the importance of the Senate vote of ratification of the world court is, in view of the reservations, mainly in the direction it points, and but little in the actual commitment it makes.

But our actual entry into the world court if the nations finally accept us on the terms we name will be so tentative that unless we ourselves ignore the reservations or abandon them; we shall not really contribute much.

What could be more absurd than to say that our entry into the court must be delayed until every one of the fifty-three nations in the court has personally assured us in the most formal way that we are welcome on our own terms? We may judge that attitude towards the court by our own feelings if Britain or Germany or any other power big or little should come to us with the same proposal.

The American answer to another nation demanding any sort of special recognition would be to go and chase itself. How many hints must we have until we understand that the United States is regarded in Europe much as European countries are regarded in the United States. The league has gone right ahead without us, and will go ahead without us. The world court is functioning in our absence and will continue to do so.

What this debate has brought out plainer than ever is the want of a sense of responsibility on our part for future world order. No real emphasis has been put on our part in securing an international code, and an international tribunal to set up civil adjudication of international disputes. We treat the matter as though we were doing the other peoples a special favor by consenting to have anything to do with a world court. It is nothing to us and everything to them.

Those who really believe in the world court are just the other way around. They feel that it is far more to America's interest and to the interest of the English speaking peoples to secure world order than to the interest of any other people or peoples. It is our part in world affairs to have civil adjustment in the place of violent outbreaks. That has been our talent as a people and that is our program. We cannot function in a world of disorder and wars. We should lead not follow in the matter of international code, of international court, of international council table.

These editorials, coming from two of the most ably conducted newspapers in the country, are well worth reading as an introduction to what followed. To their clear insight it may be added that the terms under which we proposed that the nations should accept us in 1926 were considerably less ungracious than those of 1919. Taken as a whole they still strongly suggested that worthy and wealthy Uncle Sam might be falling into a den of thieves, but there was at least a suggestion in the act as a whole of a desire to share the common responsibilities.

To be sure, we still disclaimed "any legal relationship on the part of the United States to the League of Nations or the assumption of any obligations by the United States under the Treaty of Versailles," and we still specified that we might withdraw at any time that things did not suit us.

The impression of something questionable and really risky about the proposed association would be strong to untutored readers, yet to statesmen abroad so much might be readily passed over as a concession to the feelings of the successful American objectors of 1919. So, too, might the requirement that the Court should not render any advisory opinion except publicly after due notice to all concerned and a public hearing. This was the practice of the Court and likely to continue to be.

A Free Veto Demanded. When, however, all were to be bound to agree that the Court should not even entertain without our consent "any request for an advisory opinion in which the United States has or *claims* an interest," the likelihood of our receiving a sand bagging unawares was so strongly suggested that other nations could hardly be expected to accept the terms proposed without at least some discussion.

Yet this was exactly what the Senate demanded. The signature of the United States to the protocol should "not be affixed until the powers signatory to such protocol shall have indicated, through an exchange of notes, their acceptance of the foregoing reservations and understandings." Silence was not to give consent, nor was any conference or discussion envisaged. Each and every one of the 48 powers, great and small, was to send a note to Washington, saying, "We accept you into the Court under all the reservations laid down by the Senate, without any reservations whatsoever on our part."

Reasonable to the Legislative Mind. The Senators who made the terms and who were thinking of the wrath of the isolationists, of the possibility that the question of the old repudiated state debts might be raised, of embarrassment that might conceivably come to us from the airing of some angle of our policy towards Japan or Latin America, of the possibility, even, that in some way the ethics of our war debt collection policy might be dragged into argument before the Court, the Senators pondering on these imponderables gravely added to the conditions suggested by the Executive the sweeping prohibitions of reservation 5 and directed the Secretary of State to send out 48 letters to the nations, asking for as many acceptances at the pleasure of the powers. [1] The Senate was once more attempting to seize the power to negotiate with foreign powers by the device of sending them an ultimatum, and if very many of the Senators doubted that the terms they prescribed would be accepted their doubts did not creep into the Record.

Not So Clear to the Diplomatic World. Yet the nations by no means stampeded to accept the Senate's terms. Our ward, Cuba, accepted on March 17; Greece followed on April 9, Liberia on May 11, Albania on August 11 and Luxembourg on August 21. Two of these acceptances were in part withdrawn by subsequent action. Their de-

[1] The freedom of the United States in a wicked and designing world was still further buttressed by two final resolves added by way of reassurance. The first said: *"Resolved further, as a part of this act of ratification,* That the United States approve the protocol and statute hereinabove mentioned, with the understanding that recourse to the Permanent Court of International Justice for the settlement of differences between the United States and any other state or states can be had only by agreement thereto through general or special treaties concluded between the parties in dispute." This would prevent the President from submitting any case to the Court without the consent of the Senate. Some relaxation of the Senate's views on this score was implied, however, by the possibility of general arbitration treaties which was suggested.

The final paragraph of the resolution *"Resolved further,* That adherence to the said protocol and statute hereby approved shall not be construed as to require the United States to depart from its traditional policy of not intruding upon, interfering with, or entangling itself in the political questions of policy or internal administration of any foreign state, nor shall adherence to said protocol and statute be construed to imply a relinquishment by the United States of its traditional attitude toward purely American questions."

These revered words coming down from the days of our first adventures into international politics in the Hague and Algeciras Conferences will soon begin to take on the sanctity of Washington's Farewell Address. Needless to say, they encompass the Monroe Doctrine, the phrase "purely American questions" meaning in reality Western Hemisphere questions.

fection was counterbalanced by informal assurance that Santo Domingo and Uruguay were willing to sign. [2]

The acceptance of these seven tiny states did not advance our adherence very fast. Nor did the failure of six countries, Brazil, Bulgaria, Canada, Chile, Hungary and New Zealand, to reply to the American letter in any manner whatever promote our entry, though the fact that six countries should ignore the American note need not be thought strange. That is only one-eighth of the countries concerned —not a high percentage. Anyone who sends a long ten paragraph proposition to 48 people concerning a subject of common concern to them, requesting unconditional acceptance, and gets 40 replies of any kind, may consider himself fortunate, as the irreconcilable Senators who insisted on perfecting the reservations well knew. That any Senator should have really expected that no single one of the 48 powers would demur seems strange indeed. And the objection of one only was, by the terms of the ultimatum, sufficient to keep us out of the Court.

The requirement of unanimous consent to our conditions may have been legally advisable, if not necessary. While there was no provision in the original protocol of signature of December 13, 1920, or in the Court statute governing amendments or conditional adhesions, it was probable that no considerable limitations of the Court's functions could be established without the unanimous consent of the members of the Court. Secretary Hughes had not asked for the agreement of every member because the reservations framed by him did not touch the functions of the Court or set up any special position for the United States. He therefore had no reason to anticipate that any member would object to our signing the original protocol under the understandings set down in his reservations. The protocol had been left

[2] See *United States Daily,* December 31, 1927, for a complete report of the individual action of the powers on our proposal up to that date.

open for our signature as a state "mentioned in the Annex to the Covenant" and so long as he did not question the powers or privileges of the Court he had no ground for expecting that any member of the Court would pass upon our right to adhere. [3]

When the Senate decided to question one half of the Court's work, and to challenge its continuance, a quite different situation was created. Then probably the unanimous consent of the Court members would be necessary to our admission. It was called for with little dissent, most Senators apparently assuming that it would be granted at once on their demand, others thinking about it not at all and still others, who foresaw what the effect would be, feeling sure that they had defeated our entry by sufficiently expanding the Hughes reservations.

The reaction of the bulk of the nations was as natural as that of the two small groups who accepted and ignored respectively the product of our three years of travail over what to do about the Court. Sixteen of them acknowledged the American "offer" without indicating whether they thought it acceptable or not, and never found time to decide that the American proposition was a good thing. [4] Yet again, this should not seem strange. Governments are as busy as individual men are; they likewise need to be persuaded sometimes that things offered them are better than they seem to be—and the Senate lacks both the desire and the machinery to persuade uninterested nations that what it offers them is good or acceptable. Worse than that, up to this time it seldom even stopped to ponder what the other parties might want; it was only concerned with stating forcibly what it did not want—and asserting the "sovereignty" of the United States. The "sovereignty" of the

[3] See The League of Nations, World Peace Foundation Pamphlet No. 5, Vol. 5 for the protocol of December 13, 1920, and the original statute governing the Court.
[4] United States Daily, December 31, 1927.

other nations apparently escaped it entirely, as did the fact that note writing as a method of reaching agreement among many nations is an outworn device. The foreign ministers and diplomats now settle face to face in the halls of Geneva what interminable letter writing never could accomplish at all.

THE SEPTEMBER CONFERENCE OF THE POWERS

This new method of conducting international affairs is well enough illustrated by the conference which considered the American proposal to join the World Court. On March 18, 1926, the terms of our proposal to enter the Court coming up in the Council of the League, Sir Austin Chamberlain suggested that it was not usual that rights established by an instrument which had been ratified should be varied by a mere exchange of notes. Moreover, the fifth reservation was not clear in meaning. It could be interpreted in a manner which would hamper the work of the Council and prejudice the rights of members of the League. It was not to be assumed that any such meaning was intended, but the correct interpretation should be the subject of discussion and agreement with the United States Government.

A conference of the nations belonging to the Court and of the United States was therefore called by the Council to meet in Geneva on September 1, 1926, to facilitate common action on the American reservations by all the member nations of the Court and to frame any new agreement that might be found necessary to give effect to the special conditions on which the United States was willing to adhere. [5]

This action was reported by the newspapers as being received in Washington with amazement. The irreconcilables were jubilant. Senator Reed attacked both the Court

[5] *League of Nations, Official Journal,* April 1926, 7th year, No. 4, p. 536.

and League and Senator Borah said the United States would have to go through with it and "sit with" the League. [6] Other anti-Leaguers condemned the Council for its action, as well they might, for without a real effort to arrive at a common understanding there was hardly more than one chance in a thousand that the 48 Governments would all return replies of any kind.

Participation Declined. The State Department, on receipt of the invitation to attend this conference was in a quandary. It felt itself without power to negotiate. The troublesome clause had been proposed by the Senate. The Department did not think it wise to try to explain what it might mean. Secretary Kellogg, therefore, replied, in part:

I do not feel that any useful purpose could be served by the designation of a delegate by my Government to attend a conference for this purpose. These reservations are plain and unequivocal and according to their terms they must be accepted by an exchange of notes between the United States and each of the forty-eight States signatory to the Statute of the Permanent Court before the United States can become a party and sign the Protocol. The resolution specifically provided this mode of procedure.

I have no authority to vary this mode of procedure or to modify the conditions and reservations or to interpret them, and I see no difficulty in the way of securing the assent of each signatory by direct exchange of notes, as provided by the Senate. It would seem to me to be a matter of regret if the Council of the League should do anything to create the impression that there are substantial difficulties in the way of such direct communication. This Government does not consider that any new agreement is necessary to give effect to the conditions and reservations on which the United States is prepared to adhere to the Permanent Court. The acceptance of the reservations by all the nations signatory

[6] New York *Times,* March 19 and 20, 1926.

to the Statute of the Permanent Court constitutes such an agreement.[7]

The refusal to attend the Conference was probably inevitable under the circumstances. The United States not being a signatory to the Court Protocol could hardly have a standing of equality in the conference and it could not afford to appear as a suppliant for admission. The right of the members to confer was, however, granted.

The suggestion that nothing but acceptance of the reservations was necessary can hardly be similarly justified. We asserted the right to prevent the giving of an advisory opinion whenever we claimed an interest in the subject. What would be the effect of this claim upon the advisory opinion function of the Court? American activities permeate every country in the world to such an extent that we might claim an interest in almost any question upon which the Court might be asked to give an advisory opinion. How would the right be used? Would it be used sparingly, only when we had a direct, important interest in the case, or would our impatience with the League lead us to assert it so frequently as to frustrate the pacific activities of the Council and hamstring the functioning of the Court?[8] At the very least the effects of the claim and manner in which it was to be exercised were obscure enough to require discussion and clarification.

The Report of the Conference. The conference of signatories called to consider the proposals of the United States met in Geneva on September 1, 1926, and discussed them until September 23. On that date the report of a committee of eleven, appointed to draft the results of the discussions, was received and embodied in a Final Act, which was signed by 21 powers. Two signatures were added later.

In reporting to the Conference the Committee felt that:

[7] World Peace Foundation Pamphlets, 1926, Vol. 9, No. 8, p. 622.
[8] *American Foundation Bulletin* No. 5, Oct. 7, 1927.

it was the unanimous wish of the Conference to accept the offer by satisfying the United States' reservations as far as possible. The very creation of a Permanent Court of International Justice constitutes in itself and irrespective of the existence of the League of Nations so great a progress in the development of peaceful relations between States that every effort should be made to render that act fruitful of still further results.

The greater the number of states which have acceded to the Court the greater will be the Court's authority. It is to the interest of the States which founded the Court that all the other States of the world should agree to become parties thereto, even if they feel unable to become Members of the League of Nations. In particular, the possibility of the accession of the United States of America, as a State mentioned in the Covenant of the League of Nations, was provided for in the Protocol of signature of the Statute of the Court. It therefore seems quite natural that the States signatories of the Protocol, in presence of a proposal—even a conditional proposal—by the United States of America to accede to the Court, should adopt a favourable attitude.

On the other hand, the conditional character of the proposal is sufficiently explained by the fact that the United States of America is not a member of the League of Nations and does not desire to change its attitude. This fact must be taken into account and an endeavor must be made to reconcile the working of the Covenant with the important object of increasing the number of states which have acceded to the Court and with the requirement of the position of the United States.[9]

Four Reservations Accepted. This having been admitted, the Committee recognized that it would be desirable simply to agree to the first three reservations.

[9] Report presented to *The Conference of States Signatories of the Protocol of Signature of the Statute of the Permanent Court of International Justice,* Publications de la Société des Nations, V. Questions Juridiques, 1926, V. 25.

Its recommendations as to reservation 4 were embodied in the Final Act as follows:

A. It may be agreed that the United States may at any time withdraw its adherence to the Protocol of December 16th, 1920.

In order to assure equality of treatment, it seems natural that the signatory states, acting together and by not less than a majority of two-thirds, should possess the corresponding right to withdraw their acceptance of the special conditions attached by the United States to its adherence to the said Protocol in the Second part of the fourth reservation and in the fifth reservation. In this way the *status quo ante* could be re-established if it were found that the arrangement agreed upon was not yielding satisfactory results.

It is hoped, nevertheless, that no such withdrawal will be made without an attempt by a previous exchange of views to solve any difficulties which may arise.

B. It may be agreed that the Statute of the Permanent Court of International Justice annexed to the Protocol of December 16th, 1920, shall not be amended without the consent of the United States.[10]

The original fourth reservation in the Hughes draft had said simply that the statute governing the Court should not be amended without our consent. There could be no quarrel with this condition since the Court Protocol had been adopted by unanimous consent and could only be modified in the same way. The Senate, however, had added to this reservation a provision for withdrawal.

The September Conference did not oppose this proposition but decided that it might be wise to accept the conditional American adherence under the same reservation—that if the association should not prove mutually satisfactory the members of the Court might have the same right to dissolve

[10] *The Final Act of the Conference,* Publications de la Société des Nations, V. Questions Juridiques, 1926, V. 24, p. 6.

it that the United States had. The Conference, however, was "anxious to invest the exercise of such a right with the character of a collective decision taken by a sufficiently large majority to ensure that it is inspired exclusively by objective considerations arising from the discovery of some practical difficulty." It therefore provided that a two thirds majority should be necessary to eliminate the United States from the Court and ended by hoping "that the right of denunciation will not be exercised, either by the United States or by the other signatory States, without an exchange of views first taking place with regard to such difficulties as may have arisen and, possibly, as to the means of overcoming them."

The logic of this position was difficult to attack. If the United States came in under a set of conditions which might powerfully affect the usefulness of the Court from the standpoint of the signatories, and if she even then reserved a right to flee immediately if things did not suit her, when no other power had shown so little faith in the Court, would it not be well to exercise a little counter caution and reserve the right to do without the collaboration of the United States in case the conditions of her membership proved onerous?

Should They Not Allow For Our Fears? It may be said in reply, of course, that such reasoning on the part of the signatories was not realistic, that they should have known that the United States once in the Court her fears would subside and that the conditions of her entry would probably never be applied. It may even be further suggested that the delegates were not acting in a very large spirit in hoping that the right of denunciation would not be exercised on either side in a temperamental moment—and of making it impossible that it should be so exercised on the part of the powers.

Was it not a little gratuitous to hope that the great United States would not act in this fashion? Perhaps. But when they had listened to the bitter emanations of

United States Senators for a solid year from 1918 to 1920 and had seen the policy of the United States toward them veer quickly from one of alliance and blood brotherhood to one of haughty aloofness, vituperation and disdain, under the force of the Senatorial onslaught, when they had seen the United States hesitate for three years over so small a step as joining the Court, and when they had freshly before them another six weeks of Senatorial speeches still dominated by suspicious charges and insinuations and the effort to overcome them—when the delegates had all this in mind can they be severely condemned for having their doubts about what the United States would do next? It is possible to say that they should have set all this down to the exigencies of American domestic politics and ignored it as a passing manifestation. But could they be certain what the same exigencies would next demand? And can we complain if they happen to return gently just a little bit of the distrust that we shout from the hilltops?

They would be innocent indeed if they did not make some allowance for what the urgencies of party politics will lead us to do next. We cannot play fast and loose with the greatest attempts the human race has ever made to give itself order and stability without finally finding ourselves judged as a doubtful risk in international cooperation, no matter how sound we may be at heart.

It was apparently a real uncertainty about our future permutations which dictated the decision of the conferees to embody the legislation asked by the United States in a special protocol to be signed and ratified by all concerned. If the United States should shortly decide to pull out when something unpleasant arose, the amendments to the Court statutes, made necessary by our entry, would be not only unnecessary, but perhaps disadvantageous. If they were put into a special agreement they could be easily gotten rid of in that contingency.

Again, it may be said that it certainly was not tactful of the Powers to refuse to accept and "sign on the dotted line" the terms of that august assembly, the Senate of the United States. The Senate had said, "Here are our conditions. They will please be accepted by each and every one of the 48 signatories." Was it not flying in the face of fate to have the temerity to submit a reply with reservations and risk it in the Senate? The result would seem to have been fore-ordained. Yet if there was a little unlovely desire among the other Governments to teach the Senate that the feelings about national prerogatives it preached so loudly were not entirely extinct abroad, need we continually impute to others all the weaknesses that inhabit human flesh and then complain if they return us a bit in kind?

The Reply to the Fifth Reservation. That the conference was actuated by a real desire to obtain our cooperation can hardly be doubted. Certainly the form of its acceptance of our first four reservations could not be objected to. Concerning the first part of the fifth reservation, calling for publicity for advisory opinions it simply cited the practice of the Court, enclosed a copy of its rules and agreed to consider the incorporation of these rules in a more permanent protocol.

With regard to the second part of the fifth reservation, also added to the recommendations of the Executive by the Senate and claiming the right to prevent the giving of any advisory opinion, the Committee observed that it had been the subject of long and careful examination both in the Committee and in the Conference itself. In the larger body several speakers had drawn attention to the debates in the Senate preceding the conditional accession to the Court agreed to. As near as they could tell it was desired to ensure for the United States of America equality with any State Member of the League which had, in the capacity of a Member of the Council or of the Assembly, the right to pronounce upon a request to the Court for an advisory opinion. The Committee had taken these considerations into account and had proposed a distinction between disputes to which the United States was a party and disputes to which it was not a party, together with questions other than disputes.[11]

The Final Act stated that the principle that the United States should be assured a position of equality with states represented either on the Council or the Assembly should be agreed to. "But," it continued, "the fifth reservation appears to rest upon the presumption that the adoption of a request for an advisory opinion by the Council or Assembly requires a unanimous vote. No such presumption, however, has so far been established. It is therefore impossible to say with certainty whether in some cases, or possibly in all cases, a decision by a majority is not sufficient. In any event the United States should be guaranteed a position of equality in this respect; that is to say, in any case where a State represented on the Council or in the Assembly would possess the right of preventing, by opposition in either of these bodies, the adoption of a proposal to request an advisory opinion from the Court, the United States shall enjoy an equivalent right."[12]

The sincerity of the position taken, that the practice of the League had not been settled in favor of requesting advisory opinions by unanimous vote, was questioned in the United States even by pro-Court Democratic Senators. There seemed to be no doubt about it before, they said, until our reservation came up. This was apparently true, but it did not follow that there was not an honest difference of opinion abroad as to how the point should be decided once it had been raised. Miss Esther Everett Lape has

[11] *Publications de la Société des Nations*, V. Questions Juridiques, 1926, V. 25, p. 3.
[12] *Publications de la Société des Nations*, V. Questions Juridiques, 1926, V. 24, p. 6.

demonstrated the lack of agreement by showing the different views held by some of the great jurists who had studied
the question. Dr. van Eysinga, the President of the September conference, considered that a request for an advisory opinion was a matter of substance, requiring unanimity. M. Rolin, the Belgian representative at the Conference, and Sir Cecil Hurst, Legal Advisor of the British
Foreign Office, agreed that a request might be sometimes a
matter of substance, requiring a unanimous vote, and sometimes merely a matter of procedure, requiring a majority
vote. On the other hand, M. Fromageot, Jurisconsult of
the French Foreign Office, took issue with the view that
a request for an advisory opinion might be sometimes one
and sometimes the other. The matter did not, therefore,
seem simple. Moreover, some of the leaders did not favor
forcing an early decision on a matter of such great importance to both the League and the Court.[13]

The Problem of Equality. Neither was it an easy task
to put the United States upon a position of equality with
League powers, whatever the majority required. Senators
thought they had accomplished it; others felt they had set
up a privileged position for the United States. How, practically, was a state which desired to be absent from League
deliberations, and free from all liability for League decisions, to exercise just the same veto that a League member
would have and under the same responsibilities? The Conference evidently felt that it was an important and delicate
adjustment which would have to be made with care for its
Final Act continued in the discussion of the fifth reservation:

Great importance is attached by the Members of the
League of Nations to the value of the advisory opinions

[13] E. E. Lape, "A Way Out of the Court Deadlock," *Atlantic Monthly,*
October, 1927, Vol. 140, p. 529.

which the Court may give as provided for in the Covenant. The Conference is confident that the Government of the United States entertains no desire to diminish the value of such opinions in connection with the functioning of the League of Nations. Yet the terms employed in the fifth reservation are of such a nature as to lend themselves to a possible interpretation which might have that effect. The Members of the League of Nations would exercise their rights in the Council and in the Assembly with full knowledge of the details of the situation which has necessitated a request for an advisory opinion, as well as with full appreciation of the responsibilities which a failure to reach a solution would involve for them under the Covenant of the League of Nations. A State which is exempt from the obligations and responsibilities of the Covenant would occupy a different position. It is for this reason that the procedure to be followed by a non-member State in connection with requests for advisory opinions is a matter of importance and in consequence it is desirable that the manner in which the consent provided for in the second part of the fifth reservation will be given should form the object of a supplementary agreement which would ensure that the peaceful settlement of future differences between members of the League of Nations would not be made more difficult.[14]

The advisory opinion is a powerful instrument and, aside from the inadvisability of rigid decisions early in the life of young institutions, the members of the League were not disposed to give us as an outsider a free veto on its use nor to determine that any one member of the Council possessed that veto. The mere suggestion of an advisory opinion had often been enough to bring a recalcitrant state to agreement and the possibility of its invocation by a majority vote was something for even a great power to consider. We might not like the possibility ourselves, but neither did the

[14] *Publication de la Société des Nations*, V. Questions Juridiques, 1926, V. 24, p. 6.

small powers like to give up the possible restraint upon a great power aggressively inclined which the possibility of asking for an advisory opinion by majority vote of the Assembly offered.

It is difficult to see how we can enjoy the political advantages and privileges which membership in the League gives without accepting such membership and the responsibilities that go with it. Nor is the method clear by which we can remain in the shadows watching for some development unfavorable to our interests or prestige and then step in just long enough to cast one vote that will veto the thing under way. Aside from the ethical nature of such participation in the much abhorred "political" affairs of the world, it is an impractical method of trying to assure ourselves political equality with the other great powers. The influence of a great nation sitting on the Council is not to be measured in terms of votes. If Great Britain, let us say, does not wish to have an advisory opinion asked it is not probable that the question will ever come to a vote. The issue would be discouraged long before it reached that stage, though it might possibly be successfully raised by the small powers in the next Assembly, if the rights of one of their number were seriously infringed.

Great Britain and the other great powers have a channel through which their power in international affairs may be readily and amicably exerted, their rights and prestige protected, while the small nations have a protection and a guarantee of fair dealing which they have never possessed before. We do not wish such a medium for "dabbling in the political affairs of Europe." We reject all such association. Having done so how can we claim more than the right to protest against the acts of either the Court or the League that do not suit us?

Who Would Wield the Veto? The difficulty of dealing with the League by Senatorial ultimatum is further illus-

trated by the doubt the September Conference found itself
in as to how the free veto on advisory opinions would be
imposed in behalf of the United States, if it should be
granted.   Who, they asked, would decide when the United
States was interested in a case and who would make the
claim of interest?   Would the Executive Department of
our Government in Washington make the decision or would
the Senate have to be consulted?   If so and the Senate was
not in session would a critical point in a dispute have to
wait until the Senate assembled?   Or would the Minister
of the United States to Switzerland have the power to block
or hold up an advisory opinion?

These questions may seem unnecessary to those uphold-
ing our way of dealing with the powers. Yet still another
one might have been asked, i. e., would not the Senate
presently assert the right to stop the wheels of the Court
if a few of its leading members should become alarmed
about the implications of some hearing for an advisory
opinion? The Senate would be much more likely to try to
increase the number of protests against advisory opinions,
than to try to decrease them.   And if of its own volition
it could enforce upon the nations of the world a right of
the United States to veto actions before the Court, why
should it not exercise that veto itself?

At the very least the nations may be pardoned for not
knowing just what the American Senate is going to do next
in the realm of foreign affairs.

The Fifth Reservation Accepted in Principle.   After all
this has been said, however, the September Conference did
not reject the second part of the fifth reservation.   Instead
it proposed the following as a basis for discussion and
agreement with the United States:

The manner in which the consent provided for in the
second part of the fifth reservation is to be given, will be the

subject of an understanding to be reached by the Government of the United States with the Council of the League of Nations.

The State signatories of the Protocol of December 16th, 1920, will be informed as soon as the understanding contemplated by the preceding paragraph has been reached.

Should the United States offer objection to an advisory opinion being given by the Court, at the request of the Council or the Assembly, concerning a dispute to which the United States is not a party or concerning a question other than a dispute between States, the Court will attribute to such objection the same force and effect as attaches to a vote against asking for the opinion given by a Member of the League of Nations either in the Assembly or in the Council. [15]

This reply, it has been said, was unsatisfactory and untactful because it accepted conditionally a conditional offer. It did just that, but it is difficult to say that it did not answer as definitely as it could. Perhaps it might have been more "tactful" to have accepted the pretentions of reservation 5 outright, but what puts the powers under any special obligation to be tactful to us? And if they had opposed reservations to reservations merely to return a little of the distrust and implication of grasping motives that the Senate had so freely heaped upon them, could we rise to complain?

We should recognize rather that the whole tendency of the kind of reservations that the Senate evolves whenever effective cooperation with the powers is proposed is naturally and normally to breed counter-reservations. Distrust breeds distrust, just as confidence begets confidence.

The spirit of the September Conference seems to have been much more conciliatory than might reasonably have been expected. Its President, in adjourning, frankly said

[15] *Publications de la Société des Nations.* V. Questions Juridiques, 1926, V. 25. p. 7.

that he did not know what attitude the United States would take. "We have built a bridge," he said. "Let us hope America will cross it. Our constitutional difficulties in drafting this reply certainly have been greater than was dreamed of in the United States when the reservations were formulated. We look to the United States to resume her place in the pacific settlement of international conflicts."[16]

FURTHER YEARS OF DELAY

Did we cross the bridge thus laid down by the representatives of 22 nations? We certainly did not hasten to do so. In fact we even refused to discuss the reply of the powers. On September 24 it was reported from Washington that the Administration took a "very gloomy view" of the situation created by the conference, and again, on October 1, it was announced that the President, "who has been very gloomy about the World Court situation," would make no move for the time being.[17] His uncertainty as to what could be done was so great in fact that the reply of the powers, forwarded 21 times in separate letters, as the niceties of our splendid isolation demanded, went unanswered.

The Court Abandoned by the Administration. Six weeks later, after various predictions that our terms were final and irrevocable, the newspapers generally carried large headlines on November 12, 1926, saying "World Court Entry Only On Our Own Terms." That caption headed President Coolidge's Armistice Day speech dedicating the World War Memorial at Kansas City. After denying that we profited by the War, and extolling the spiritual power found in peace, he advised against any national spirit of suspicious distrust and hatred toward other nations. "The Old World had for generations indulged itself in that form of luxury." The re-

---

[16] New York *Tribune*, September 24, 1926.
[17] New York *World*, February 8, 1928.

sults had been ruinous, though it was not for us to pass judgment.

In reply to our reported unpopularity in Europe he thought it exaggerated, but explained it as follows: "We are a creditor nation. We are more prosperous than some others. This means that our interests have come within the European circle where distrust and suspicion, if nothing more, have been altogether too common. To turn such attention to us indicates at least that we are not ignored." Yet we should not fail to appreciate their trials and sufferings and extend to them "our patience, our sympathy and such help as we believe will enable them to be restored to a sound and prosperous condition."

Then after a strong statement pointing out the necessity of institutions in securing justice and the misrepresentation to which the World Court had been subjected he came to this final paragraph but one: "While the nations involved cannot yet be said to have made a final determination, and from most of them no answer has been received, many have indicated that they are unwilling to concur in the conditions adopted by the resolution of the Senate. While no final determination can be made by our Government until final answers are received, the situation has been sufficiently developed so that I feel warranted in saying that I do not intend to ask the Senate to modify its position. I do not believe the Senate would take favorable action on any such proposal, and unless the requirements of the Senate resolution are met by the other interested nations I can see no prospect of this country adhering to the court." [18]

In this fashion our second great effort to join with the peoples for world pacification seemed to end. After years of effort we had at length made a highly conditional offer to take one of the smallest possible steps in uniting with the nations for peace. They in turn had ventured to question our

[18] Kansas City *Star,* November 12, 1926.

terms and to invite discussion of one point only, with a view to mutual agreement. Whereupon we retorted that we would play upon our own terms or not at all. Not a comma would be varied or a line discussed. The sin so much attributed to Woodrow Wilson—and so questionably—of demanding signature "without the crossing of a t or the dotting of an i" became the virtue of the Senate and Mr. Coolidge.

We had travelled far indeed from the day when our name was the symbol in households of every land of unselfish and fearless championship of right to the day when a President of the United States attributed our unpopularity abroad to the fact that our former allies in arms owed us money and were distrustful and suspicious of us, "if nothing more," because of our prosperity. Yet it was only seven short years from the time that the moral leadership of the world had been securely in our grasp to the day when the best that Calvin Coolidge could say was, "at least we are not ignored!"

The President was no doubt right, however, in concluding that there was little desire in the Senate to have its terms discussed with the powers, particularly the League powers acting in concert. Yet that body refused to retire in the opposite direction by rejecting, on February 9, 1927, a motion of Senator Trammell, of Florida, to rescind the resolution of adherence to the Court. The vote was 59 to 10, 26 not voting.[19]

The Gillett Resolution. The matter then slumbered another year, until February 6, 1928, when Senator Gillett, of Massachusetts, introduced the following resolution:

Whereas, the Senate on January 27, 1926, by a vote of seventy-six to seventeen, gave its advice and consent to the adherence of the United States to the Permanent Court of

[19] *Congressional Record,* Vol. 68, Pt. 3, p. 3328.

International Justice, upon certain conditions and with certain reservations; and

Whereas the signatory States in transmitting their replies referred to "such further exchange of views as the Government of the United States may think useful:" Therefore be it

Resolved, That the Senate of the United States respectfully suggests to the President the advisability of a further exchange of views with the signatory States in order to establish whether the differences between the United States and the signatory States can be satisfactorily adjusted.[20]

Explaining the purpose of his resolution Mr. Gillett later said:

The conference of the nations upon our reservations was finished in September, 1926, and they sent us the result of it with courteous expressions of hope that the differences between us could be accommodated and that there might be such further exchanges of views as the Government of the United States might think useful.

There negotiations ended, and the subject has slept for a year with no attempt toward further adjustment. It seems to me the next move is up to us. Unless we make some response the question will lie dormant indefinitely. I presume the Secretary of State, who received the communications from the other nations, felt that as he did not originate the reservations, but as they were framed by the Senate, he could not presume to interpret them or to answer the messages from the other nations by telling them whether their interpretations of the reservations were correct or their suggestions of changes acceptable. And so, not knowing what answer would correctly represent the views of the Senate, he prudently answered nothing.

And there the matter has rested. Thinking that so momentous a matter should not be allowed to die from inaction

[20] *Congressional Record,* Vol. 69, Pt. 3, p. 2503.

so long as there was a chance of agreement, particularly when I believed that both parties sincerely desired some agreement, I introduced my resolution.

My hope is that the debate on that resolution will disclose clearly the attitude of the Senate toward the suggestions of the other nations, or possibly the resolution might be so amended as to indicate exactly the position of the Senate, and that then the President will respond to the long unanswered letters referring perhaps to the proceedings of the Senate, and with this new light as to the meaning of the reservations and the probable attitude of the Senate the other powers will again consider whether a satisfactory agreement cannot be reached.

It certainly would be disheartening if the United States, which has always been the leader in the movement for submitting disputes to arbitration, should not become a member of the Court, and I hope the other nations really want us enough to accede to the conditions which we think necessary to protect us." [21]

Reiterating his original belief that we would never need to exercise the veto power asked, even if we had it, he granted that the Senate would be "unwilling to take any chances at first," and thought the Senate would insist upon its point, but a further exchange of views was in any event desirable.

Further Action Demanded. The Portland *Oregonian,* one of the greatest Republican papers of the West, seemed to express in restrained form the feelings of the supporters of the Court, saying, on February 12, 1928:

A resolution by Senator Gillett of Massachusetts urging that negotiations for adherence of the United States to the World Court be resumed has drawn forth expressions of approval from so many representative men and women in all occupations and of both parties that it may well be said to

[21] New York *Times,* March 11, 1928.

voice a widespread public demand. Mere courtesy requires that the other nations signatory of the World Court protocol be given an opportunity to smooth out differences, even by those Senators who believe they cannot succeed.

A deadlock has arisen because the Senate attached to its resolution of approval conditions which it put in the form of reservations, though these might better have been given the form of recommendations to the Secretary of State as matters for negotiation. A reservation of ratification to a treaty leaves no opening for further negotiations, therefore it is in the nature of an ultimatum. It in effect says to the other party: "Take it or leave it," and the natural impulse of the other party is to leave it. Notwithstanding this brusque manner of asking admission to a Court which the other nations established and put in successful operation, they frankly accepted some reservations, attached conditions to acceptance of another and left the one regarding advisory opinions in such shape that by negotiation we could gain all that we can reasonably ask.

There is a studied effort to suppress discussion of this subject, as there was between the date when President Harding recommended action and the date when President Coolidge obtained action by the Senate. During that period several tests proved public opinion to be nine to one in favor of the Court, and the pressure became so strong that the Senate yielded, even against the will of influential members who are determined enemies of the Court. The Gillett resolution gives opportunity for another such expression of public opinion and for another exertion of pressure on stubborn Senators who cherish the delusion of American isolation.[22]

The 26 Scripps-Howard newspapers had already demanded a renewal of negotiations on December 14, 1927, in commenting on the nation-wide petition presented to President

---

[22] A score of leading newspapers scattered throughout the country joined in support of the Gillett Resolution. See *Bulletin No. 6, American Foundation*, April 10, 1928, and the collection of editorials issued March 1, 1928. Published at 565 Fifth Avenue, N. Y.

Coolidge urging that action, under the title "Coolidge and the World Court."

After first quoting from the President's inaugural address that "We ought not to barter away our independence or our sovereignty, but we ought to engage in no refinements of logic, no sophistries and no subterfuges, to argue away the undoubted duty of this country, by reason of the might of its numbers, the power of its resources and its position of leadership in the world, actively and comprehensively to signify its approval and to bear its full share of the responsibility of a candid and disinterested attempt at the establishment of a tribunal for the administration of even-handed justice between nation and nation," the Scripps-Howard editorial concluded:

> In no state paper does the logic of President Coolidge appear to better advantage than in this. And it is to be hoped, as the petition of Monday suggests, that the President will indicate his willingness to continue along the same line. The Senate, in framing the conditions upon which the United States would adhere to the World Court, deliberately or otherwise threw the President's recommendations to the winds and indulged in so many refinements of logic, sophistries and subterfuges that we were finally finessed out of the Court.
>
> These reservations were more sounding than sound, more superficial than fundamental, and one of the most useful acts the President could do before he leaves the White House, as he has expressed his intention of doing, would be to tell the Senate so.[23]

A New Approach

The President maintained silence, for another year, until shortly before the opening of Congress in December, 1928. The Gillett resolution was discussed in the Foreign Relations

[23] Ibid.

Committee several times in the Spring and eventually a motion to postpone until the first meeting in December was carried by a vote of 9 to 8, indicating that it was likely to be strongly supported before the Senate. A few days before the Committee met, President Coolidge invited a number of Senators, including Senator Gillett, to luncheon and expressed a willingness to renew negotiations with the powers.[24]

Shortly after, Mr. Gillett stated that he was delighted by the President's intention. He presumed the President recognized that the general treaty renouncing war having been concluded it was important that a substitute for war be found. He would let his resolution lie dormant until the result of the new negotiations was known.[25]

The Kellogg Reply. No news of renewed negotiations reached the public until February 20, 1929, two weeks before the close of the Coolidge administration, when Secretary Kellogg made public a note just delivered to each of the nations belonging to the Court. In it he recalled his note of February 12, 1926, transmitting the Senate's reservations and frankly recorded that he had received five unconditioned acceptances out of forty-eight.

After a brief but fair review of the reply returned by the September Conference he stated that "The Government of the United States desires to avoid in so far as may be possible any proposal which would interfere with or embarrass the work of the Council of the League of Nations, doubtless often perplexing and difficult, and it would be glad if it could dispose of the subject by a simple acceptance of the suggestions embodied in the final act and draft protocol adopted at Geneva on September 23, 1926."

There were, however, some elements of uncertainty in the bases of these suggestions which seemed to require further

[24] November 24, 1928. N. Y. *Times,* November 25, 1928.
[25] N. Y. *Times,* November 28, 1928.

discussion. The powers of the Council and its modes of procedure depended upon the Covenant, which might be amended at any time, and the rules of the Court, including the one adopted in the Eastern Karelia case, were also subject to change. For these reasons it appeared that the protocol submitted by the powers would not furnish adequate protection to the United States.

He was gratified to learn from the proceedings of the Conference at Geneva that the considerations leading to the adoption of the second part of reservation five were appreciated by the powers and thought that "Possibly the interest of the United States thus attempted to be safeguarded may be fully protected in some other way or by some other formula. The government of the United States feels that such an informal exchange of views as is contemplated by the twenty-four governments should, as herein suggested, lead to agreement upon some provision which in unobjectionable form would protect the rights and interests of the United States as an adherent of the Court Statute, and this expectation is strongly supported by the fact that there seems to be but little difference regarding the substance of these rights and interests." [26]

Developments abroad, as well as the pressure of American public opinion, indicated that the time had come to reopen the closed matter of the Court. On September 8, 1928, M. Motta of Switzerland had placed a resolution before the Council of the League asking it to decide whether a majority or a unanimous vote was necessary to request an advisory opinion of the Court. In case such a decision should be made favoring a unanimous vote the United States would no longer be in the position of seeking a special position. A similar effort to obtain a ruling upon this matter was also made in the Assembly.[27]

[26] *United States Daily,* February 20, 1929.
[27] N. Y. *Times,* September 9, 21, 26, 1928.

This movement was apparently not in the interest of bringing the United States into the Court. On the contrary the small powers, led by Switzerland, desired a determination in favor of a majority vote which would make it easier to request advisory opinions and practically impossible to give the United States the veto demanded by the Senate. The big powers favored a unanimous vote.[28]

Mr. Hughes on the World Court Bench. While this discussion opened up the moot question and gave a chance for a settlement in League circles, especially if we could influence it in favor of unanimity, the election of former Secretary of State Charles E. Hughes to a judgeship on the World Court was probably of more importance in arousing a renewed appreciation of the anomaly of our abstention from the Court. On June 23, 1928, both Cuba and Brazil placed Mr. Hughes' name in nomination to fill the vacancy caused by the resignation of Judge John Bassett Moore. Sweden, England, France and the other nations rapidly followed and by August 6 twenty-six nations, or more than enough to elect, had nominated him. Italy and Poland added their approval on the same day. Mr. Hughes was accordingly elected on September 8, by a unanimous vote in the Council and by a vote of 41 states out of 48 in the Assembly. Mr. Hughes telegraphed in reply that he felt highly honored by his election and would feel it a privilege to serve.[29]

Returning to the United States from a trip abroad he was given a part of great prominence in the campaign to elect Mr. Hoover to the Presidency, an activity which reminded millions of Americans, indirectly at least, of the matter of the Court. His willingness to undergo the labor, now almost continuous, of hearing its cases, be they advisory opinions or judgments, indicated a degree of faith in the workings and

[28] N. Y. *Times,* December 11, 1928.
[29] Ibid., June 24, July 10, 20, September 9, 11, 1928.

purposes of the Court which contrasted strongly with the timidity of the Senate in approaching it and the lukewarmness of the outgoing Administration in its advocacy.

The same League Assembly which elected Mr. Hughes also took another step which facilitated a reexamination of the American attitude toward the Court. On the motion of the French delegation the Assembly adopted a resolution creating a committee of jurists to consider possible changes in the statutes of the World Court, in view of the approaching general election of judges, and on January 7, 1929, it was announced from Geneva that Mr. Elihu Root had accepted membership on the committee.[30]

Mr. Root in Geneva. Thus another great American, and leading Republican, signified his willingness to do what he could personally to assist the Court in becoming established. This desire was natural in Mr. Root since he had played a vital part in drawing up the original statutes of the Court, now to be amended, but it was not usual that a man four score years of age should be glad to undertake an arduous mission of this character in mid-winter.

Before leaving for Europe, Mr. Root visited Washington and had conferences with the President and Senate leaders, which were believed to have resulted in Secretary Kellogg's cordial reply of February 20 to the 1926 communication of the powers. Mr. Root could hardly attempt to compose the difficulty created by the Senate reservations while the reply of the members of the Court went unanswered.

As he sailed, on February 15, he issued a statement explaining that there had been no suggestion of any fundamental changes in the statute or anything more than minor adjustments of the machinery. Nor had there been any suggestion of any desire that the committee should deal at all with the relations of the United States to the Court. He characterized the Court as a great success. He did not see

[30] N. Y. *Times,* January 8, 1929.

how the many problems left by the War could have been liquidated without its aid and thought it equally needed in the future.[31]

Though disclaiming any official status or mission Mr. Root began to confer individually with the members of the Council soon after his arrival in Geneva and to explain to them the formula which he hoped would solve the difficulty. After these conferences the Council considered the proposal and, on March 9, voted unanimously to authorize the committee of jurists to take up the matter of American adhesion.[32]

A Channel For Our Protests. Mr. Root's plan attempted to solve the quandary raised by the Senate's claim of a veto over advisory opinions by re-affirming that claim both for cases touching any dispute to which the United States is a party, and for all other disputes (or matters besides disputes) to which the United States is not a party but claims an interest, and by then laying down rules governing the exercise of such claims which would be likely to reduce them to a minimum. After asserting again the full claim his plan provided for the notification to the United States of every request for an advisory opinion and for discussion between the American Government and "the proponents of the request." The Assembly or the Council might also invite an exchange of views with the United States before submitting the request. If finally the discussion should bring out

(1) that no agreement can be reached as to whether the question does touch an interest of the United States within the true meaning of the second paragraph of this article; and (2) that submission of the question is still insisted upon after attributing to the objection of the United States the same force and effect as attaches to a vote against asking for the opinion given by a member of the League of Nations

[31] Ibid., February 16, 22, 1929.
[32] Ibid., March 10, 1929.

either in Assembly or Council; and if it also appears that
the United States has not been able to find the submission
of the question so important for the general good as to call
upon the United States to forego its objection, in that particular instance leaving the request to be acted upon by the
Court without in any way binding the United States; then it
shall be deemed that owing to material difference of view
regarding the proper scope or practice of requesting advisory opinions, the arrangement now agreed upon is not
yielding satisfactory results, and that exercise of powers of
withdrawal provided in Article XII hereof will follow naturally without any imputation of unfriendliness or unwillingness to cooperate generally for peace and good will. [33]

In explaining the scheme to the Committee Mr. Root
frankly said that he didn't suppose the complicated machinery he proposed would ever come into use, but if it did
he felt sure the result would be agreement. He did not think
the apprehensions that had been aroused in both Washington
and Geneva well founded, but both had to be guarded
against.[34]

The solution seemed to meet with favor everywhere except
in Latin America where it was felt that the United States
might still attempt to veto, under the Monroe Doctrine, any
settlement by the Court (or the League) of any question
to which a Latin American state was a party.[35] The delegates of these countries did not, however, oppose the adoption of the plan as redrafted and somewhat simplified by
Sir Cecil Hurst, the British Delegate, and the report was
adopted by the Committee on March 18. It assured the
United States a right of protest at every stage of an advisory
opinion proceeding. [36]

[32] N. Y. *Times*, March 7, 1929.
[34] Ibid., March 12, 1929.
[35] Ibid., March 9, 1929.
[36] See the accounts of Mr. Root's mission by Philip C. Jessup, "Mr.
Root, the Senate and the World Court," *Foreign Affairs*, July, 1929.

The Hurst Report. The official report drafted by Sir Cecil Hurst to accompany the revised protocol for the adherence of the United States after giving an account of the proceedings to date stated that the Committee felt the advisory opinion too useful in the solution of disputes not otherwise approachable to permit of its abandonment. [37] Neither did the committee feel able to recommend that requests for an advisory opinion require a unanimous vote of the Council or the Assembly. It would be inexpedient and premature to attempt to force a decision upon this issue. All that was possible was to guarantee the United States a position of equality in this matter with the members of the League and leave the issue of unanimity to be settled "by the gradual evolution of recognized and obligatory practice." [38]

It would not always be possible, the report continued, to consult the United States in advance before requesting an advisory opinion, for the need for an opinion often became apparent near the end of a session of the Council when it would not be possible to complete an exchange of views before the members separated. It was for this reason that conference with the United States at later stages was provided for. Proceedings before the Court might even be interrupted, if necessary, to permit a full discussion with the United States.

The conclusion of the report recognized the difficulty of mobilizing 48 states for the purpose of acquiescence by urg-

---

Vol. 7, pp. 585-99. The new protocol was drawn to contain words that might satisfy everybody. Its first article stated that the Signatory States "accept the special conditions attached by the United States in the five reservations. . . . upon the terms and conditions set out in the following articles." pp. 592-3.

[37] As more and more nations accept the jurisdiction of the Court over all disputes affecting them the need for the advisory opinion will correspondingly diminish.

[38] This decision was made necessary by the insistence of the small powers that the possibility of asking for an advisory opinion by a majority vote might enable one of them to bring a big power before the Court when it would be otherwise unable to get its dispute before that body.

ing the states to send delegates to the 1929 Assembly empowered to sign the protocol, if the states approved of it,
and if further discussion was desired to participate in a special conference so that the matter might be settled before
the end of the Assembly. [39]   If, therefore, the revised protocol is accepted by the Council, the Assembly, the United
States Senate and the governments of the 49 states without
a single demur, the United States may enter the Court during the year 1930.[40]

Settlement in Prospect. The right of the United States to
withdraw if its protests against an advisory opinion are not
heeded, which according to the formula agreed upon "will
follow naturally without any implication of unfriendliness
or unwillingness to cooperate generally for peace and good
will," is likely to be the point most discussed both in the
Senate and abroad. It will appear to many non-Americans
that the veto has been granted, since the nations would
hardly oppose the United States to the point of withdrawal.
All the United States need do, therefore, to have its way is
to insist long enough. On the other hand, to the irreconcilables, the veto claimed has been denied because, they say,
we would never dare go to the length of pulling out of the
Court to block an advisory opinion, and, in truth, it would
take a deal of explaining to convince world opinion that we
were justified in any such withdrawal. In actuality, probably few discussions of advisory opinions between the
United States and the League would ever come up and in

[39] N. Y. *Times,* March 20, 1929.
[40] *United Press* dispatches of September 4 and 5, 1929, reported that
the Root-Hurst protocol had been unanimously approved by the special
conference of Court members convened to receive it, after that body
had been informed that Secretary Stimson would accept the instrument
and submit it to the Senate.

It would not be sent to the Senate, however until the governments of
all the signatory states had formally ratified it. In view of the lukewarmness of the Latin American states and others toward it it was not
considered improbable that one or more might forget to ratify, in which
case the whole effort would fail. See also *The Literary Digest,* September 14, 1929, Vol. 102, No. 11, p. 12.

all likelihood neither side would ever care to push a disagreement over one to the point of a break. [41]

The danger is likely to come from the insistence of Senators that the Senate censor requests for advisory opinions and tell the League and the Court whether the United States consents to the proceeding or not. The Senate has quite successfully asserted the right to scrutinize every proposed arbitration before permitting it to go to court. Why should it not also pass upon all advisory opinions of the World Court if the American Government is empowered to do so? The usual loud cry will be raised to change something or specify something. How can we "sign on the dotted line," especially when the line has been drawn in Geneva? What demand more natural and appealing to the Senate than one to give it whatever power over advisory opinions is granted the United States?

However, the prospective settlement of our relation to the World Court will find a man in the Presidency who not only has a full comprehension of the powers of his office but also a broader view of world conditions than any other President ever had on coming into power. Mr. Hoover should be adequate to the task of concluding the long effort to bring us into the Court, so far, at least, as the United States is concerned.

Mr. Root's diplomatic statesmanship found full support in the President's inaugural address in which he said: "American statesmen were among the first to propose and they have constantly urged upon the world, the establishment of a tribunal for the settlement of controversies of a justiciable character. The Permanent Court of International Justice in its major purpose is thus peculiarly identified with American ideals and with American statesmanship. No more potent

---

[41] Whether the other members of the Court possess a right of withdrawal is a matter of some controversy. Presumably they do. Yet no one of them claimed any such right, either at the time the Court was created or since, so many contend that the right does not exist.

instrumentality for this purpose has been conceived and no other is practicable of establishment.

"The reservations placed upon our adherence should not be misinterpreted. The United States seeks by these reservations no special privilege or advantage, but only to clarify our relation to advisory opinions and other matters which are subsidiary to the major purposes of the Court. The way should, and I believe will, be found by which we may take our proper place in a movement so fundamental to the progress of peace." [42]

[42] Chicago *Tribune,* March 5, 1929.

CHAPTER XI

INTERPRETATIONS OF THE PARIS PEACE PACT

WHEN President Coolidge announced, on Armistice Day, 1926, that we would not join the World Court, unless the Senate's terms were accepted as delivered, the great body of Americans who wished to see their country have some positive part in the movement to limit warfare found their efforts again nullified. Twice within ten years they had labored long and valiantly to put the tremendous weight of American influence actively behind machinery created to adjust the disputes which had heretofore led to war and in both cases the effort had ended in failure. To a movement backed by less conviction the ensuing sense of frustration would have been fatal. Men do not like to labor repeatedly and long for negative results. The disappointment in the outcome was naturally widespread. What could the United States do to ally itself with the movement to create a safer and more stable civilization? If we could not have a part in either the League or the Court, what was there to do?

To some who refused to believe that the organization of peace could be blocked, the next approach seemed to be one which would give the American aversion to war a chance to express itself without involving directly the use or approval of any of the machinery already set up for keeping the peace. They believed moreover, that it was time to advance in principle from the original position taken in the Covenant.

It was, therefore, only a few months after the apparent

close of our effort to join the Court until, on April 6, 1927, the tenth anniversary of American entrance into the War, Foreign Minister Briand, of France, acting upon the advice of American friends, offered to make with the American people a "mutual engagement tending to outlaw war, to use an American expression," as between the two countries. "The renunciation of war as an instrument of national policy," he continued, "is a conception already familiar to the signatories of the Covenant of the League of Nations and the Treaties of Locarno." [1]

Two months later, on June 20, Mr. Briand proposed to the United States Government the following treaty:

> Article 1.   The High Contracting Powers solemnly declare, in the name of the French people and the people of the United States of America, that they condemn recourse to war and renounce it respectively as an instrument of their national policy towards each other.
>
> Article 2.   The settlement or the solution of all disputes or conflicts, of whatever nature or of whatever origin they may be, which may arise between France and the United States of America, shall never be sought by either side except by pacific means.

The proposed treaty appealed at once to many opponents of the League and the Court.   One of the earliest and bitterest of these, a Chicago lawyer, Mr. S. O. Levinson, had decided that the thing to do was not to try to prevent, limit or suppress war, but simply to outlaw it completely by mutual international agreement. [2]   Beginning with the irreconcilable Senators in 1919 he had gained powerful individual advocates for his alternative thesis, including Senator Borah, and by 1926 he had received the support

---

[1] James T. Shotwell, *War as an Instrument of National Policy*, New York, 1929, p. 41.
[2] Wm. Hard, "The non-stop Peace Advocate," *World's Work*, March, 1929, pp. 76-77.

of a considerable wing of the peace advocates. It was a forthright idea. It didn't temporize with war as an institution but proposed to banish it from civilized society without further parley. If possible what could be more desirable? It was especially attractive to those who hoped the United States could do something for peace without agreeing to do anything positive.

Extended Negotiations. Yet notwithstanding the appeal which M. Briand's offer made to the outlawry advocates the proposal was received with considerable skepticism in Washington and went unanswered for nearly six months. It was widely held to be only an effort of France to put the power of the United States, morally at least, back of her nationalistic undertakings. However, the principle proposed by M. Briand won such outstanding support in public discussion throughout the country that the opening of Congress in December found an unusually widespread and united demand that negotiations looking to its acceptance be opened.[3] Senator Capper, of Kansas, and Senator Borah both introduced strongly worded resolutions in the Senate urging the proscription of war,[4] and, on December 28, 1927, Secretary Kellogg replied to M. Briand with the rather startling proposition that the two governments join "in an effort to obtain the adherence of all the principal powers of the world to a declaration renouncing war as an instrument of national policy."

This broadening of the stage led the French Government to propose that only wars of aggression be outlawed and months of negotiation ensued before there came to be a general agreement on both sides of the ocean that the new treaty did not invalidate or weaken the obligations of the

---

[3] Shotwell, *War as an Instrument of National Policy,* chapters 6 and 8. These chapters especially give an illuminating account of the surprising spread of opinion favorable to such a treaty.

[4] Senator Capper's resolution was introduced on December 8, and Senator Borah's on December 12, 1927.

powers under the League Covenant, the Locarno Treaties or any others of a similar nature. Many notes were exchanged and understandings stated before, on August 27, 1928, the representatives of fifteen nations signed the Pact of Paris in the French Foreign Office.[5]

By the time President Coolidge transmitted the treaty to the Senate, on December 4, forty-four additional states had signed it or expressed their intention to do so, though they showed an almost unanimous disposition to wait until the Senate had ratified the pact before taking that step themselves. This was probably one reason why the President hoped, in his covering letter to the Senate, that it might come into force with the least possible delay.[6]

The Treaty Signed. The multilateral treaty followed exactly the original bilateral proposal of M. Briand saying:

ARTICLE I

The High Contracting Parties solemnly declare in the names of their respective peoples that they condemn recourse to war for the solution of international controversies, and renounce it as an instrument of national policy in their relations with one another.

ARTICLE II

The High Contracting Parties agree that the settlement or solution of all disputes or conflicts, of whatever nature or of whatever origin they may be, which may arise among them shall never be sought except by pacific means.

If these few words were to come into actual working effect they marked indeed a revolution in international rela-

---

[5] The original signatories were: Germany, the United States, Belgium, France, Great Britain, Canada, Australia, New Zealand, The Union of South Africa, The Irish Free State, India, Italy, Japan, Poland and the Czechoslovak Republic.

[6] *Congressional Record*, Vol. 70, p. 20.

tions. In Mr. Coolidge's view, expressed in his annual message, "the observance of this covenant, so simple and so straightforward, promises more for the peace of the world than any other agreement ever negotiated among the nations." He commended it to the Senate as superseding in no way our inalienable right and duty of national defense or of undertaking to commit us to any action if the treaty should be broken.

Reservations Proposed. These assurances did not satisfy the irreconcilable Senators who proceeded, in a resolution introduced jointly by Senators Moses, of New Hampshire, and Reed of Missouri, to ask the Senate to say, as usual, all the things which the treaty did not mean. The resolution, introduced on December 14, read:

Resolved: That the Senate of the United States declares that in advising and consenting to the multilateral treaty it does so with the understanding:

(1) That the treaty imposes no obligation on the United States to resort to coercive or punitive measures against any offending nation.

(2) That the treaty does not impose any limitations upon the Monroe Doctrine or the traditional policies of the United States.

(3) That the treaty does not impair the right of the United States to defend its territory, possessions, trade or interests.

(4) That the treaty does not obligate the United States to the conditions of any treaty to which the United States is not a party.[7]

In addition to desiring a free hand to do all the things we might find it to our interest to do in the future, these Senators feared that they were again approaching from another angle the obligations of that "treaty to which the

[7] Ibid., p. 623.

United States is not a party." Thus Senator Robinson, of
Indiana, a strong opponent of the League and the Court,
asked if the other signatories, practically all members of
these two bodies, could not by pacific means decide a question
in which we were vitally interested to our disadvantage and
against our best interests, and, "assuming we should object,
would not the United States in that event be placed in the
position, so far as world opinion is concerned, of opposing
pacific means and would not all of those, so far as the moral
effect is concerned, be leagued in opinion against the United
States?"

The reply which Senator Borah made was that the World
Court might decide a controversy in which the United States
had a very great interest without the new treaty.[8] The implication in Mr. Robinson's question seemed to be that we
had better remain free not only to reject decisions of the
Court but to fight all the members of the League if need
be. To many other Senators the treaty was attractive because it seemed to offer a way to keep out of the League
and still others favored it in the belief that it was a sure step
toward the League. One party or the other seemed headed
for disappointment.

Two Monroe Doctrines. The case for the treaty was first
presented by Senator Borah on January 3 and 4, 1929.[9] It
seemed a novel spectacle to find Mr. Borah defending a peace
plan in the Senate, but his defense appeared to be as whole-
hearted as his criticism of former efforts had been. He first
insisted that no mention or reservation of self defense was
necessary because the right of self defense was inherent and
implicit. It was a right which could not be bartered away,
abrogated or surrendered. All the signatories had agreed
that each nation was left free to determine for itself what
self defense meant. He conceded frankly that there was a

[8] *Congressional Record,* Vol. 70, p. 1145.
[9] Ibid., pp. 1267–89.

weakness in the treaty here but thought it was a condition about which nothing could be done.

Similarly he thought there was no need for mention of the Monroe Doctrine because it rested on the principle of self defense. We retained complete freedom to say for ourselves what the Doctrine meant and to go to war to protect our rights under it. Several Senators asserted that Secretary Kellogg had scrupulously avoided any mention of the Monroe Doctrine either in the treaty or in his correspondence with other powers in order to secure the adhesion of the Latin American states,[10] and there was a lack of the tendency so pronounced in the debate over the League to magnify the Doctrine into an assertion of our right to do as we pleased in this hemisphere that was distinctly encouraging. The disposition, on the contrary, was to squeeze the Doctrine back into something like its original proportions. Mr. Borah said he believed in it as originally announced and not as too often misconstrued. Senator Barkley, of Kentucky, and other Senators agreed that we had wandered far from the original conception of the Monroe Doctrine.[11] A more numerous group, however, insisted that we ought to say something about it or somebody might assume that we had waived it and in the end it was proclaimed anew. A hundred years of rather constant assertion did not seem to give it standing and security enough to permit of one opportunity for its intonation to be missed.

It must be admitted, however, that the numerous understandings which the various nations had stated in their letters to Secretary Kellogg had given the Senators ground for feeling that we ought to do some interpreting ourselves. Certainly when everyone else was following the Senate's custom of saying what the treaty didn't mean it was almost out of the question for the Senate to fail to join in. This

[10] Ibid., pp. 1218, 1276, 1465, 1521.
[11] Ibid., 1277, 1520.

was particularly true when the British Foreign Secretary had enunciated a British Monroe Doctrine that seemed to anti-British Senators even more expansive than our own.

In his note of May 19, 1928, Mr. Chamberlain had said:

> 10. The language of Article I, as to the renunciation of war as an instrument of national policy, renders it desirable that I should remind your excellency that there are certain regions of the world the welfare and integrity of which constitute a special and vital interest for our peace and safety. His Majesty's Government have been at pains to make it clear in the past that interference with these regions can not be suffered. Their protection against attack is to the British Empire a measure of self-defense. It must be clearly understood that His Majesty's Government in Great Britain accept the new treaty upon the distinct understanding that it does not prejudice their freedom of action in this respect.

Here, said Senator Blaine, of Wisconsin, was the missing link in the Covenant of the League of Nations. Its Article 10 had guaranteed the British Empire against external aggression; now this new article 10 sought to secure it against internal aggression—to "complete the chain which binds 400,000,000 lives to the dominion and tyranny of the British Government." He therefore offered a resolution which declined to recognize this doctrine.[12] Other Senators, too, thought that this new British Monroe Doctrine covered a lot of territory. It was said to apply primarily to Egypt and the Suez Canal, but its terms covered the five continents and the seven seas. Should we not at least remind them that our doctrine was paramount in the American continents? It was a little amusing to hear one of the group of Senators who had expanded the Monroe Doctrine so passionately in 1919 complain about the breadth of the British doctrine, but when

---

[12] *Congressional Record*, Vol. 70, pp. 1068, 1463. The British Note of May 19 may be found in Shotwell, *War as an Instrument of National Policy*, 291-95.

he quoted the statement of the British Foreign Secretary that "His Majesty's Government have been at pains to make it clear in the past that interference with these regions cannot be suffered" it seemed logical that we should restate our own doctrine once more by way of caution.

The Effect of the Negotiations Upon the Treaty. Senator Borah maintained throughout the discussion that neither the British notes nor any of the others had changed the treaty in the slightest. They simply described rights and obligations which everybody must agree existed and must be respected. They neither added anything to the treaty nor took anything away from it. They had no legal effect whatever. He accordingly resisted the making of any amendments or reservations or interpretations on our part to the last day of the debate.

The critics of the treaty contended, however, that these negotiations did modify the scope of the treaty and that in case of future dispute "every explanatory word and comment and every condition of acceptance that was reduced to writing by the official negotiators before the treaty was approved" would be published and have their effect on public opinion, [13] which in the minds of some Senators was to be the only tribunal with any authority to pass upon the observance of the treaty. Others apparently envisaging some kind of judicial interpretation, held with Senator Reed that it would be a gross breach of faith for the nations to ignore the interpretations given to the treaty by our Secretary of State, whether in his open declarations or in his silent acquiescence to the interpretations given by other governments. Similarly we could not obtain the consent of other nations under stated conditions, permit the nations to sign the treaty under expressed understandings and then repudiate them afterwards.[14] Therefore the Senate had better set down its understandings also.

---

[12] Senator McLean, *Congressional Record,* Vol. 70, p. 1218.
[14] *Congressional Record,* Vol. 70, p. 1214.

This was the view notably of Senator Bingham, of Connecticut, and others who were interested in the effect of the treaty upon the protection of American citizens in foreign countries.   Mr. Bingham had often traveled abroad as a member of scientific expeditions and had felt the hostility of peoples who doubted the pure scientific mission of the explorers.   His own experiences, including arrest in countries where evidence of guilt was not necessary to trial, and observation of the plight of other Americans in China before the armed forces of the United States came to their relief, had given him a very lively interest in maintaining protection for Americans abroad.   He wanted to be sure that the right of self defense was to be construed to include the right to use force in protecting Americans in foreign countries. [15]

Senator Borah explained that the protection of the lives and property of our citizens in other lands was not war and never had been regarded as war.   To this Senator Bingham agreed, but he felt that there were a great many people in the country who did not understand this and who would be likely to look askance hereafter at warlike measures in behalf of our citizens in foreign countries.   He was much more interested in seeing American opinion in the future willing to stand behind the Government in protecting the lives and property of its citizens abroad than he was in what foreign opinion was going to say. [16]

---

[15] *Congressional Record,* Vol. 70, p. 1543.

[16] Ibid., 1272, 1535.   In attempting to smooth the way for the treaty, Mr. Borah agreed with his questioners to such an extent that the doctrine of self defense was given wide scope indeed.   In addition to covering all activity to protect the lives and property of our people abroad, he agreed that if a European nation and a South American nation amicably settled a dispute between them with a result that we disapproved of under the Monroe Doctrine we could still go to war with both countries to upset the settlement agreed upon by them.

He held also that after the sinking of the *Maine* we could have gone to war with Spain under the right of self defense without violating the treaty, though he qualified this statement by adding, "but only on the theory that we acted in good faith in defending against any further attacks." pp. 1272-74.

There was little disagreement as to the power of the public opinion supporting the treaty. There seemed to be agreement that to an unusual degree this treaty had been negotiated in response to and in accordance with public demand. It was so difficult to say also that it committed us to any positive action that it was hard to show the necessity of attaching amendments or reservations directly to it. Moreover, in its multilateral form it was "an American proposal" and it was generally recognized that if it were not ratified in good faith by the United States Government it would not be by the other nations. The rejection of the Covenant by the Senate had not killed the League, but the alteration of the Pact in the Senate would almost certainly prevent its acceptance elsewhere.

A Committee Report Demanded. Those criticising the treaty, either in principle or in detail, therefore united in demanding that the Foreign Relations Committee submit a formal report rejecting the implications that the various Senators feared might reside in the treaty. Some desired that the report be adopted by the Senate, though not as a part of the resolution of ratification, and sent along with that document to the powers for their information, until Secretary Kellogg refused to send the proposed interpretative report to the other signatories and began to line up Senators on the Committee against such a procedure.[17] Mr. Kellogg did not believe that his treaty needed any further explanations or reservations. He had discussed it with the Committee[18] before submitting it to the world and now felt that on this ground as well as others he was entitled to support.

The majority of the Senators seemed convinced that no qualifying action was necessary on their part. Meeting this

[17] N. Y. *Times,* January 9, 1929; *Congressional Record,* Vol. 70, pp. 1538, 1717.
[18] *Congressional Record,* Vol. 70, 1267.

situation the reservationists modified their demand to require only a report from the Foreign Relations Committee
which might be adopted by the Senate, but not transmitted
to the powers. When this did not meet with greater favor
they stood for a report from the Committee which would
neither be voted upon nor transmitted, but merely filed in
the Senate.

They had retreated about as far as they could and still
record something about the treaty, yet there was strong
opposition even to this minimum proposal. Senator Norris,
of Nebraska, never noted for subserviency to the Executive, asked Senator Bingham: "Does not the Senator
know that there would be just the same opportunity to disagree with the conclusions of the committee as there is to
disagree with the treaty itself? Would there not be just
as much dispute about what the committee meant as there
is about what this treaty means? We cannot do anything
that will prevent men from disagreeing, and honestly so, as
to what certain words mean, and if there is a disagreement
as to what the treaty means now, there would be a disagreement as to what the Foreign Relations Committee
meant if they undertook to re-write the treaty." He was
not in favor of construing a treaty that was already plain
and then giving two opportunities for misconstruction and
misinterpretation afterwards instead of one.[19]

A great peace treaty seemed about to pass the Senate
without any protest more formal than the speeches of individual Senators. The dissenters thereupon took a leaf
from the objectors of another year and let it be known in
the press, on January 13, that 25 Senators had signed a
round robin demanding formal interpretation of the treaty.
This group would not be strong enough to defeat the treaty
but it was added that about 10 other Senators had expressed
themselves in sympathy with the statement, though they did

[19] Ibid., 1537.

not care to sign it. The names of the signers were not published, nor were they given to the Senate when the round robin was read by Senator Bingham to that body on the following day. Was there a suggestion here that some of the signers of the round robin of 1919 had regretted their action, or only recognition that the current round robin was likely to be more unpopular than the earlier one?

In any case its signature did not please President Coolidge, who called Senator Bingham into conference immediately and labored vainly in "an effort to dissuade him from advocating attaching an interpretative report to the treaty." [20] Like President Wilson, Mr. Coolidge was unable to see why the United States should be super-safeguarded against his peace treaty.

The Effect of Reservations Abroad. Senator Borah, also, was as concerned about the effect of the proceedings in the Senate upon foreign opinion as Mr. Wilson ever was. The sober mantle of responsibility hung somewhat more heavily upon him than the carefree cloak of criticism had in earlier years, though no one had been more open and fair in the previous contests than Mr. Borah. He had drawn up a report embodying his interpretation of the treaty, as requested, but when it was proposed to have it adopted by the Senate he "felt at once that that would result in what would be practically a reservation, and even if it was not technically so, the foreign governments would all regard it as a reservation." He felt, furthermore, that in fact it would be a reservation and so could not agree to it. He had "never been willing at any time to do anything that could be construed into a change of the treaty or constitute a reservation." Neither was he ever "willing to do that which could be represented abroad as a change or reservation."

He was not only opposed to any action of the Senate as a body that would cloud the ratification of the treaty abroad,

[20] N. Y. *Times,* January 14, 1929.

but he was keenly alive to the effect of even tentative proposals and rumors of reservations upon the other signatories to the treaty, all of whom, without exception, were waiting to see what the Senate would do with the pact before ratifying it themselves. Speaking of the proposal to have the Committee report not only adopted by the Senate but transmitted to the other governments, he said, "That thing alone has been used to our detriment abroad." It was true that the proposal was afterwards abandoned. But, he continued, "it is also true that before any of this happened the matter had gone to the public both here and in Europe and the situation was such that it was being construed as effectuating reservations through a report, and that is what caused the embarrassment. It has produced a serious situation."[21]

Evidently the attitude of the world toward Senate reservations to multilateral peace treaties had changed since 1920 when Senators had loudly assumed that the Covenant would be everywhere accepted with any changes they saw fit to make in it. Apparently, too, there was no longer the supreme disdain as to what other peoples might desire that there had been in the earlier year, for no Senator arose to proclaim that it was the Senate's job to make the thing wholly safe for the United States regardless of what anybody else thought about it.

Instead of the strident assertions of the former period Senator Robinson, of Arkansas, observed that "The mere fact that a newspaper—or some garrulous Senator, for that matter, if there be such a Senator (laughter), desiring to save his face and make it appear that he had won a gallant fight with odds against him—should circulate a story or give publicity to the declaration that the submission of a committee report constitutes reservations or qualifications of the treaty does not justify this body in wasting day after day over a subject about which there is no substantial differ-

[21] *Congressional Record,* Vol. 70, pp. 1717-19.

ence." For his part he was willing to give the Senator who wanted the report that gratification.

The demand for a report had been justified on the ground that it would protect the country from charges of bad faith in the future. This has grown to be the orthodox defense of Senators endeavoring to qualify multilateral treaties. It protects them, they feel, from the charge of bad faith in changing or limiting what the representatives of many nations, including our own, have agreed upon.

There is always the reasoning, too, that the Senate must make certain that the fundamental rights remain intact and undisturbed. To this claim, reiterated near the close of the debate, Senator Fess, of Ohio, replied, "Mr. President, I wish to observe that if anybody hopes that any statement can be made in language sufficiently clear so that 96 Senators will agree to it, I think it is a vain hope." He hoped the treaty would be ratified and "that any complicated or embarrassing interpretations that might cause its defeat or result in a charge of bad faith on our part in Europe" would be avoided.[22]

Senator Bingham thereupon read the statement to which twenty-five Senators had assented, saying: "We believe in the purposes and objectives of the Kellogg multilateral treaty. We believe that clarity of understanding regarding its inherent and declared functions is vital to its usefulness at home and abroad. To avoid reservations we believe the Foreign Relations Committee should report its official interpretation."

The Committee Report. When presented with this notice the majority leaders capitulated and the next day Senator Borah brought in the desired report. Practically every Senator had promised privately not to move the adoption of the report and no one did. It first defined the treaty as a pledge not to resort to war "save in bona fide self-defense."

[22] Ibid., 1719, 1724.

It was added, however, that each nation was "the sole judge of what constitutes the right of self-defense and the necessity and extent of the same." The United States Navy and marines might thus continue to protect American lives and property abroad as before.

Including the Monroe Doctrine as a part of our national security and defense, a series of definitions of it were given which tended to reduce it to a principle of self defense and nothing more. The original statement of President Monroe was about the broadest one quoted. It said: "It is impossible that the allied powers should extend their political system to any portion of either continent without endangering our peace and safety." The reader was left to understand that "the allied powers" meant the great autocracies of 1823, all of which have ceased to exist. The statement of President Cleveland seemed also to point back to the earlier period rather than to the future when it was said that the Doctrine was "essential to the integrity of our free institutions and the tranquil maintenance of our distinct form of government." The despotic powers threatening armed conquest of American lands are not evident upon the horizon of 1929, though they may be somewhere beyond it.

Nevertheless, milder statements of the Doctrine were probably difficult to find before 1900 and that of Elihu Root made in 1914 expressly declared that it rested on no basis other than the safety of the United States. Professor Theodore Woolsey in the same year had grounded it upon the same principle and had added "Whenever it oversteps the principle of self-defense, reasonably interpreted, the right disappears and the policy is questionable, because it then violates the rights of others."

Altogether the definitions of the Monroe Doctrine selected by Mr. Borah were distinctly liberal, so much so as to fall, probably, considerably short of the desires of some of the reservationists.

Two following paragraphs stated as strongly as words could that there was no obligation express or implied to engage in punitive or coercive measures against a nation violating the treaty. The only effect of violation admitted was that it would take the offender "from under the benefits of the treaty and relieve other nations from any treaty relationship with the said power." The phrase "from any treaty relationship" was perhaps one of the phrases of the interpretative report that would need to be interpreted in the future. The words obviously meant to relieve the nations from any treaty relationship under the Pact, but they are broad enough to cover the denunciation of all existing treaties with the offending nation, a course which future Senators are likely to demand, for no possible meanings are overlooked by them in construing our international rights and duties.

The final stipulation said: "This treaty in no respect changes or qualifies our present position or relation to any pact or treaty existing between other nations or governments." This statement was as mild as anyone could have written. It made the usual disclaimer without even mentioning the name of the League and there was no suggestion whatever of the good fortune of the United States in being free from such a questionable institution or of resentment toward it. Ten years time had both softened the feelings against the League and established it to such an extent that one wondered whether the disavowal of any relationship with it might not soon cease to be made at all.

The treaty having been duly interpreted to everybody's partial satisfaction at least, the Committee closed its report with the declaration that "This report is made solely for the purpose of putting upon record what your committee understands to be the true interpretation of the treaty, and not in any sense for the purpose or with the design of modifying or changing the treaty in any way or effectuating a reservation or reservations to the same." [23]

Thus were reservations made with apologies and in such a form, indeed, that they were not reservations at all, nor even an official expression of opinion on the part of the Senate. They would constitute, however, a possible defense against charges that we violated the treaty in the future and they permitted some Senators to feel that they had discharged their function as the preserver of the country's fundamental liberties.

Approval Voted. Following the reading of the Committee report the treaty was approved by a vote of 85 to 1, on January 15, 1929. Compared with the League of Nations and World Court debates this one was short, lasting only two weeks.

Does the brevity of the debate together with the failure to attach any reservations to the Pact indicate a new tendency on the part of the Senate to refrain from altering great international peace treaties? Perhaps, to a degree. It must be borne in mind, however, that this treaty provided for no action on the part of the United States. If it had done so the amendments and reservations offered by the preservers of "the traditional policies of the United States" and by the defenders of the Senate's power over treaties would doubtless have been many and varied.

[23] *Congressional Record,* Vol. 70, p. 1783.

CHAPTER XII

SOME CONCLUSIONS ON THE LEGISLATIVE CONTROL OF
TREATIES

As noted early in Chapter IV the number of treaties rejected by the Senate has not been quantitatively large. Have the results of the treaties failing in the Senate been correspondingly negligible? It will hardly be contended that they have. The contrary proposition that the results have been out of all proportion to the number of rejections is more likely to be accepted.

Whether the results have been more good than bad will depend, of course, somewhat upon the temperament and views of the person replying to that question. One who has little belief in the causes that have met defeat in the Senate, or an antipathy toward the men identified with them, will see little harm flowing from the failure of the treaties killed by the Senate. He may even feel the Senate's role to have been genuinely conservative. On the other hand, a student who sympathizes with the chief measures rejected by the Senate, and the men who stood for them, may conclude that the checks to progress resulting have been of fundamental importance.

Opinions will vary as to the responsibility for and results of the failure of the treaties for the suppression of the slave trade with Great Britain in 1824 and Colombia in 1825. One may believe either that the Senate erred in proposing unnecessary amendments or that the British Government mistakenly refused to agree to the withdrawing of concessions which the American Government never should have made. Whichever be true, long years of controversy resulted from which the slave traders, at least, profited largely.

Certainly no blame for the failure to solve the Panama Canal problem can be laid on the American Senate. The treaties of 1869 and 1870 with Colombia were rejected by the Colombian Congress, with the result that it was later "necessary" for our Government to guarantee a revolution in Panama that would give us the canal, all sovereign rights of Colombia to the contrary notwithstanding.

The repeated defeat of the Convention for Reopening and Retrying the claims of Benjamin Weil and the La Abra Mining Company against Mexico by a minority of the Senate undoubtedly perpetuated a great fraud which had been engineered at the expense of Mexico.

Evidence that the claimants exercised effective pressure on the Senate is lacking, but there can be no doubt that the Gadsden Purchase treaty, which was rewritten by the Senate, was long at the mercy of a bitter contest between the two groups of speculators, the Garay and Sloo companies, who were fighting over the right to build a railroad over the Mexican isthmus. The Garay group managed to influence the negotiation of the treaty, but the Sloo grantees won in the Senate, with the result that "The Gadsden Treaty immediately became the basis for new diplomatic issues between the two nations, and it proved a failure as an instrument for a better relationship between the sister republics, and a definitive settlement of the Mexican questions." [1]

---

[1] These are the final conclusions of the Doctoral dissertation written by Mr. P. E. Garber, *The Gadsden Treaty*, University of Pennsylvania Press, 1923. Some of his further conclusions are that the treaty had no direct connection with the expansion of the institution of slavery and that it would have been neither negotiated nor accepted by the Mexican Government of Santa Anna except for its dire need of money and for fear of war with the United States. The money received was squan-

The opposition to the Gadsden Treaty included eleven Northern Senators who opposed it throughout on the ground that it would increase slave holding territory, if only in small degree. Similar feeling caused the defeat of the treaty for the annexation of Texas in 1844, together with the unpopularity of President Tyler. This rejection had small result, however, since Texas came into the Union in 1845, by joint resolution of Congress.

The defeat of Secretary Seward's proposed annexation of the Danish Islands in the West Indies did not prove so easily rectified. The failure of the treaty left us in an awkward position since we would not wish to let them fall into the hands of another great power, yet refused them ourselves. This became more acutely true after the building of the Panama Canal so that finally we carried through a treaty with Denmark during the Great War whereby we acquired the islands for $25,000,000.

The failure of President Grant's Dominican Annexation Treaty seems better justified in view of the much greater ethnic and administrative problems involved. There may be some who feel that annexation would have been preferable to the protectorates we have exercised over this island since, but it would appear difficult to substantiate this view.

Similarly the defeat of several extradition treaties has not had important consequences and the same might be said of the numerous reciprocity treaties vetoed by the Senate. From the position of those who believe that all protective tariff duties are good this will be true. It appears probable, however, that the mutual lowering of duties and admission of goods which these treaties provided for would have benefited the country as a whole. The fact that three of the greatest Republican exponents of protection, Blaine, McKinley and Roosevelt, made themselves responsible for

---

dered at once and the people of Mexico received no benefit from the treaty.

them would seem to be sufficient evidence of their advantage to the nation.

THE SENATE RETARDS UNDULY THE PEACEABLE ADJUSTMENT OF INTERNATIONAL RELATIONS

To the writer it seems clear that the greatest losses from the negative action of the Senate, both from the standpoint of national interest and from that of better international relations, have undoubtedly resulted from the slowness of the Senate to accept machinery for the peaceable settlement of international disputes. This may not be a surprising conclusion when one remembers that the principal object of treaties is to adjust international relations in an orderly fashion. This conclusion, moreover, will not be shared by those who believe that, destructive as it may appear at times, the Senate does well to hold us far back from a position of leadership in organizing international relations. It must be recognized that time and experience may show that the nations generally will not submit to law without further periods of bloodshed and that we should remain free to protect our interests in future great wars as we see fit. In the interim it may possibly prove to be wise to put small trust in the arbitral or judicial settlement of disputes.

From the view of the present, however, it seems apparent that the negative action of the Senate upon measures designed to secure the peaceable settlement of international disputes has had the effect of leaving us in a highly equivocal position to say the least. Furthermore, the fact that a large part of the Senate's activity in this connection has been motivated by a desire to extend its own power over our foreign relations, as they expand in importance, rather than to hamper international intercourse, does not alter the situation, though it largely explains it.

The rejection of bilateral arbitration treaties by the Senate has not often led to serious situations, though in two cases dangerous disputes were aggravated and prolonged. The failure of the Johnson-Clarendon Treaty of 1869 for the settlement of our claims against Great Britain growing out of the Civil War aggravated a tense state of feeling which might readily have led to war if the Senate's temper had existed in the other parts of the two governments. We were fortunate that soberer counsel eventually made the Geneva arbitration possible.

Likewise the Senate's refusal of the Canadian Fisheries Treaty of 1888 served only to embitter and prolong a dispute which had been settled honorably and fairly. The dispute consequently continued another twenty years before it was finally arbitrated by a Hague tribunal, in 1910, on substantially the terms of the treaty of 1888. [2]

The Senate's attitude toward general arbitration treaties has surely had the effect of placing us at the tail of the procession of nations advancing toward the judicial settlement of international disputes. Much of the stimulus and brains of that movement have been supplied by individual American statesmen and publicists, but the Senate for thirty years after 1897 consistently refused to permit any appreciable advance in the development of arbitration. The League of Nations and other post-war peace movements brought about a great increase in the number of arbitration treaties among the rest of the civilized nations, and a steady widening of their scope, but the United States remained quite isolated from this forward movement.

From 1910 to the middle of 1927 some 160 treaties of arbitration and conciliation were concluded, yet the United States was a party to only two, namely one with Liberia and one with Sweden. [3] Most of these treaties came after the War, and omitted the old phrases that made them largely

---

[2] W. F. Johnson, *America's Foreign Relations*, II, 331. Compare with President Cleveland's message of February 23, 1888, given in Chapter IV above.

[3] J. W. Garner, *American Foundation Bulletin No. 3*, June 30, 1927.

gestures, but until the Kellogg-Briand treaty of 1928 the United States remained entrenched behind "vital interests, independence or national honor." The dropping of these expansive prohibitions is a real gain, even though it comes years after the rest of the world has abandoned them. But who can foretell when the Senate will give up its insistence upon scrutinizing the *compromis* of each arbitration case? Until it does so we can never really agree to arbitrate even the narrowest class of disputes; we merely agree that after a dispute has reached the point where diplomacy cannot settle it the Senate will consider whether to arbitrate it or not. If the dispute is of sufficient importance to arouse the feelings of any vocal minority of our people the reader of these pages may judge as to what assurance of arbitration any of our arbitration treaties gives. We can be quite certain that the Senate will approve the *compromis* when it is reasonably sure that we shall win the proposed arbitration, but what will it do when our case is questionable, or when it is so bad that we are almost sure to lose? And how could law ever be established among the nations if all of them used it only to gain advantages? The great purpose of law, civil or international, is not to satisfy all disputants but to settle disputes without violence.

The Soundness of the Rejected Principles Proved by World Adoption. In the meantime, the world goes on using the principles and formulas developed by American statesmen, and rejected by the Senate, in building its arbitration system, its Locarnos, its World Court and its League of Nations. Primarily it is the distinction made by the Taft treaties of 1911, with the Bryan additions, that is the backbone of the movement which has transformed the policy of the nations since the War. [4] These ideas, crystallized dur-

---

[4] Denys P. Myers, "America Lost Leader of World Peace," *Independent,* January 21, 1928, Vol. 120, pp. 57-58. See also *World Peace Foundation Pamphlets,* "Arbitration and the United States," 1926, Vol. 9, Nos. 6-7.

ing the War, were gathered together into Article 12 of the Covenant of the League of Nations which says: "The members of the League agree that, if there should arise between them any dispute likely to lead to a rupture, they will submit the matter either to arbitration or judicial settlement or to judicial inquiry by the Council and they agree in no case to resort to war until three months after the results are known."

The acceptance of this obligation by more than nine-tenths of the nations certainly took the novelty from such engagements. States decided to provide for arbitration in advance of being compelled to submit to it. Consequently, Norway, Sweden, Denmark, Germany, France, Switzerland, many of the Latin American States, Persia, Siam and sundry others are making arbitration agreements with their neighbors without any limits as to jurisdiction. Sixty such bilateral treaties have been made since 1919 providing for the settlement by arbitration, conciliation or judicial settlement of all disputes whatsoever.[5]

Short of this binding and unequivocal outlawing of war, Germany, Great Britain and twenty-six other states, by ratifying the optional clause of the Court statute, have given that body complete jurisdiction over all classes of legal disputes concerning "the interpretation of a treaty, any question of internationl law, the existence of any fact which, if established, would constitute a breach of an international obligation, and the nature or extent of the reparation to be made for such a breach." [6]

[5] Ibid. Only Colombia and Switzerland have agreed to send all their disputes to the Court without any attempts at arbitration or conciliation.

Mr. Myers' conclusion that "The Senate has always been for arbitration when it was up for academic discussion, and has regularly mustered votes against it when it was the actual issue" would doubtless be modified by the ready acceptance of the Kellogg series to the extent that that event indicates a different attitude of mind.

[6] These nations are: Austria, Belgium, Brazil, Bulgaria, China, Costa Rica, Denmark, Dominican Republic, Esthonia, Ethiopia, Finland, Germany, Great Britain, Guatemala, Haiti, Latvia, Liberia, Lithuania Luxem-

The reader has no doubt formed his own conclusion as to the wisdom of the Senate's action in prescribing the terms of our entry into the Court. He may feel that some sinister machination or malevolent purpose among the powers justifies the asking of the veto which the Senate has demanded. He may even feel that in the absence of any such conspiracy simple caution and the desire for "equality" in an organized world justify the demands.

Whatever the conclusion may be, while we are waiting for that assurance of complete safety and perfect equality which some Senators must have, the world moves rapidly ahead, developing machinery for the peaceable settlement of disputes in advance of the time when they shall occur. It does not wait on even its greatest nation but builds both international law and international relations around the Court and the League.

As early as 1923 some fifty treaties existed providing for the reference to the Court in some manner of disputes arising under the treaties. Only five years later, more than 200 such treaties had been made, the signatories including practically all the nations on the globe except Mexico, the United States and Soviet Russia. In view of these matters of fact the conclusion does not seem overdrawn that "it is difficult to see how the United States can take a constructive part in the development of treaty relations with the rest of the world if it continues to ignore the Court to which the rest of the world is intrusting the final disposition of its international relations." [7] Furthermore, becoming a

---

burg, Netherlands, Norway, Panama, Portugal, Salvador, Sweden, Switzerland, and Uruguay. *American Foundation Bulletin* No. 6, April 10, 1928; *Literary Digest,* September 14, 1929, Vol. 102, No. 11, p. 12.

[7] It is equally difficult to see how it can be done by the making of negative promises only. The campaign of the nations to limit war is a cooperative one. It could not exist without some positive obligations. If we still refuse to bear any burdens whatever it may well develop that the only result of our effort to enter the Court has been to partially cover our failure to join the League, and the result of the effort to outlaw war to

member of the Court will not alter our situation greatly unless we make treaty provision for sending our disputes to it.

Just how keenly the situation is recognized by the American people is a question, but there is recurring evidence that their leaders are uneasy. Out of the world's great need a system for the orderly settlement of all kinds of international disputes has been developed. The rest of the world trusts it and seems likely to continue to use it "with increasing frequency and growing faith."

Are We to Assist or Oppose the League? The results of our abstention from the greatest of all efforts to organize the world against war—the League of Nations itself— cannot yet be wholly estimated. If a weakening of prejudices and the force of our interests bring us into the League system before another great war is due, or if the League unaided is able to establish a stable world, the results will be by no means as calamitous as they will be if we drift ultimately into a position of permanent hostility to the League.

The probabilities may not be confined to this alternative. It may be that we can stand aside uninterested, neither actively sympathetic nor hostile, while the great experiment is being worked out. Pursuing such a course it may be, as many aver, that if a major threat against the world's peace develops we will unerringly throw our might behind the League, save it and restore the peace. This third development may occur. Yet who can say that we would have gone into the Great War if our commerce had not been attacked? Who can say that the Germans could not have won the War without bringing us into it by unrestricted submarine warfare, if on two critical days counsel had taken a little different turn in Berlin? In that event

cover partially our failure to enter the Court. If this proves true, what must be said of our statesmanship as dominated by the Senate?

there would be no League of Nations to which we might give support. Or who can say even that we would not have decided the War in favor of the Germans if the Allies had happened to interfere with our Commerce the more ruthlessly? We had some grave moments with them as it was.

Any thoughtful answer to these queries must cast doubts upon our always pursuing the rôle of the righteous judge unswerved by the play of circumstances and undeterred by the weight of inertia or minority protest. Surely the responsible statesmen of the League states cannot predict with assurance or safety what our free and irresponsible will or the defense of our trade may lead us to do. The League members know that we have entered the last two world wars on the side that interfered with our commerce the most. We also at times give signs of building a navy which can dominate the seas.

What are we going to do with our power if the League finds itself compelled to blockade an aggressor nation? This question is sometimes solved of late on this side of the water by denying that an aggressor can be defined. But granted that the League acts upon its own definition, what attitude will we take? Will we insist that our commerce go through the blockade and thus make it ineffective? This is by no means a light matter to the naval powers in the League, especially in view of the repeated evidence we have given that our excursions into international "politics" can be predicted with no certainty.

Will Negative Assurances Discharge Our Duty? As a step toward removing this distinctly paralyzing doubt from the minds of the League members Dr. Nicholas Murray Butler has proposed that we say to Great Britain, to France, to Italy, to Germany and to Japan, that is, to the great League powers, "If you find yourselves under obligation, either as members of the League of Nations or as signatories of the pact of Locarno, to establish a blockade against an aggressor nation as defined, we shall accept your good faith, and shall ourselves respect that blockade, with the proviso that no such blockade shall be effected against any nation on the Western Hemisphere." [8]

Even with the rather large reservation of territory at the close of this suggestion the step proposed would be of great importance in preventing us from paralyzing or frustrating the action of the League to keep the peace. We assume no positive responsibility under it, but how long can, or should, the most powerful nation of all continue to assume no responsibility for the peace? Can there be any true neutrals in the effort to organize the world for peace? Is not the saying of the great Peacemaker that "He who is not for Me is against Me" applicable to the business of organizing the peace?

But, say those desiring to uphold our foreign policy as framed in the Senate, "We do not believe in organizing the peace; nations must not be organized for anything. We will renounce war for ourselves, and when all others do so, nothing more is necessary," and this reasoning so far controls us.

We take the position of relying on organization to accomplish every conceivable purpose until we come to the greatest task of all—establishing the peace. In any American village there are dozens of organizations working to accomplish stated ends, schools, clubs, churches, etc. In any American city there are literally hundreds of organizations set to accomplish every sort of objective from almsgiving to hi-jacking. The typical state of the American Union contains scores of state wide organizations with thousands of federated or subordinate units which wield influence in proportion to their numbers. These are not enough, however, for the national area is covered by hundreds of organizations which bring to bear weight of all

[8] New York *Times,* April 23, 1928.

the undertakers, or teachers, or manufacturers, or what not, upon the problems of the group.

Yet the tens of thousands of permanent organizations working in the United States, the names of which alone would fill a volume, are not enough. We annually create yet other thousands of temporary organizations to accomplish limited objectives. We organize a drive a week in the average city for some purpose or other. As a people, in short, we positively worship organization. We do not attempt to do anything without it and the bigger the job the bigger the organization.

The same thing is true also of the world's work. As Americans we participate in hundreds of unofficial international organizations and in many official ones, such as the International Postal Union. We put our faith in organization to accomplish any and all objectives until we come to the greatest problem of all—the problem of world peace. Then we stop and say, "No, we refuse to trust any organization for world peace. We will renounce war ourselves and when all other men get peace in their hearts, then we shall have peace!"

The unorganized city or state or nation is ineffective, if not helpless, or chaotic—in fact it is impossible. How long will we maintain that the nations must solve their greatest and oldest problem without instituting any effective organization for the purpose?

The superiority of the new method of collective international action over the old way of haphazard agreement is strikingly shown by considering that the effect of the acceptance by twenty-six states of the obligatory jurisdiction of the Court for certain classes of justiciable disputes is the same as if 351 bilateral treaties had been concluded for the same purpose. Again, the obligation of Article 12 of the Covenant, which is the power house back of the current arbitration movement, has the effect of 1485 bilateral treaties. [9]   It would take that number of treaties to provide the same amount of agreement. How long would we have had to wait for them to be signed one at a time?

The conclusion is difficult to escape that the inhibitions set up by the contest over the League of Nations, and still perpetuated in the Senate, have seriously delayed in the United States the change of mind which must accompany a world diminishing daily in size and increasing hourly in international contacts. Consequently we have refused to recognize that "The rule of law—the peace and quiet and justice and fair play—which are essential to the fulfillment of the purposes of individual human lives, can no longer be guaranteed by separate governments with no authority outside small geographical areas—governments, moreover, accustomed to behave like masters who maintain splendid order and discipline within their workshops and then feel free to go out and racket in the streets. The rule of law is becoming a question of all or none." [10]

The spread of the Industrial Revolution to new countries and its further development in the older lands brings home this realization to more people every year. Eventually we shall not need to be reminded that when the raw materials which we use in our daily work come from the ends of the earth and our very livelihood depends on the ability of distant peoples to buy what we produce the stability of the international order must be maintained. [11]

Due to our fortunate economic position this realization is not now so widespread in the United States as it will be as we become ever more industrialized. Our statesmen understand that war in an industrialized world means the bankruptcy and collapse of governments, the wiping out of

[9] D. P. Myers, *Independent,* Vol. 120, pp. 57–8.
[10] J. C. Maxwell Garnett, in *Problems of Peace,* Oxford, 1927, pp. 344–5.
[11] See the stimulating exposition of this development by James T. Shotwell in the New York *Times,* Sunday, April 22, 1928.

whole classes of people and the impoverishment of the masses; our politicians still preach a self-sufficiency which multitudes of insular Americans would like to believe can be maintained.

THE POWER OF SENATORS TO OBSTRUCT TREATIES SHOULD BE REDUCED

To Americans hoping to remain isolated from world politics and to others of generally conservative tendencies, the stoppage in the Senate of our efforts to cooperate and unite with the nations of the world is a good thing. To others no less patriotic and no less desirous of advancing the power and glory and influence of their country the constitutional provision which puts it in the power of a rather small minority of the Senate to paralyze any proposed association with the nations is little short of a calamity. To them it leaves us impotent to adapt ourselves to a rapidly changing world, much less lead it. "A body of ninety-six men," says former Attorney General G. W. Wickersham, "of such diverse characteristics and opinions as the members of the Senate is almost hopeless as an executive force. But it is ideal for the purposes of obstruction." [12]

To the complacent isolationist the constitutional provision giving one-third of the Senators plus one the right to veto or alter any treaty is one of those wise, far seeing flashes of wisdom that make "the fathers" immortal forever. To others it is the greatest mistake in the Constitution, the one that has cost us the most and the one that will be hardest to eliminate. Indeed most people doubtless feel that it is all but hopeless to expect the Constitution ever to be modified in this particular. Because, therefore, a dozen men in the days of the sailing vessel and the ox cart thought that

[12] "The Senate and Foreign Relations," *Foreign Affairs*, December 15, 1923, Vol. 2, p. 192.

international agreements should be few and difficult to make must we ever remain in the days of air travel and television —and beyond—at the mercy of any determined group of men in the Senate who happen to decide to block the way of progress?

It may be that because arbitrary monarchs were hated and feared before 1789 we must continue to conduct our foreign relations under a leadership which always tends to become two headed and antagonistic within itself whenever a real issue of foreign policy is to be settled by agreement. It may be that we must permanently reconcile ourselves to conflict and the blocking of action whenever we have a strong President and to inactivity and the attempt of the Senate actually to dictate foreign policy when we have weak Presidents. It may be that we must permanently leave it in the power of a handful of men representing perhaps a single racial minority or powerful economic interest, or a few thinly settled states—or a combination of such restricted interests—to nullify the efforts of the President, representing the whole people, to advance their interests.

It must be granted at once that a constitutional amendment to reduce the power of the Senate to obstruct treaties is not now within the limits of practical politics—but neither was the popular election of Senators for many years. The Senate resisted that reform until a long campaign compelled its submission. It will take even longer no doubt to lead the Senate to modify its power over treaties.

Recognizing the great difficulty of achieving such a change, many students who agree as to its desirability feel that it is wiser to urge upon the Senate and the President the necessity of getting together and agreeing than it is to advocate an impractical constitutional change. This view harmonizes with the undoubted fact that conventions and ways of doing things grow up about any rigid constitution which get around its restrictions. Yet the need for a method of approving treaties that is less subject to deadlock seems likely to become greater rather than less as the need for international agreement and unity grows. When our treaties were few, bilateral and limited in scope, obstruction did not often occur in the Senate and when it did its effects were not often far reaching. It was possible for Story to say after half a century of experience with the Constitution, "It is difficult to perceive how the treaty-making power could have been better deposited, with a view to safety and efficiency."[13]

As the necessity for international adjustments increased, as points of friction multiplied and the necessity of settling them grew, the number of rejections in the Senate increased also, as perhaps might have been expected, but the need was for exactly the opposite development—a readier acquiescence in creating the processes and methods of agreement. It was, however, not strange that an important American diplomat, Mr. John W. Foster, should feel at the turn of the century, even after the arbitration and reciprocity treaties of Cleveland, McKinley and Roosevelt had been killed in the Senate, that the two-thirds majority for treaty approval was an evidence of wise conviction on the part of the fathers that no stipulations with a foreign power should be entered into unless supported by a large majority of the American people. [14]

---

[13] Story, *On the Constitution* (Cooley Edition), 1873, p. 355.

[14] W. B. Munro, of Harvard University, has commended the Senate since 1919 as follows: "All things considered the Senate has not abused its power or used it arbitrarily. There is something to be said for reducing the two-thirds vote to a mere majority in the case of treaties, but the arguments in favor of this change are not convincing. The present plan is not working badly. It has at least saved the United States from some serious mistakes, for example, the San Domingo Treaty of 1869, which would have annexed this territory and added to the nation's troubles. On the whole it is wise to let well enough alone." *Current Problems in Citizenship*, N. Y., 1924, p. 493.

The San Domingo case is perhaps the clearest example of a treaty that should have been rejected. The two-thirds majority was, however, not necessary to save us from that error. The treaty did not command a simple majority.

His further conclusion that experience had, in the main, justified giving the Senate a share of the treaty making power would be generally granted, though his opinion that the Senators generally forsook partisan considerations and considered treaties in a high spirit of patriotism might be questioned.[15]

Party Strife No Longer Stops at the Ocean. Certainly in the twenty years since Mr. Foster wrote, partisanship has ceased to stop at the water's edge. During most of the period it has hardly even halted at the ocean. It exercised no visible restraint on the campaign to destroy President Taft politically which was chiefly responsible for the mutilation of the Taft arbitration treaties. To accomplish their purpose the Senators and the politicians back of them did not hesitate at all to attack his treaties and defeat them regardless of the beneficent ends in view or of the feelings of foreign powers.

A little later, when a President of the opposite party was to be destroyed, his bitter partisan and personal enemies were never deterred for a moment in seeking to frustrate and defeat him in the field of foreign policy.[16] They exerted every influence at their command to try to determine how he should conduct the negotiations and from where, who his negotiators should be and what they should attempt. Failing to deter him at the start they warned him not to follow the supreme aim of his diplomacy and not only him but the Peace Conference itself was warned that no League of Nations must be created.

Failing to heed the warning the Conference was admonished again and again from the platform of the Senate in an effort to swing it against the American President who led it. At one high point in this effort an ultimatum was

[15] J. W. Foster, *The Practice of Diplomacy*, N. Y., 1906, pp. 263 and 283.

[16] It is not meant to include in this category, by any means, all those who came to oppose the League of Nations.

signed by more than a third of the Senators warning both Conference and President to desist. When they still persevered the campaign continued with increasing bitterness for four months, culminating in a final effort to scotch the League in the Conference just before it signed the treaty and adjourned.

While granting the right of every citizen to oppose any foreign policy which he believes detrimental to his country we can never doubt again that partisanship is likely to follow the flag wherever it goes, no matter how high or sacred its errand.

This is the chief vice of the two-thirds requirement for treaties. It puts practically every administration at the mercy of its political enemies in making treaties. It almost never happens that either of our parties gets a two-thirds majority. Even the anti-Wilson landslide of 1920 did not give it. Most of the time the parties are almost evenly balanced in the Senate, and the minority only needs the promise of reasonable political capital to make the conclusion of the most beneficent treaties impossible.

Minority Control Tends to Increase. But the difficulty goes deeper than that. The two-thirds requirement not only puts it in the power of the opposing party to sabotage our treaties if it thinks the policy will pay in winning the votes of certain states or minority groups, but it enables a small faction of the Senators to dominate the Senate and the country when a crucial treaty is proposed. The group may be composed of a dozen confirmed radicals, or a handful of determined reactionaries, or, if a President has been long in office, of his personal enemies, men who have been crossed in previous political campaigns or disappointed over the distribution of patronage.

They may not be numerous, but if they are determined they can not only prolong consideration of the treaty while passions and prejudices and fears are aroused in various quarters of the country, but they can so intimidate the majority that damaging concessions will be given them out of fear that they may wean away just a few votes from the pro-treaty side and gain the necessary third of the Senate. Some Senators are sure to be uneasy about the effect of the continued fulminations on their constituents, and they may at any time decide that it would be easier to vote for the proposed amendment than to explain to the folks at home why it was unnecessary or inadvisable.

The power of a small number of men to imperil a treaty or kill it by amendments is further augmented by the most powerful customs of the Senate. The practice of "Senatorial Courtesy" has grown to the point where any Senator can hold up consideration of a measure if it affects "my state." The favor is usually granted as a matter of course. And unless a treaty is of great importance the fact that any Senator does not want it passed is a real consideration. The tendency of each Senator to become a sovereign is such that his wishes are by no means to be ignored. If he objects to a vote the vote must wait until the Senate reluctantly brings itself to adopt closure. It is likely to attempt to persuade him privately and publicly for days before it does so, and when several Senators are in the group the reluctance is intensified.

Thus our treaty ceding the Isle of Pines to Cuba was held up in the Senate for 21 years not because it lacked Executive endorsement—it was urged by President after President—nor yet because the Senate Foreign Relations Committee smothered it—it was favorably reported many times—but because some Senator representing the American sugar planters on the island demanded further consideration or requested an additional committee of investigation. [17]

[17] See New York *Times* editorial, February 27, 1925. Objections prevented a vote at the close of that session of Congress, and the matter went over again.

On January 24, 1926, the *Times* said of the tendencies of the Senate:

This is an extreme example, but it is symptomatic of the influence a single Senator, representing himself alone, or some financial interest, may have upon an international engagement entered into in good faith by the Executive Department of the United States Government. It certainly does not "contribute to National influence or prestige or safety that the process of ratifying or rejecting treaties should degenerate into an effort to discover some qualifying formula acceptable to a minority." [18] The abolition of the two-thirds majority would not of course destroy this dangerous tendency, but it would check it.

The Senate Can Defeat Treaties With Impunity. Furthermore, the step would bring the Senate into a little closer touch with the popular will. As it is the position of the Senate in opposing treaties is impregnable. The people cannot reach it. They may be strongly in favor of a treaty, but they can change at most only a third of the Senate in any election. If a simple majority could ratify treaties it might be possible to swing the balance over in one election. Under the present practice it can rarely be done in less than two elections, and how often can Senators be punished for

---

"For years the rules, or lack of rules, of the Senate, have tended to exalt the importance and privileges of the individual Senator. If he is only obstinate enough, rude enough, remorseless enough, he can, especially if he is able to get up a combination with others like-minded, hold up the proceedings of the Senate and impose his will upon the larger number. It is plain that this process could not have been going on for a long time, as it has been, without bringing forward a class of Senators who appear to be headstrong, willful, domineering, and utterly unreasonable. But they, on their part, have come to think that they are merely exercising the rights of a Senator. They presume upon the courtesy of the Senate to be discourteous. They have long been bred to the idea of dictating, and so they proceed to tell the Senate and the country what legislation they will permit and what they will veto. It cannot be said that they are bad men, but they are certainly bad Senators. They do more than anybody else to bring into disrepute the very body to which they belong, and which they profess to honor."

[18] Quoted from the Presidential Address of Mr. John W. Davis to the American Bar Association in 1923. G. W. Wickersham, "The Senate and Foreign Relations," *Foreign Affairs*, December 15, 1923, Vol. 2, p. 190.

narrow or personal action on a treaty after the lapse of four years?

In the campaign of 1920 Mr. Taft urged that the best way to forward American entry into the League was to vote for Republicans on the ground that holdover Republican Senators would still block entry into the League even if there were a Democratic sweep in the elections. [19] The appeal seems a strange one but it was based on a good deal of reality. And the possibility of entry into the League by the Republican route existed only because enough Democratic Senators were so strongly committed to the League that the two-thirds majority would be made up if the bulk of the Republicans could be brought into agreement.

EXPERIENCE SUGGESTS THE TRANSFER OF THE POWER TO THE HOUSE

The position of the Senate is so secure in resisting pressure in favor of treaty ratification, indeed, and it is so likely to become intolerant of attempts to move it toward the approval of treaties, that former Governor S. W. McCall, of Massachusetts, has proposed that the power to approve treaties be taken away from the Senate entirely and given to the House of Representatives. [20] Then it would be possible for the real wishes of the American people with regard to an important treaty to be indicated in a single election, before other issues and events completely covered the question up.

The very existence of such a possibility, even though imperfectly realized, would be of tremendous assistance to us in our efforts to find our place in a shrinking and organized world. Such a change should be approved by

[19] S. W. McCall, "Again the Senate," *Atlantic Monthly*, September, 1920, Vol. 126, p. 395.
[20] Ibid., p. 402.

all those who really believe in the popular control of foreign relations. Many who profess this belief really do not have it. What they want is oligarchical control, group control, minority control. Such control in the Senate therefore suits them well and they extol it as a gift of democracy to the American people and to the world.

The Qualities Expected of the Senate Have Not Developed. The original arguments advanced in 1789 in favor of giving the Senate the treaty power have ceased to have any real validity. The House was excluded from the treaty function then because "accurate and comprehensive knowledge of foreign politics; a steady and systematic adherence to the same views; a nice and uniform sensibility to national character; decision secrecy and despatch, are incompatible with the genius of a body so variable and so numerous." [21]

Of all these points in which the Senate would be supposedly superior, the matter of secrecy was made the most of. Yet there never was much of it in the Senate and for many years there has been none at all, except that the exact language the Senators used in debates was not officially quoted. But now that the Senators have given up this privilege in the case of the two most important treaty considerations in our history in order to use the Senate as a forum from which to attack the treaties, the advantage of secrecy can no longer be claimed for the Senate, even if secrecy had not become positively undesirable. Nor can the Senate defend the imputation to it of decision and despatch; the House is distinctly more noted for these qualities.

Further, "accurate and comprehensive knowledge of foreign politics" is at least as likely to be found in the House as in the Senate. Of the League of Nations debates of

[21] "Publius" in *The Federalist*, No. 74 (Dawson's Edition), N. Y., 1867, p. 523.

1919–1920 Professor Lindsay Rogers says: "It was literally true that the strength of convictions and the length of speeches were directly proportional to the ignorance and tyrociny of Senators in foreign politics. Too many Senators made addresses based on the knowledge of a mediocre college undergraduate, increased by resort to a couple of war books and the Encyclopedia Britannica, and presented with the argumentative skill of the average lawyer. This will be evident to anyone with sufficient leisure to read the speeches in the Senate debate. . . Senatorial imaginings were uncurbed; terrible threats to American institutions were discovered—threats, it may be added, which were not peculiar in their application to the United States, and which, strange to relate, were not discovered in foreign parliaments. The art of imagining dire possibilities if American isolation is abandoned was so successfully nurtured in the League debates of 1919 that more horrendous international goblins were seen in the World Court proposals. These fears did not come from transitory Senatorial nightmares; the phobia was more serious. It results in part from ignorance of foreign politics and international relations, and from inexpertise in discussing them." [22]

The House would at least do no worse in handling treaties than the Senate has done from the standpoint of parochial and partisan speechmaking. Election to the House, too, does not seem to have the effect of making a man at the same time "more opinionated and more timorous."

Our Representatives Less Bound By Legalism. The same writer is also of the opinion that the members of the House of Representatives are much less intensely legalistic than the Senators. If this be true, as seems probable, it is one of the strongest reasons that could be advanced for turning the scrutiny of the treaties over to the Representatives.

[22] Lindsay Rogers, *The American Senate*, Knopf, N. Y., 1926, pp. 73-4. Reprinted by permission of the publishers.

Whether because the House members are more often non-lawyers or because they do not get so used to interpreting everything by some written rule of Constitution or law the chances of securing a greater reliance upon good sense and less upon rigid legislative methods are worth careful scrutiny. The limitations of the Senatorial mind in this respect are serious. Words mean everything to many of them.

The Senators, "habituated to legalistic manoeuvers, want nothing left to the good sense of a World Court, a League Council or anyone else, even the President. The provisions governing advisory opinions must be written in treaties; illegality, rather than impropriety being relied upon to prevent the Court from usurping the authority and extending its jurisdiction. That a body like the World Court, with its future utility dependent on its own wisdom and discretion, would be restrained by fear of acting improperly or unwisely is a consideration in which Senators find scant comfort. . . The Senatorial view is that liberties may suffer if good sense is relied upon and that they are unaffected by wars over words." [23]

It will not be denied that the original germ of popular control over foreign affairs is to be found in the giving of a check over treaties to the Senate, but the makers of the Constitution had no idea of establishing anything like real popular control. That was one reason why they denied the power to the House; they wanted to keep it in select hands, as far removed from the people as possible. So they entrusted our good name and reputation to a minority of the Senate and gave us no way to make the popular will effective upon it. The "irreparable mistake" [24] of the Constitution was coupled with its most fundamental omission.

[23] *The American Senate*, pp. 75–6.
[24] The phrase is Secretary John Hay's.

The Senate Has Balked Our Best Statesmanship. The result of the irreparable mistake has been a long series of defeats and failures in our efforts to cooperate with the nations for the common good, broken only by an occasional advance by indirection, as in the case of the Bryan treaties and the Peace Pact, or a very tardy recognition of established world practice, as in the Kellogg arbitration treaties—all secured when the Senate was off guard or temporarily quiescent politically. The further result has been the amazed and reluctant conclusion on the part of the other civilized peoples that the American people are incapable of adopting a positive foreign policy or of carrying it through if one be temporarily indicated. Warned by premonitory deadlocks early in our history and again by an outbreak of hatreds after the Civil War that killed several treaties, they have seen our Executive struggle manfully to recognize the trend of the times, to help direct it or place us in harmony with it, and almost always at the end there have been long sustained and violent eruptions from some determined group in the Senate that paralyzed the effort and brought it to naught—except as other hands abroad took it up and carried it on.

The President, standing for advance along the path of orderly progress in international relations, might be Republican or he might be Democratic; the result was the same. The step he stood for might be small or great; it might be dictated merely by a statesman's vision of what the ordinary conditions of the future would require or it might be a cause sung by the nation, dedicated in blood and consecrated on the field of battle. Whatever the circumstances, the result has been the same whenever a group of Senators decided that the political destruction of a President was more important than international friendship or the good name of the nation in the future.

And finally, the Senate, left largely to its own devices except for the stimulation of a universal public opinion, has reluctantly proffered the cooperation through the World Court of the greatest nation on the globe in such terms that only a handful of the weakest nations honored them by acceptance. We were at last brought to the final humiliation that if Liberia and Uruguay took us seriously we were lucky.

The House Is More Amenable to Popular Control. Yet that is scarcely the worst of it. How can the American people lead a body whose *amore propre* is so extensive to reverse itself? It sits secure behind its long terms, seniority control of committees and its own feeling of the finality of wisdom in its decisions. Nothing short of death and time seem likely to change its direction perceptibly, once it has fulminated a position.

It can not be claimed, of course, that giving the power to approve treaties to the biennially elected House would give us a perfect reflection of the popular comprehension of our duties and responsibilities as the world's greatest nation. Domestic issues, small district politics, partisan feeling and super-patriotic appeal would usually prevent a clear cut expression on foreign policy. But we ought to come closer to it than we do, and after the election it would be much easier for the responsible sentiment of the people on a treaty to be made effective. Members of the House are closer to the people than the Senators, and much easier to reach. They are not so likely, either, to condemn an expression of public opinion as mere propaganda if it happens to conflict with a position previously assumed by themselves. Moreover, in the by-elections between Presidential contests there would be an opportunity to get some expression of sentiment on foreign affairs apart from Presidential politics.

On the other hand, these elections would sometimes give control to the opposite party, and thus make the blocking of an administration's foreign policy likely, yet in the absence of an abnormal majority for treaties this result would be no more certain than it is at present. The stricter control exercised over the members of the House by their leaders would no doubt often defeat a President's treaties when the opposing party controlled the House, and it would often prevent desirable debate, but the same condition would at least enable a President to carry out his foreign policy when his party controlled that body.

Our Method of Treaty Approval Rejected Abroad. On broader grounds still, the removal of the power to approve treaties from the Senate to the House would put us in agreement with the trend of democracy elsewhere. Nowhere else does a second chamber retain predominate control over either domestic or foreign affairs. In the fluid conditions resulting from the War, when many new governments were created and constitutions studied as never before, the merits of a dominant position for a second chamber had full chance to be copied if they commended themselves, but no new Senates were created abroad.

In Germany, the Bundesrat was reduced to the usual secondary position. It is permitted to share in the declaration of war and the conclusion of peace, by assenting to national law for those purposes. Alliances and treaties with foreign states which relate to subjects of national legislation require the consent of the Reichstag only; the upper house is not even consulted. [25]

If anything could have induced the Germans to admire and reproduce our Senate, either as a legislative organ or a power in treaty making, surely the assaults of the Senate upon the Treaty of Versailles, the treaty under which all Germans groaned, and the Senate's presentation to Germany of a separate treaty of peace in the hour of her abasement, must have produced that result.

[25] See McBain and Rogers, *New Constitutions of Europe,* N. Y., 1922, p. 185.

In Austria, also, the new constitution provides that "all political treaties, and all other treaties only in so far as they provide for an alteration of existing laws, shall require for their validity the consent of the Nationalrat." Again it is the lower house which must approve; the upper is not consulted. Bulgaria alone of the enemy powers admitted its upper house to a share in scrutinizing treaties, but only an equal share. [26]

Perhaps the failure of the former enemy countries to see the virtue of the Senate check may be explained by some as growing out of feelings connected with the war. The merit of our procedure would be much more likely to be sympathetically appreciated in the new countries made possible by the strength of our leadership and the force of our arms. Yet in Poland the consent of the Sejm only is required, and then only for commercial and customs treaties, treaties imposing a permanent financial burden on the state, containing legal rules binding on the citizens, changing the frontiers of the state and making alliances. Other treaties are simply to be brought "to the notice" of the Sejm. The Polish Senate is not to be consulted at all. [27]

Czecho-Slovakia has similar constitutional provisions regarding treaties, except that the affirmation of certain classes of treaties takes the form of a constitutional law. In these laws the Senate, strictly subordinated to the Chamber of Deputies in all matters, participates. Esthonia requires parliamentary ratification of all treaties, and Finland of certain classes. Neither of these countries have any upper house in their legislature. This is also the case in the important country of Jugo-Slavia where certain treaties must be referred to the single chambered national assembly, though purely political agreements, not contrary to law, need not be so approved. [28]

---

[26] *New Constitutions of Europe,* 269, 413.
[27] Ibid., 361-2.　　　　　[28] Ibid., 324-5, 462, 473.

Surveying the new constitutions as a whole, we find general, if not complete, agreement that the upper chambers far from being superior to the lower houses are not even coordinate with them. They are both second and secondary. They may impede and delay, but no more. Deadlocks are carefully guarded against. Repassage by the lower house, or referendum approval by the voters overrides them in practically all cases. [29]

Should Not We Too Have More Direct Responsibility?
From this steady development it is not necessary to draw the conclusion that we should attempt to go over to the par-

[29] Ibid., 38. Nearly all of the earlier Nineteenth Century constitution makers followed the example of the United States in establishing some legislative check over treaties. Thus the Belgian Constitution of February 7, 1831, limited the right of the Crown to make treaties in certain cases. Under it treaties dealing with individuals directly, laying financial burdens on the state, or effecting either its territory or commerce, must be approved by both Houses of Parliament. Other treaties, even of alliance, may still be made by the Crown on its own responsibility and the Houses need be advised only when the interests and safety of the state permit. W. E. Dodd, *Modern Constitutions*, Vol. 1, p. 137.

A law supplementing the Ausgleich between Austria and Hungary took the Belgian enumeration of four classes of treaties that must have legislative approval, but the Italian Constitution of March 4, 1848, required the submission of only two kinds of treaties, those laying financial burdens on the state or altering its territory. The French Constitutional Law of July 16, 1875, added peace treaties to the list. Dodd, *Modern Constitutions*, II, 5; J. E. Hartley, *American Journal of International Law*, 1919, p. 394; Ponsonby, *Democracy and Diplomacy*, p. 141.

The Constitution of the German Empire required that treaties having reference to affairs belonging to that domain of Imperial legislation should have the consent of the Bundesrat for their conclusion and the sanction of the Reichstag for their coming into force. Presumably the Bundesrat advised and the Reichstag consented. This provision, however, left the Kaiser free to make treaties of alliance, cede colonial territory and take other important steps without legislative consent. Fiske, *Germany's Constitutions of 1871 and 1919*. Cincinnati, 1924, pp. 33–38; Ponsonby, *Democracy and Diplomacy*, pp. 136–38.

Only one European country, so far as can be discovered, had given its parliament a right to review all treaties. The Portuguese constitutional charter of 1852 made such provision. The Constitutions of Argentina, Brazil and Chile gave the Congress the right to pass upon all treaties. The Chilean Constitution of 1833 is apparently the first one which followed our example. Hartley, above citation, p. 396; Dodd, *Modern Constitutions*, I, p. 165; *The Chilean Constitution Promulgated May 25, 1833 as amended to May 1, 1899*, Urbana, Ill., 1899.

In all these cases the right to consider treaties was granted to both houses of parliament or congress and no unusual majorities were required for approval.

liamentary form of government, but certainly such an equali-
zation of power between the Senate and the House as the
removal of the power to approve treaties to the latter body
might be a wholesome adjustment. The step would have the
double advantage of reaffirming our belief in representative government and of preventing small groups of men
from keeping us perpetually in deadlock with foreign
powers, or out of touch with them.

It should be difficult, too, for the Senators who have done
most to block our treaties to object logically to this broadening of popular control over them. They are fond of nothing
more than inveighing against the exercise of power by small
groups of men far removed from the people. Nothing is
worse to them than the idea of "nine men sitting in Geneva,"
or "eleven sitting on the destinies of mankind at the Hague."
How can they insist upon the right of a small group of
Senators, varying in number from a dozen to thirty-three, to
rule the foreign affairs of the American nation?

Our arrangement permitting a minority of the upper house
to veto or alter treaties has been studied and observed by
foreign statesmen and students of government for a century
and a half without commending itself, so far as can be
learned, in a single state other than our protégé, Liberia.
Nearly all of the governments now existing have been
created in that period, but none of any importance have
seen fit to repeat the "irreparable mistake" of our Constitution. The device has commended itself no more to
the recent additions to the family of nations than it did
to the group of American states modelling their governments after ours a century ago. Copied only by the Confederate States of America, [30] it is highly probable that not
even an offshoot from our body politic would now adopt
it. Is it not time to abandon it ourselves?

[30] *Virginia Law Review*, May, 1914, p. 602.

Our present system, says Ray Stannard Baker, leads to "utter weakness, muddle and delay; it forces both sides to play politics. . . . The deadlock between the Executive and the Senate every time we face a really critical foreign problem is intolerable. It not only disgraces us before the nations, but in some future world crisis may ruin us." "At one time in our history," adds Dr. R. L. Buell, "deadlocks over treaties made little difference. But with the growing complication of international affairs, the obstructive nature of the American constitution may be increasingly harmful."[31]

OTHER SOLUTION MAY GIVE ADAPTABILITY AND DIRECTION TO OUR FOREIGN RELATIONS

If it be held that nothing except a revolution would induce the Senate to abandon its power over treaties to the more representative branch of our national legislature, there are other less thorough-going reforms which would greatly liberalize the present situation.

A Majority Vote of Both Houses Widely Favored. Admitting the House to an equal share in the approval of treaties and requiring only a majority vote in each house would be an immense gain for responsibility. This is the step favored by Dr. Quincy Wright in his recent study "The Control of American Foreign Relations." Though reluctant to recommend a constitutional amendment, Mr. Wright comes to the conclusion that this change would bring us into line with the practice abroad, that it "would obviate the complaint of the House of Representatives and eliminate the ever present possibility of inability to execute a treaty, valid at international law, because of refusal of the House to agree to appropriations or necessary legislation," and that it would make deadlocks less frequent.[32]

[31] R. S. Baker, *Woodrow Wilson and the World Settlement*, N. Y., 1922, Vol. I, p. 316; R. L. Buell, *International Relations*, N. Y., 1929, p. 757.
[32] Quincy Wright, *The Control of American Foreign Relations*,

Professor J. T. Young, in a recent book also favors this change. Although feeling that the original grounds for requiring a Senate majority of two-thirds were strong, he concludes that "In later years, however, the needs of the people have changed considerably and the treaty-making power must be considered from a different standpoint. We now need more treaties, and we must regard our treaty-making machinery more with a view to producing results than of merely preventing action. It is hard to believe that our Executive is to be less trusted than those of other nations. In no other great world power is a majority of two-thirds of the upper House required for the approval of international agreements.

"This requirement together with the right of unlimited debate in the upper House seems to give to a small group of men too much power to delay and block action on important measures and as it becomes more necessary to enter into trade arrangements with other countries we require a more effective method of treaty-making. To this end the suggestion has been made that treaties be approved by a simple majority of both Houses. This would be an easier method than the present two-thirds rule in the Senate and yet it would fully safeguard all interests concerned." [33]

The same judgment has been expressed by other political scientists including Professor J. W. Garner, Dr. James Brown Scott, and Professor H. L. McBain. Approval by both houses was also advocated by W. J. Bryan at the 1920 Jackson Day banquet and by John W. Davis in his campaign for the Presidency in 1924. [34]

N. Y., 1922, p. 368. A reciprocity treaty with Mexico made in 1883 and duly ratified did not become operative because the House refused to pass a law to carry its provisions into effect. This is believed, however, to be the only case of its kind. Chalfant Robinson, *Two Reciprocity Treaties*, New Haven, 1904, pp. 163–4.

[33] J. T. Young, *The New American Government and Its Work*, N. Y., 1924, pp. 47–8. Reprinted by permission of the Macmillan Company.
[34] J. W. Garner, *American Foreign Policies*, N. Y., 1928, p. 30; H. L. McBain, *The Living Constitution*, N. Y., 1924, pp. 47–8; *Congressional Record*, Vol. 59, p. 1292.

It is difficult to see how majority approval of treaties by both houses can be reasonably opposed. By the constitution itself all treaties are the supreme law of the land. They often require the concurrence of the House to make them effective. The reasons for confining the function to the Senate no longer apply, and its practical operation in the Senate has made us unique among all the nations of the world, if not in all history, in being unable to agree upon or carry out a foreign policy.

Considering these facts, what ground can be advanced for continuing to refuse four-fifths of our national representatives any voice on treaties? To oppose it is to contend, describing the situation as favorably as it can possibly be described, that the vote of every objector should continue to be as powerful as the votes of two Senators favoring a treaty. Almost nowhere else, if anywhere, do we submit to minority control in ordinary affairs, let alone those of supreme importance. Why should the United States Government continue to wear a ring in its nose in matters of international relationship. [35]

We may have an able, farseeing leader in the President's chair, surrounded by a Cabinet composed of men of real statesmanship and vision, but unless the President be absolutely fearless the whole Executive Department is likely to be so dominated by the ever present threat of Senate obstruction in international affairs that it must remain inactive or follow the Senate whither it listeth. [36]

No matter how strongly wisdom and information may impel toward a policy or a settlement the impulse to act for the larger and longer good is likely to be stifled or frustrated.

[35] The phrase is taken from the Springfield *Republican*, February 4, 1926.
[36] If a strong and rash President should seek to commit us to unjustified ventures a simple majority could surely be mustered against him in one of the two houses.

Why Should the Senate Be Sovereign? Thus after the Franco-American war debt negotiations, a leading French publicist, Stephen Lauzanne, explained the situation during the negotiations to the French people as follows:

> Theoretically, it would seem that the present government—or administration as they say in Washington—should control the great majority of the commission. It includes in fact, three cabinet officers, and Messrs. Hurley and Olney are accustomed always to follow the opinion of Mr. Hoover. Thus, there are five votes out of eight for the administration, but, practically, the sole vote of Mr. Smoot is almost preponderant. He represents, in fact, the Senate, the omnipotent Senate. And we know, since the treaty of Versailles, that it is necessary always to reckon on the omnipotence of the American Senate.[37]

After noting that our own best correspondents agreed that Senator Smoot really blocked proposals which both the Secretary of the Treasury and the President favored, the Des Moines *Register* in commenting on the incident, observed that the puzzled foreigner had a multitude of other illustrations before him to justify the notion that the Senate is sovereign.

"But," asked the *Register,* "what of the thing from our own standpoint? Why, in fact, should the Senate grow into a place of greater importance in our governmental scheme than the House of Representatives? Why should it encroach upon the executive and, exceeding its function of final review, as one of our numerous 'checks' take mastery of negotiations? Why, even more importantly, should a minority of the Senate, and often a small minority, have the power,

---

[37] Des Moines *Register,* February 11, 1926. Some will take the view that some direct representative of the American taxpayer should have had a veto in the conference, regardless of larger considerations in the minds of the statesmen.

by virtue of the two-thirds rule, to nullify any action in foreign affairs that may be thoroughly approved by the President, the majority of the Senate itself, and the majority of the people?

"Nobody can deny that Senate minorities have exercised that power. Amazingly, they have been applauded for doing it, by those more concerned about political aims of a domestic kind than about foreign policy."

Approval By a Simple Majority of the Senate. For those who admire the Senate for its great obstructive power over our foreign relations, as demonstrated in the last eight administrations, and who believe it should often reduce us to immobility in foreign affairs, the admission of the House to the treaty check will be undesirable. To those who disapprove of the leadership which the Presidents of the period from Cleveland to Coolidge have attempted to give us the recalcitrance of the Senate will seem so justified as to call for no reform.

Others may have enough doubts as to what has been right that they would favor a reduction of the Senate majority required for treaties as a safe step in a situation that calls for some amelioration, but not for a real break with precedent. Many somewhat similarly minded may approve of more basic reform, but, recognizing the great belief of the Senate in its own competence, they may doubt that the Senate could ever be brought to surrender even a part of one of its "prerogatives" to anybody.

To these groups the proposal to leave the power in the Senate, but reduce the requirement for treaties to a simple majority should appeal. As proposed in a Senate Joint Resolution introduced by Senator Owen of Oklahoma, on March 22, 1920, the Constitution would be amended to read: "The President shall have power, by and with the advice of the Senate, to frame treaties, and, with the consent of the

Senate, a majority of the Senators present concurring therein, to conclude the same." [38]

If this had been the rule from the beginning the Convention for Reopening and Retrying the Claims of Benjamin Weil and the La Abra Silver Mining Co. would have been approved by the Senate, instead of rejected, and the wrong done to Mexico corrected, in all probability, years before it was. This convention was rejected in the Senate by votes of 33 for to 20 against, on January 15, 1883, and 32 for to 26 against, April 20, 1886. Similarly, four commercial treaties rejected by minority votes would have gone into effect. They are: the Cuban Claims Convention of 1860, rejected by a vote of 28 for to 18 against; the reciprocity treaty with the German Zollverein, lost April 17, 1854, 26 to 18; the Hawaiian reciprocity treaty of 1870, defeated 20 to 19; and the Lausanne Treaty of Amity and Commerce with Turkey which failed January 18, 1927, with 50 votes for it to 34 against. None of these treaties were of vital importance to the country, yet in every case their passage would have notably improved our relations with a foreign state.

Whether the approval of the Olney-Pauncefote Arbitration Treaty of 1897 and the Treaty of Versailles of 1919, as amended by the Senate, would have had the same result cannot be stated as confidently. The Olney-Pauncefote Treaty rejected May 5, 1897, with 43 Senators for and 26 against, had been so changed by the Senate that its value was highly questionable. Still, its passage in any form would have prevented the bad feeling between Great Britain and the United States which resulted from its total rejection. Likewise the Treaty of Versailles, as qualified by the Lodge Reservations and rejected finally March 19, 1920, by a vote of 49 yeas to 35 nays, might have been dropped by the Presi-

[38] J. M. Mathews, *The Conduct of American Foreign Relations*, N. Y., 1922, p. 162.

dent or if he had submitted the Senate's terms to the Powers they might never have been accepted. It seems highly probable that our entry into the League of Nations under the Lodge Resolution would have been long delayed, if it ever came about. Nevertheless, the conditional approval thus voted by the Senate, in the absence of the two-thirds rule would have had some chance to be considered by the members of the League, and we might have known positively what the world thought of the Senate's action. [39]

The principal objection to approval by an ordinary majority which was made in the Constitutional Convention was that Senators representing a distinct minority of the people might vote approval of treaties. This objection still applies. It would be possible for a combination of the Senators from small states to pass a treaty over the protests of Senators representing two-thirds of the people of the country. To most students of the question, however, this danger is not to be compared with the ever present one of blocked action by Senators representing only small racial, sectional or occupational groups.

What is more likely is that in times when attendance in the Senate is low, treaties would be approved by an affirmative vote smaller than a majority of the Senators elected, by votes ranging, say, from 30 to 50.

The Minimum Proposal—Approval By a Majority of the Whole Senate. To those to whom this possibility is a real objection the admission of the House would provide the proper corrective. To those, however, who want to make the smallest possible break with tradition, the suggestion of Professor J. M. Mathews should commend itself. Mr. Mathews writes that "A minority of the Senate should not be allowed to block action; and it should be possible for the Senate to act by vote of a majority of all the senators

[39] The citations for all the votes here given will be found in the earlier chapters.

elected—at all events provided that such a majority represents states having more than half of the total population of the country." [40]

This is the solution which narrowly missed finding its way into the Constitution. It was rejected by the vote of six states to five. The change of one state delegation, probably of one man in a divided delegation, would have given us this provision instead of the two-thirds vote, and we should have revered that arrangement as an expression of the Convention's great wisdom instead of looking up to its inspired action in fixing the higher majority.

Reducing the vote required for treaties to a majority of the whole Senate is the minimum of reform that would make any appreciable difference in the present situation. It would merely substitute a necessary minimum of 49 affirmative votes for the possible maximum of 64 as at present required. The change would be of great aid in the case of important treaties, even though in most cases it would make no difference at all.

It suffers, in less degree, to the objection against a mere majority vote, as Mr. Mathews' qualification indicates. Responsible and representative government would seem to be best advanced by admitting the House to a share in the check on the basis of ordinary majority votes. Setting up a second barrier for treaties may seem to many a questionable way to advance, but it should usually be possible for most treaties to scale two moderately high hurdles easier than one very high one. This reform seems distinctly preferable to the further limitation of debate in the Senate. It would be a great loss indeed if we should be deprived of the free forum for the criticism of executive policies, both domestic and international, which the Senate provides. Let us guard it jealously, assuring to minority groups of Senators every right of protest. What is needed is a limitation of their

[40] Mathews, *The Conduct of American Foreign Relations,* 162.

power to nullify the judgment of the majority by threatening
a veto, or perhaps actually mustering one, when they cannot prevail by reason.

The Alteration of Negotiated Treaties is Not a Proper Legislative Function

As an essential part of any reform there should be an
abatement of the Senate's custom of proposing amendments
or binding reservations to important treaties.

No legislative body should have the right arbitrarily to
add to or subtract from a compact which two or more governments have made; none of any importance have asserted such
a right outside our own country. If other legislatures did
so, international relations would become capricious and uncertain, if not chaotic, except as the situation would be ame-
liorated by the unity of parliamentary governments.

Yet instead of abandoning a custom which has been uni-
versally disapproved, we have reached the point in the United
States that it is taken for granted in the Senate that when an
important treaty reaches it there must be amendments or
reservations or both. Senators even feel offended if this assumption is questioned and ask indignantly if they are to be
only rubber stamps. If they can do nothing to the treaty,
how can they maintain their sovereign dignity and "equality"
in the treaty making power? Does the treaty not need perfecting? Surely it is not perfect. Ergo, we will perfect it!
And the work of impressing the President, foreign powers
and the country with the ability of Senators to detect possible
flaws in any document begins.

The results of this practice are known to everybody concerned. Why should it continue? It rests upon the mistaken
notion, as Premier Ramsay MacDonald has pointed out, that
a treaty must be the best conceivable bargain, whereas it
can never be more than the best possible bargain under the

circumstances. [41] The consequences are not wholly disastrous to us because of our relative self-sufficiency and independence of others. They would be fatal if the necessity to give as well as take were greater. As it is, the amending habit not only provides a method of defeating treaties under pretence of "perfecting" them, but it leaves the Senate in the position of habitually insulting both the President and the foreign powers, and, adds Professor Howard Lee McBain, "perhaps naturally but none the less regrettably, it is being used with more contumely as the United States, sitting smug in the family of nations, becomes more and more puffed with prosperity, pride and power."

The Practice is Offensive. "The situation is this," says Professor McBain, "The American and the foreign negotiators have sat. They have exchanged ideas. They have come to hand to hand agreement. They have drafted a document. This document the Senate receives. That body is securely isolated from the other party to the proposed agreement. It debates in spurious secrecy. It adds or subtracts or otherwise alters and sends the proposal back to the President, saying, in effect: 'We give you our constitutional consent with these changes which we have made.' The President has the choice of dropping the disfigured proposal in disgust, (which he has rather frequently done) or of going back to the foreign negotiators with the word that 'My overlord, the American Senate, demands these words or nothing', which the foreign power may, or may not be willing to accept.

"The point is not that the Senate should abrogate its power or conceal its views—it is immensely important that a legis-

---

[41] New York *Times,* November 1, 1925. The Labor Prime Minister will not be accused of lack of sympathy for popular control of foreign relations. His solution for Great Britain is that treaties be scrutinized by a House Committee so composed that it can neither be hostile to the Government nor independent of it.

lative body should pass upon treaties, which are nothing more nor less than law. It is rather a question of international good manners. Why should not the Senate, without either giving or refusing consent, send the proposal back to the President with its suggestions, leaving the matter of drafting to the joint representatives of the countries whose joint law this is to be?"[42]

The practice of submitting treaties to legislatures for their approval or rejection is growing in Europe, but no European legislature has copied the Senate's custom of proposing amendments. This is an adherence to the fundamental amenities of international intercourse, under repeated provocation, which should give food for thought.[43]

It is Especially Destructive to Multilateral Treaties. There is much to contemplate, too, in the consideration that multilateral treaties, especially those of a political nature, could never be agreed upon if the negotiators could settle nothing, and if their tentative agreements could go into force only after interminable parliamentary dickering. Reservations to multilateral treaties dealing with technical matters, such as sanitary and radiotelegraphic conventions, are only feasible if understood during the discussions and stated at the time of signature. Otherwise the object of the convention might

[42] H. L. McBain, *The Living Constitution,* copyright, 1927, by The Worker's Press Bureau Inc., pp. 196–98. Reprinted by permission of the Macmillan Company.

[43] Ibid. The Constitutions of two small Central American States give the Congress the right to modify treaties. That of Nicaragua says that the Congress may "approve, modify or renounce" treaties and that of Honduras "approve, modify or disapprove." These two acceptances of our practice offer, it is submitted, little support of it.

Others of the Latin American states specifically bar amendment by the Congress. The constitutions of Guatemala, Peru and Panama specify that the Congress may only "approve or disapprove," that of Costa Rica that it must "approve or reject," and that of Paraguay "reject or ratify." The Chilean Congress likewise has power only "to approve or reject" treaties.

In all the cases cited action by the entire legislature is called for. *The Treaty Making Power in various Countries,* Government Printing Office, Washington, 1919.

be defeated or the considerations on which it was signed impaired, if not destroyed. [44]

Since multilateral treaties are fast becoming the chief means of adjusting international affairs and seem likely to become even more necessary, the United States should not continue to insist on a privilege which can be tolerated only because we alone of all the powers demand it.

It Leads to Subterranean Diplomacy. International agreements will continue to be made in ever increasing number, objectors in the Senate to the contrary notwithstanding. The business of regulating the rapidly increasing international contacts must go on. The Senate can add greatly to the difficulty of making these adjustments by peaceable processes but it cannot stop the effort to make them. What it does do is to drive our diplomacy into irregular channels. Our Executive, faced daily with the need of accommodating conflicting national interests, is continually put under the necessity of making private understandings and unofficial arrangements with foreign powers. [45] The proper scope of executive agreements with other countries is likely to be stretched beyond what the Constitution contemplates. Declarations of policy are likely to be made orally, which should be embodied in treaty form. Personal representatives of the President, and "unofficial observers" must be sent to diplomatic conferences. [46] Things must be done in underground fashion or not at all.

[44] See H. M. Malkin, "Reservations to Multilateral Conventions," *British Yearbook of International Law, Oxford,* 1926, pp. 146–62. Reservations had been made to 17 multilateral conventions since 1883. In all except three or four cases the treaties dealt with non-political matters. With two exceptions the number of powers making reservations was small, usually one to three, and the consent of the other powers to the reservations was either given or fairly implied by the other signatories at the time of signature.

[45] See Rogers, *The American Senate,* 79–81.

[46] This evasion of the Senate in turn nettles the Senators deeply. Thus in the debate on Japanese immigration in 1924 Senator Swanson, of Virginia, said: "I am tired of the State Department entering into agreements fixing the foreign policy of the country except by treaty. The Constitution determines how the foreign policy of this country

The Power to Negotiate Treaties Belongs in the Executive. The qualification of treaties under the guise of approving them is an attempt to seize the power to negotiate, a power which long experience has shown should be left to the Executive. Its assertion implies an equality between the Senate and the President in treaty making which is not feasible. Coordinate control of foreign policy by two independent bodies is not possible nor desirable. One must have the initiative and exercise the power; the other should ask only the right to encourage and to warn and to veto the result when grave reasons of public policy demand it. Public policy requires that there be a legislative check on treaty making, but when the Senate attempts to grasp the power itself it violates all experience.[47]

---

shall be fixed. I am tired of people making understandings of the force and effect of treaties and committing us in foreign matters so as to avoid coming to the treaty-making power. I am certainly opposed to it." *Congressional Record,* April 8, 1924, Vol. 65, Pt. 6, p. 5829.

Senator Swanson of course understood clearly the place of the President in treaty making. His opinion, however, of the share of the Senate in that function would not seem to differ much from that of Senator Borah who stated repeatedly with regard to the World Court matter "The Senate has advised and the sole duty left is that of communicating with foreign governments—that is peculiarly the duty of the President." *Congressional Record,* Vol. 69, p. 6317 ff. Having performed his peculiar duty the President, added Senator Reed of Pennsylvania, had "no power to vary to the extent of one comma the reservations as outlined by the Senate." No doubt both Senators would have agreed with Mr. Swanson that the President ought not to avoid coming to "the treaty-making power."

⁴⁷ The principal exception to the usual practice of leaving treaty making to the executive, that of ancient Rome, does not appear to argue for legislative treaty making.

During the period of the Roman Republic treaty making was in the hands of the Senate. It sent and received ambassadors and controlled all negotiations. In the whole field of foreign affairs nothing was done without its consent. For a considerable time treaties, particularly peace treaties, were also submitted to the popular assembly, the comitia. This practice ceased during the third and second centuries B.C., when the Senate gathered executive, administrative and legislative powers in its hands and ruled the state. The Empire followed. See: Harper's *Dictionary of Classical Literature and Antiquities,* p. 1440; Taylor, *Constitutional and Political History of Rome,* p. 227; Phillipson, *International Law and Customs of Ancient Greece and Rome,* Vol. 1, p. 416; Walton, *Introduction to Roman Law,* p. 125.

There are, moreover, other effective ways by which Senators may express their views both during negotiations and afterwards. The device hit upon by the Senate in approving the Pact, a committee interpretation filed in the Senate but not acted upon, might well be used in the future to permit a small minority of Senators to record their fears. If the apprehensions about the future effect of the treaty be more general the report might be adopted by the Senate and thus serve as an authoritative interpretation of its meaning from our standpoint in case of future dispute. If the doubts of the Senators be still more grave such a resolution of the Senate might even be forwarded to the other signatory powers as a separate document for their information, but not binding upon them.

If it be contended that in the rare case of doubts of real gravity being shared by a majority of the Senators some further alternative of action, short of complete rejection, must exist, the right of the Senate to say to its own Executive, "If you can secure substantially the following changes in the treaty, we will accept it," may well be granted. In fact the prospect of securing amendment by this means should be better than by direct action of the Senate on the treaty itself, for the Executive, approaching the other powers with at least some little discretion maintained, would be much more likely to secure the desired results, and if it did not wholly succeed the Senate would not find itself in the position of having publicly delivered terms from which it could not readily recede.

The scrutiny of treaties by Parliamentary Committees is highly desirable. The problem is to secure such examination without endangering the larger interests of the state or sacrificing its ability to work effectively and amicably with other nations. A unified form of government naturally facilitates this kind of study for treaties. The French Commission on Foreign Affairs exercises as constant and effective supervision over treaties as is exercised by the parliamentary body of any other country. [48] It can summon ministers and have policies explained at any time.

Following this model the new German constitution provides for a standing committee on foreign affairs which may act while the Reichstag is not sitting. [49] Norway also has a system based on custom which compels all treaties to be submitted to full scrutiny by special parliamentary committees before going into effect. [50]

The fact of a unified parliamentary government in these countries of course makes a solution much easier than here where the theory rules that independent branches of the Government must watch and check or block each other. In the countries mentioned all concerned come into office together and stand or fall together. There is therefore no motive to play politics or try to put the Executive in a hole when treaties come up. The aim is rather to prevent one's own colleagues from making mistakes that the country would disapprove and for which it might perhaps sweep both negotiators and reviewers out of office.

This is a situation so totally different from the one we commonly find ourselves in that the proper working of popular control over treaty-making will probably be much more difficult to accomplish here, but the difficulty of the adjustment should not prevent us from attempting to work it out.

The development of the habit of informal conference between the Secretary of State and the Senate Foreign Affairs Committee will give us much greater harmony in the conduct of our foreign affairs, under normal conditions. The Senators are very human. They greatly appreciate

[48] McBain and Rogers, *New Constitutions of Europe,* 150.
[49] Ibid., 183, Articles 34 and 35.
Its sittings are secret unless two-thirds of the members vote otherwise.
The English also look with favor on treaty supervision by a carefully constituted committee of the House of Commons.
[50] Ibid., 149.

being consulted and informed by the Secretary about his leading projects. When so considered they are not nearly so likely to take highly critical attitudes toward his treaties, and they may also give him valuable suggestions. When there is personal or political hostility between the Senators and the Secretary or the President such contact may be of little value, if it is not out of the question entirely. Then an easier method of ratifying treaties will be indispensable if we are to make treaties. The persistent use of the method of conference is likely, however, to prevent some impasses between the Senate and the Executive from developing while we wait for a more flexible constitutional arrangement.

Education Requisite for Effective Popular Control. A more efficient and reliable method of legislative review for treaty making is not likely to be worked out in the United States until the American people become aware of the permanently increased importance of their foreign relations. Writers of all shades of opinion unite in agreeing that the great bulk of our people tend to be simply uninterested and indifferent to what our foreign policy is. "The essential fact," says a former Consul General of the United States, "is the indifference of the public to matters which are so often removed from their immediate interest and understanding. Only the later and more acute stages of foreign problems can be counted upon to command any general attention, and interest is then directed to the ends to be attained rather than the means. Respecting many situations, especially in their initial stages, there is, as we have previously noticed, no public opinion at all, and the responsible officers of government must proceed in their discretion and in accordance with such guidance as they may find in tradition and precedent." [51]

The necessity of putting faith in our responsible repre-

---

[*] D. C. Poole, *The Conduct of Foreign Relations*, N. Y., 1925, 193.

sentatives in foreign affairs, and of giving them our support is one that we can well be reminded of in closing this study. It will long continue. There is much evidence, however, that the sections of the American people which furnish its leadership, if not an actual majority of the people themselves, are rapidly becoming both informed and interested in the problems and responsibilities of foreign affairs. There is corresponding reason to hope that what the writer believes to be the real power in the life of his country, "the spirit of orderly progress," will give increasing adaptability and direction to our foreign relations.

INDEX

A

Adams, Charles Francis, 61
Adams, John, 22
Adams, John Quincy, quoted, 19; 52, 53; q. 117
Advice and consent, original meaning, 46
Advisory opinions, danger of suggested, 182; reservation proposed, 182; upheld by President Coolidge, 189–190; original reservation on, 191; prevalence of, 192; reservation on, expanded and adopted, 209–211; majority necessary for request of, 243, 247; attitude of small powers toward, 243, 247
Alabama, cruiser, 60
Alaskan Boundary Commission, 30
Aldrich, Nelson W., 28
Alliance, treaties of, 7
Amendments to treaties, origin, 33–34; number of, 36; refusal to agree to, 40–43; sources of, 47; undesirability of, 47; results of, 48; substitutes for, 48–49; to British slave trade treaty, 53–54; not a legislative function, 307 ff.; effect on multilateral treaties, 309; leads to underground diplomacy, 310
American Foundation, 187
Anglo-Japanese Alliance, 106
Annexation, treaties of, rejected, 61–67, 271, 284
Anti-War Pact, 251 ff.
Anzilotti, Dionisco, 206
Arbitration, 48, 91; treaties for, 48, 59, 61, 76–123; post-war increase of treaties for, 273; unlimited, 275
Argentina, power of Congress over treaties, 297
Arthur, Chester A., 22, 57, 71
Article 10, origin of, 131–132; 134; discussed, 145; scope of, 148; text of reservation on, 160
Asquith, Herbert H., 92

Association of nations, sketch of, 169
Aves Island, 36

B

Bacon, Augustus O., 24, 101
Baker, Ray Stannard, quoted, 299
Balfour, Sir Arthur, 92
Baltimore *American*, quoted, 99
Baltimore *Sun*, quoted, 99
Barkley, A. W., 257
Bavaria, treaty with, 34
Beckham, J. C. W., 144
Behring Sea Arbitration Treaty, 35
Belgium, treaty with, amended, 35; extradition treaty rejected, 67; treaty making practice, 297
Benes, M., 207
Bingham, Hiram, 210; views on Peace Pact, 260; and Peace Pact round robin, 263, 265
Blaine, James G., 73
Blaine, John J., 258
Blease, Cole, 200; World Court resolution, 202
Bok, Edward W., 172, 187, 206
Bonds, repudiated, 79, 87, 95, 98, 182; in World Court debate, 209; description of, 209–210
Borah, William E., opposed internationalism, 130; 133, 142; views on League reservations, 145; for a court, 176; opposed consideration of World Court, 184; against a League court, 185, 192; quoted, 199–200; 201, 207, 221, 253, 256; things not to be defined as war, 260; opposed to Peace Pact reservations, 263–264
Boston *Herald*, quoted, 99
Boycott, economic, 163; relation of U. S. to, 278
Brazil, 64; power of Congress over treaties, 297
Brent, Bishop, quoted, 178–179

Briand, M., offer of anti-war treaty,
252; received skeptically in Washington, 253; text of Briand proposal, 252; final form, 254;
negotiations for extension of, 253–
254; reservations to, proposed,
255; and Monroe Doctrine, 257;
effect of negotiations on, 259
British Dominions, votes of, in
League, 165
British Monroe Doctrine, 258
Brookhart, S. W., quoted, 201
Bruce, Wm. Cabell, quoted, 197–198
Bryan Treaties, 109–113; submitted
to Senate, 110; approved, 111;
analyzed, 111; not tested in the
war, 112; signatories to, 112;
administration of, 113
Bryan, W. J., 80; supported treaty
of Paris, 122; 124, 156, 300
Buchanan, James, 22
Buell, R. L., quoted, 299
Bullitt, W. C., 152
Burton, Theodore, 97
Bustamente, Antonia de, 206
Butler, Nicholas Murray, on League
blockade, 278
Butler, Pierce, quoted, 10

C

Calhoun, John C., 53, 66, 72
Campaign of 1920, result of, 169
Campaign of 1924, World Court in,
183. See also Election of 1918
Canada, and Halibut Fisheries
Treaty, 42; 68–72; failure of
reciprocity treaties with, 73; and
the League, 168
Canadian Fisheries Treaty, 68–72,
273
Canning, George, 41, 55
Capper, Arthur, 253
Caribbean islands, British, 64
Carnegie, Andrew, peace conference
called by, 124; 206
Catholic Church, 119
Chamberlain, George E., 101
Chamber of Commerce, 92
Checks and balances, applied to
treaties, 47
Chicago Record Herald, quoted, 100
Chicago Tribune, 99, 188
Chile, power of Congress over
treaties, 297, 309
China, treaty with, amended, 36;
immigration treaty, 82

Claims commission, Mexican, 57
Claims, court of, 58
Clay, Henry, quoted, 42
Clayton-Bulwer treaty, 40
Clemenceau, Georges, 131
Cleveland, Grover, 68; on the fish-
eries treaty, 69; 73, 80, 266
Cleveland Plaindealer, quoted, 100
Cloture, in behalf of World Court,
209
Colby, Everett, quoted, 180
Colombia, canal treaties, 56–57, 270
Colt, L. B., 143
Commerce, treaties of. See Trea-
ties of Commerce
Commission of Inquiry, in Taft ar-
bitration treaties, 91, 93, 101;
principle of Bryan treaties, 109;
in League covenant, 275
Committee on Foreign Relations.
See Foreign Relations Committee
Commons, House of, 77
Compromis, in Hay treaties, 86;
record of Senate in approving,
88; practice of other countries in
making, 89; Root compromise on,
90; under Taft treaties of arbitration, 92, 104; 274
Confederate States, belligerent
rights of, 60; cruisers of, 61;
methods of making treaties, 298
Confederation, Articles of, 4
Confirmation of commissioners, 103
Congo, treaty concerning, 35
Congress, U. S., under the Articles
of Confederation, 4; resolution on
arbitration, 77
Constitution, U. S., provision governing treaties, 43; intended
meaning of treaty clause, 46
Coolidge, Calvin, 48, 173; concerning the League, 177; World Court
in inaugural address, 184; on the
necessity for concession, 190;
World Court dropped by, 234–
236; interest in World Court renewed, 241; views on interpreting
the Peace Pact, 263
Costa Rica, treaty making in,
309
Crawford, William H., 53
Crittenden, John J., 119
Cuba, claims convention rejected,
59; reciprocity treaty with, 73;
reciprocity treaty approved, 75;
accepted World Court reservations, 217

Ransdall, Joseph E., 147
Reciprocity, with Hawaii, 36; treaties defeated, 72–75
Reed, David A., 311
Reed, James, 133, 142, 205–206, 220, 259
Reparation Commission, authority limited by Senate reservation, 163
Republican Party, and fisheries treaty, 70; and League, 169; and World Court, 183
Republicans, thirty-one, 169
Reservations, on Monroe Doctrine, 97; effect of, 144; need of, debated, 153; to treaty of Versailles, 158–167, probability of acceptance, 158; the utility of, 204; to World Court, 173, 191, 194, amended 209, adopted, 211, nations ignoring, 218, nations failing to take action on, 219; and counter reservations, 233; to Peace Pact, 255, effect of proposals abroad, 263–264
Richmond *Times-Dispatch*, quoted, 99
Riddleberger, Harrison H., quoted, 70
Robinson, Arthur R., 256
Robinson, Joseph T., 144, 264
Rogers, Lindsay, quoted, 291, 292
Rolin, M., 229
Rome, treaty making in, 311–312
Roosevelt, Theodore, 35, 48; on reciprocity, 74; 86, 87; position on Hay arbitration treaties, 88; on Taft arbitration treaties, 92, 94; quoted, 94; alarm over opposition to treaty of peace with Spain, 120; 124; advocacy of a league of peace, 125; mediator, 125; opposed Fourteen Points, 128
Root, Elihu, arbitration treaties negotiated, 89–90; 94; advice to League opponents, 142; World Court mission of 1929, 244 ff.; plan for American adherence to World Court, 245–246; concerning Monroe Doctrine, 266
Round robin, on League of Nations, 136; on Peace Pact, 262, text, 265
Rush, Richard, 41
Russo-Japanese war, effect on peace movements, 124
Rutledge, John, quoted, 10

S

Salisbury, Lord, 82
San Domingo, treaty for annexation of, 63–65, 271, 284; reciprocity treaty with, 73
San Francisco *Chronicle*, quoted, 99
Santa Anna, 270
Schurman, Jacob Gould, concerning an association of nations, 169
Schurz, Carl, 64
Scott, J. B., 300
Scripps-Howard newspapers, editorial, 239–240
Search, right of, 52–53
Secrecy and despatch, in negotiations, 12, 290
Self defense, inherent, 256
Senate, United States, original power over treaties, 7; as a council, 16–21, 46; place of meeting on treaties, 20; consulted during negotiations, 21–22; power to negotiate, 23 ff.; power to propose amendments to treaties, 307–313
Senatorial courtesy, 44; and treaties, 287
Senators, as negotiators, 27–32
September Conference, *see* World Court; origin of, 220; report of, 222 ff.; four reservations accepted, 223; reciprocity suggested, 224; discussion of reservation 5 desired, 227, 232
Seward, William H., 60, 62, 64, 271
Shantung, settlement, 143; reservation to treaty of Versailles on, 162
Sherman, L. Y., 135, 142
Sherman, Roger, quoted, 9, 11
Shipstead, Hendrick, quoted, 198
Slave trade, British campaign against, 51; treaty for, with Colombia, 51, 55; treaty with Great Britain, 51–55; suppression of, 268
Slavery, 64–65
Sloo Co., 270
Smith, John Walter, 154
Smith, Marcus A., 145
Smoot, Reed, 170
Spencer, Selden P., 153
Spooner, John C., 26
Springfield *Republican*, quoted, 100; editorial, 213–214
States, sovereignty of, 3
Stephens, H. D., 212

Epilogue
for the 1971 Edition

Out of the terrible agonies and devastation of World War I a League of Nations was born. Our own President Woodrow Wilson, and other great Americans, led in creating this life-giving attempt to end such pitiful tragedies. The other nations, except the defeated ones who had to wait a while, flocked into the new house of peace, undeterred in a single instance by the American reservations—fifteen of them—which asserted the right of the mighty U.S.A. to do as it pleased, as determined by the Congress, in almost every conceivable contingency.

Yet these all-seeing preservative provisos, adopted by majority votes, could never command the two-thirds majority and the unamended Treaty of Versailles could not either. We never had a chance to see whether the other 32 signatories of the treaty would have accepted some of them, bearing in mind that just one rejected reservation would have kept us out of the League of Nations.

Into World War II
But in the absence of our indispensable leadership we saw the United States stand outside in isolation while the League of Nations faltered and failed to restrain new expansionist aggressors—Japan, Italy and

1

EPILOGUE

Germany—as in successive crises they plunged the world toward World War II. During these crises: over Manchuria in 1931-32; Ethiopia in 1935 and during the fatal appeasement slide into World War II (all of which I observed from Geneva); our Secretary of State Stimson did what he could to voice sympathy and support for the League from outside, but he could not halt the deadly progression by these gestures.

So within two decades, during which we had gambled our way through the great boom of the twenties into the greatest of all economic collapses in 1929, a still greater and more destructive world war engulfed us and much of mankind for another six-year orgy of slaughter and destruction. At its end, too, our hasty incineration of the Japanese city of Hiroshima and 100,000 people by an A-bomb forecast the end of all humanity in a third and final world war.[1]

Executive Dominance and World Empire

Then in mid-1945 a new and better league of nations was formed, the United Nations, of which we became a member. But the death of President Franklin D. Roosevelt in the spring of that year had

[1] *For the author's studies of what followed the failure of the League of Nations, first in Washington and then in Geneva, see:* The United States and the League of Nations, 1918-1920, *revised edition, 1968; and* The United States and the World Court, *revised 1968, both by Russell and Russell, New York. Also* The United States and World Organization, 1920-1933, *revised 1966, published by the AMS Press, Inc., New York.*

2

abruptly left the Presidency in the hands of Harry Truman, a man who was quite ready to plunge into a new balance of power contest with the Soviet Union and to make the United States the paramount power of the world, pushing the United Nations to one side.

Thus almost instantly the negative power of the Senate gave way to the positive power of the Executive. As Eric Sevareid of CBS said on March 1, 1971, a constitutional crisis began about twenty years ago. Specifically, it began with the Truman Doctrine of March 12, 1947, which in sweeping terms proclaimed the "containment" of both the Soviet Union and Communism, shortly before China went Communist in 1949, and Truman plunged into the Korean War promptly after June 25, 1950, to defend his Doctrine, without any declaration of War by Congress. Fighting the Cold War could not wait for such formalities.

During the Eisenhower Administrations the belligerencies of Secretary of State John Foster Dulles were held in check by the President, and the short Kennedy Administration turned toward peace after an initial period of heavy armament. Then President Lyndon Johnson, elected overwhelmingly on a peace platform in November 1964, plunged into the bombing of North Vietnam early in 1965 and the shocked reactions at home and abroad led to his withdrawal from standing for re-election. He had run the Cold War into tragic absurdity in the jungles and rice paddies of Vietnam, and started a dangerous

3

internal disintegration at home, while a horrified world watched the destruction of a poor peasant country.[2]

Then came President Nixon, who was of sterner stuff and long dedicated to holding South East Asia. Under the guise of protecting withdrawal of most of our half million troops, he widened the war first in Cambodia and then into Laos, in early 1971; in the first case acting solely on his own authority and in the latter by circumventing Congressional prohibitions with circumlocutions and the use of every kind of armed power except infantry, or very much of it.

Attempts to Correct the Balance

In a long, careful review of the constitutional crisis, John W. Finney of the New York Times described, on January 23, 1971, a stiffening mood in the Congress, evidenced by the Cooper-Church amendment which sought to establish the principle that the President should not involve the nation in war without the consent of Congress, and by a new Senate Subcommittee on Security Agreements and Commitments Abroad which has sent its staff travelling into 23 countries, and which "more by accident than design" is "establishing its own foreign service." The House of Representatives has also passed a resolution requiring the President to submit a written report on

---

[2] *D. F. Fleming,* The Cold War and its Origins, 1917-1960, *2 volumes, fifth printing 1970. Published in New York, London, Milan and Tokyo.*

the commitment of American troops to foreign hostilities. Other efforts attempt to require Executive officials to appear before Congressional committees when summoned and to forbid the invasion of North Vietnam which President Nixon often threatened. However, Mr. Nixon being ready to veto all of these Congressional efforts, a two-thirds vote of both houses would be required to make them legally effective. Thus again a righting of the constitutional balance was blocked by a two-thirds vote requirement.

As this was written, President Nixon was proceeding both to withdraw troops in large numbers and to sustain a war covering nearly all of South East Asia, in the face of stern warnings from China and the Soviet Union, both of which are strongly committed on the other side. The sad lesson of General MacArthur's dash to the Yalu frontier of China during the Korean War is ignored.

Presidential Dictatorship

The basic situation in early 1971 was described by Townsend Hoopes, former Under Secretary of the Air Force, as follows: "Like several predecessor Presidents, Mr. Nixon had shown himself possessed of the raw power—unrestrained by congressional guidance or public debate—to make events and deepen commitments, leaving the American people and countless others to cope with the consequences as best they could. He alone bestrode the scene,

5

reducing senators, scholars, journalists and the rest of us to impotence. No reasoned criticism or moral protest made any difference. Senator Fulbright summed it up in one pathetic sentence: 'There is nothing we can do.'" [3]

Thus the isolationist negativism of the Senate up to the first publication of this book in 1930 has been succeeded since World War II by an Executive-led outthrust into the world which cost more than a trillion dollars; fastened a vast military machine on the country, whose dominance it could be impossible to reduce; and raised the astounding prospect that the role of America in the world may end dismally by the close of this century. Our never-ending South-East Asian exploit could well be the catastrophe which brings the American Dream to a close.

Crucial Questions

Do the checks and balances of our system of government fail to function? Can we work out rules for team work between the Presidency and the Congress that will enable us to deal with our many dangerous internal sicknesses and recover a place in the world's esteem? Or should we seek decisive change by going over to the parliamentary system, under which power is centralized and much more amenable to the will of the people?

These are questions which cry out insistently for

---

[3] *"The President is the Problem,"* The New Republic, March 6, 1971, p. 23.

6

EPILOGUE

solution in the seventies and beyond.

Nashville, Tennessee   D.F.F.
March 8, 1971

7